WRVS IN SCOTLAND
Seventy Years of Service

WRVS IN SCOTLAND

SEVENTY YEARS OF SERVICE

NORMAN WATSON

BLACK & WHITE PUBLISHING

First published 2008
by Black & White Publishing Ltd
99 Giles Street, Edinburgh EH6 6BZ

1 3 5 6 7 9 10 8 6 4 2   08 09 10 11 12

ISBN: 978 1 84502 201 3

Typeset by Ellipsis Books Limited, Glasgow
Printed and bound by MPG Books Ltd, Bodmin, Cornwall

CONTENTS

ACKNOWLEDGEMENTS

Sincere thanks are due to WRVS staff at Milton Hill, Oxfordshire, where archivist Matthew McMurray was particularly helpful. Rachel Cackett, lately of WRVS in Scotland, guided my efforts and smoothed my path on several occasions. I am indebted to the welcome and expertise provided by curators, archivists and scholars at the British Library and National Archives of Scotland, and to librarians and archivists at institutions across Scotland who cheerfully offered help and advice.

I am deeply indebted to Shirley Blair of D. C. Thomson & Co Ltd of Dundee for her scrutiny of the text and her expert eye for style and detail, and to Anne Swadel and Gwen Kissock of that firm for their valuable research assistance. I am grateful to various newspaper groups for allowing the use of photographs, not least D. C. Thomson & Co Ltd.

I must also thank Yvonne Nicolson, the sister of my sister-in-law. In 2006 I met her on the North Inch park in Perth, coincidentally opposite the house where I was born and brought up. Yvonne was hurrying away for her WRVS Meals on Wheels shift. 'What are you writing now?' was her parting shot. The rest, as they say, is this history.

In particular I wish also to thank present and past members of WRVS who volunteered their stories in the same spirit in which they have, for decades, offered their services to the vulnerable and needy. Special mention must be made of former National and Scottish chairman Dame Mary Corsar for writing the foreword, former Emergency Services organiser Kirsty Smith for charting recent tragedies in which WRVS in Scotland excelled, and honorary archivist Elaine Ross for her valuable input. Many others helped and while they may not see their names listed here, I thank them for their influence and contributions, which are identified and referenced at the end of the book.

This is their story, as much as it is mine.

Norman Watson,
May 2008

FOREWORD

BY DAME MARY CORSAR

Service beyond self.

This is the real motto of members of WRVS. Daily, weekly, monthly or in emergency this dedicated band of women and men work selflessly and tirelessly for others. When a member has undertaken a task it is carried out whatever the cost to her or himself, failing which a replacement is found. The reputation of the Service is founded on these volunteers.

But this is no one-sided giving. When I visited Lockerbie after the horrendous air crash I was vexed to find that a member of the team was working over both Christmas and New Year. I said that we would find a replacement for her. "Oh no," she replied, "I lost my husband this autumn and now it will be all right." In helping others and in working with friends she found comfort in her sorrow. This is a large part of what makes volunteering so enjoyable – we meet old friends, make new ones and have a common interest.

In his meticulous research for this book Norman Watson has shown how WRVS originated and developed until it became a huge umbrella organisation. But nothing stands still. During the years other groups have taken over much of the work, notably meals on wheels and victim support. Different bodies dealing with specific issues have been formed so inevitably the work covered by the Service has narrowed. If in the fullness of time WRVS becomes redundant and vanishes like the smile of the Cheshire cat there will be no shame in this and I am sure many members will transfer their allegiance to these other organisations.

At my local hospital a young schoolteacher mans the shift on a Sunday. So seventy years on the original spirit is still alive. Volunteering continues to exist.

The Honourable Dame Mary Corsar DBE, FRSE

Chairman WRVS 1988–1993
Chairman Scotland WRVS 1981–1988

INTRODUCTION

Memories. I was one of the first journalists to reach Dunblane after the news of terrible happenings there reached our newspaper office in 1996. The wider police cordon had yet to be established and the wailing of distraught parents learning of the unfolding tragedy will remain a harrowing memory of that March morning. Another memory . . . I had expected to be at my desk that day. I was wearing only a lightweight suit. It was bitterly cold. Later, a woman wearing a fluorescent orange tabard approached offering hot tea in a plastic cup. "There you are, son," she said warmly. I mumbled thanks through numbed lips, but she had moved on. On her back were the initials WRVS. I put down the cup on a wall, made a mental note to remember her kindness, and smiled my only smile of the day. I couldn't stand the taste of tea – and had never had a cup in my life.

It was memories of Britain's unpreparedness for bombing in the Great War and the dread of worse to come from aerial attacks that inspired the Government to recruit women volunteers to boost air raid precaution work on the eve of the Second World War. Out of that concern for home defence was created the Women's Voluntary Services in 1938, thereafter Women's Royal Voluntary Service and now WRVS. By the end of the war it had a million members in 2,000 centres and was a household name.

For seventy years WRVS has been Britain's unsung emergency service. Its heroic deeds during the Blitz, when its spirit defied fatigue and falling bombs, won it the reputation as The Army that Hitler Forgot. Post-war it has served at every major British disaster and broadened its activities to pioneer projects now landmarks in the country's welfare map, not least Darby & Joan clubs and meals on Wheels.

The story of WRVS in Scotland has never been told, yet WRVS

in Scotland was everywhere, plugging gaps in services wherever they occurred. To many of these volunteers it formed a hugely important part of their lives. It is thus time to recover and reconstruct their memories and to rescue their story. And as this history shows convincingly, whenever there was a job of any kind that was nobody's particular responsibility, it was handed to WRVS – and always done in complete disregard of difficulties.

I also hope the general reader will understand what it might have been like to have been a WRVS volunteer and thus part of what has been called the most remarkable women's organisation in history.

"There is always on hand that great soother of nerves, that great assuager of griefs, tea."

1

NEVER SAY NO

High on the wall on Edinburgh Castle Rock hangs a plaque commemorating the only aerial bombardment of the First World War in Scotland. It records an attack in April 1916 in which two German airships dropped high explosive and incendiary devices across the city. A child was killed in a crib in Leith. A bomb killed a man in the Grassmarket. Six died in Marshall Street, another child perished in a tenement on St Leonard's Hill. In total 13 people lost their lives. Confused inhabitants rushed out to point excitedly at the Zeppelins, unaware of the deadly cargo they carried. Edinburgh's One O'Clock Gun, turned for the first time on an enemy, could fire only impotent blank shells. What was evident was the lack of defence against the devastating new tactic of aerial attack – and furious letters peppered Edinburgh newspapers asking why the city had been so badly prepared.

The psychological implications of mass bombing for a country without an effective deterrent were startlingly clear. People would be exposed and unprotected. In the event of another war, an uncontrolled and hysterical mass exodus from targeted areas was anticipated. In 1924 the newly-constituted Air Raid Precautions Committee produced figures estimating that in London alone there would be 9,000 casualties in the first two days of an attack, and then a continuing rate of 17,500 casualties a week. The Scottish Health Department suggested that 12,000 beds should be set aside for victims in the first week of a war, and predicted that 1,500 people would die in the first air raid on Glasgow.[1]

So when the dark clouds of war gathered again in 1938 the fear that major cities would be utterly destroyed from the air led the government to prepare the civilian population for the suffering which would inevitably result from aerial bombardment. Shelters were prepared, gas masks distributed and sirens tested as Britain braced itself. However, continuing fears over the civilian population high-lighted in a report by Sir John Anderson, MP for the Scottish Universities, led to the Air Ministry upping the weekly casualty prediction to 65,000 from aerial attack. Ministers concluded that nothing could make a government look more helpless than the prospect of no defence against falling bombs. Facing "inevitable panic" plans were announced to evacuate two million people from danger areas in the event of war.

And so it was to Stella Isaacs, Dowager Marchioness of Reading, the widow of the late Viceroy of India, that Home Secretary Sir Samuel Hoare turned in the spring of 1938 to carry out his idea of building a reservoir of women volunteers to support air raid pre-caution efforts and to assist with evacuation if required. After her husband's death in 1935 Lady Reading had continued in a number of influential positions with charities and good causes. She was a member of the BBC's Advisory Council and the Overseas Settlement Board. She was a magistrate and also led the Personal Service League, which helped people into employment. Sir Samuel called on Lady Reading at her home in London, telling her that no existing organ-isation was suited to the job of recruiting women into the Air Raid Precautions service, a role that women appeared disinclined or unwilling to carry out. He also confided to her that several city councils appeared reluctant to be placed on a war footing and that a reservoir of women volunteers could best deliver the necessary message of ARP.

Hoare followed up this meeting with a letter to Lady Reading in which he warned of the "heavy burden which would fall on women" in the event of a war. He told her that he believed that if air attacks were to be met effectively it would be "essential" that a women's service "should be organised and trained beforehand." The aim, he told her, was that every woman should be given the opportunity to contribute to home defence.

The letter set out three key objectives for such a service:

1. The enrolment of women for the ARP departments of local authorities.

2. To bring home to every household in the country what an
   air attack meant.
3. To make it known to every household what it could do to
   protect itself and the community.[2]

Sir Samuel asked Lady Reading to think over the proposals, which
she did as she thumbed through ARP manuals bought hurriedly at
Victoria Station prior to a journey two days later on the Orient
Express to Bulgaria. She cut short her stay in Sofia after which she
produced a memorandum for the Home Secretary outlining a new
women's organisation which would provide a channel through which
women could enrol to work with local authorities on air defence
duties. Its aim, she said, would be to stimulate the recruitment of
female civilians for ARP, but also to educate women – "especially
women in the household" – on the impact and aftermath of air
raids.[3]

Stella Reading's memorandum set out the skeleton of the proposed
service. An advisory council comprising representatives of the nation's
leading women's organisations would oversee its development from
London, with a similar council in Scotland drawing on the experience of relevant groups north of the border. The service would have
a national executive committee. Britain would be divided into twelve
regions – each under the control of a regional figurehead. Within
each region there were to be districts following local authority boundaries, each with a district organiser. Within districts there would be
town and county centres, under the leadership of centre organisers.
Regional representatives and district organisers would be the points
of contact with local authorities preparing schemes under the Air
Raid Precautions Act.

The organisation would be overwhelmingly voluntary, strictly
non-political and non-sectarian and completely flexible to enable
government departments, local authorities and other agencies to
draw upon its volunteers as required. From the outset women gave
what time they could spare. "If we succeed in getting the women
interested," Lady Reading told Sir Samuel Hoare, "they will feel that
the whole thing belongs to them in a real sense, more so than if it

were run for them by paid people and officials." Thus, apart from Home Office funding for the proposed London headquarters and financial support for administration work, the proposed organisation would be largely unpaid. It would also have to be, she told Sir Samuel, a service which emphasised "training and levels of proficiency" – one in which it "should be possible to introduce a little of the atmosphere of a disciplined force without militarising."[4]

With Sir Samuel Hoare's encouragement, Lady Reading assembled representatives from women influential in the welfare sector to discuss the proposed organisation and to examine the reasons why women had been reluctant to take an interest in the Air Raid Precautions service. She learned that few women had responded to national appeals to help ARP schemes because "either they were interviewed by an office boy, or that they were directed from one local or municipal authority to another in a seemingly endless series of queues." Some women said they had not the time, nor in some cases the courage, to be air raid wardens, which often involved solitary night-time duties. Others claimed they had been refused ARP training simply because they were female. Several said they had found local authorities ambivalent about the prospects for war and lukewarm over diverting resources to air raid preparations. Memories of the slaughter of the Great War also acted to prevent women enlisting for ARP duties . . . "They wanted nothing to do with it."[5]

Lady Reading was installed in a single-room office at the Home Office in Horseferry House, Westminster, with the status of Deputy Under-Secretary of State. A civil servant, Mary Smieton, was seconded to help steer her path through officialdom and was given the title General Secretary. Smieton arrived and saw Lady Reading "sitting in a small room in the Home Office designed for one person, with her secretary typing in one corner and two other young women in two other corners, all evidently working under pressure." It was Smieton, the unflappable civil servant from the Ministry of Labour, who recalled on that first day "never having been more confused in my life as to what was expected of me," who stuck it out amid the bubbling enthusiasms and drove forward the fledgling service in the difficult first months. One founding member said of her: "She never let us see her sufferings as we slashed through the red tape, and we shall always be grateful to her." Five years later another member of the team could still visualise the room, with its blue carpet, and how five in the team "became six, then seven and then eight and the chairs were exhausted and I, being the junior, felt obliged to give up my seat and sit on that carpet."[6]

Charged with the mobilisation of womanpower against a day of national emergency, Lady Reading liaised with organisations such as the Girl Guides, Women's Institutes and church groups and gathered around her influential figures and friends, seeking their views and widening the base from which the still-anonymous service would be launched. There were no precedents. No voluntary organisation had ever before been used as an official arm of government. No nationwide network of women volunteers had previously been formed for war work. Some were sceptical if such an entity was required. The Civil Service Clerical Association, for example, was troubled by the new body's seemingly autocratic leadership and its political links to the Home Office. It advised members to steer well clear of it.[7] There was still a question over the organisation's name. "This had to be something easily remembered that looked good on a badge, did not have initials that spelt something rude, did not provide the possibility of a vulgar nickname and was not already taken."[8] Eventually, 'Women's Voluntary Services for Air Raid Precautions' was chosen – WVS in shorthand – and the new organisation was agreed in principle at a meeting with Sir Samuel Hoare at the Home Office on 16 May 1938.

Today's WRVS was born.

A new and larger office was required and the women took up an offer from the Office of Works of premises in Queen Anne's Chambers, Tothill Street, Westminster, "but womenlike, we had to alter it to 41 Tothill Street, which, after all is easier to remember."[9] For the next 30 years 41 Tothill Street was the nerve centre of Women's Voluntary Services' ever-broadening spectrum of activities. Stella Reading's next task was to find among friends and contacts a dozen leading women to become regional representatives across the country. In England and Wales she was able to use the powers invested in her to appoint women already prominent in public life, virtually all of them high social status individuals well known in their localities. They were mostly women like herself – titled, influential, often wealthy and with impressive 'contacts', known for their indomitable spirit and used to getting things done. It was their task to make known to every household what it could do to protect itself and the community in the event of war.

In Scotland, however, Lady Reading was under obligation to be advised by the Secretary of State for Scotland, John Colville. After considering various luminaries, Colville recommended Lady Ruth Balfour of Balbirnie, near Glenrothes in Fife. Ruth Balfour was the daughter of the 2nd Earl of Balfour, an aristocratic Scottish family claiming descendancy from William the Conqueror. The second earl and his wife, Lady Betty, the daughter of Lord Lytton of Knebworth, had brought up Ruth, her three sisters and brother Robert on the sprawling Whittingehame Estate near Haddington, the home of the Edwardian prime minister A. J. Balfour. After studying medicine, Ruth had married Brigadier Edward Balfour of Balbirnie, a much-decorated First World War soldier, who had commanded the 1st Battalion of the Scots Guards between the wars.

Intelligent, practical, a founding member of Save the Children's Scottish Council, with a formidable profile as a public figure, Lady Balfour had been invited to represent Scotland's ARP region at the women's meeting at the Home Office on May 16 to carry out the groundwork for WVS. In her private correspondence to the Home Secretary, Lady Reading noted, "Saw Colonel Colville at the Scottish Office . . . we agreed that I should write to Lady Ruth Balfour to head Scotland." Thus on 21 May 1938 Reading wrote to Lady Balfour further outlining her plans for the service and inviting her to chair a Scottish Advisory Council. She told her: "The Home Secretary is very hopeful that you may agree to come on to this organisation as the Scottish representative and I am wondering if there could possibly be a chance of seeing you in the near future to try to persuade you to say yes." Persuasion was unnecessary. Lady Balfour accepted immediately.[10]

Ruth Balfour was formally confirmed as Scottish chairman on May 30 and a small clerical team moved into an office at 7 Coates

Gardens in the West End of Edinburgh. This became WVS head-quarters in Scotland, which was designated Region 11 in the national WVS structure. From here began the process of developing the women's service north of the border under the watchful eye of the civil servant Mary Mackie, seconded from the Ministry of Labour to fill a role similar to that of Mary Smieton at Tothill Street. Under Lady Balfour's chairmanship the WVS Scottish Advisory Council met for the first time on 24 June 1938 in the Queen's Club, Frederick Street, Edinburgh. A total of 46 organisations were represented, indicative of the breadth of voluntary work carried on north of the border. They included SWRI, the British Legion (Women's Section), the British Red Cross Society, YWCA, the Salvation Army, St Andrew's Ambulance Association, the Church of Scotland's Women's Guild and the Girl Guides Association, and smaller organisations, such as the Scottish Matrons' Association and Soroptimists. Voluntary work was not a new phenomenon. Many groups existed across Scotland fulfilling a wide range of roles and remits. The SWRI, for example, founded after the First World War, boasted hundreds of rural insti-tutes by 1938. Churches, the Salvation Army, the Girl Guides and the Red Cross were among organisations with a pedigree in welfare work. And it was to such groups that WVS turned initially for its leaders – Lady Reading appointing more WVS administrators from the Women's Institutes and Girl Guides than from other organisations.

The council was intended to act as the co-ordinating advisory board for all Scottish matters relating to ARP work. It also had direct representation to, and positions on, the WVS Advisory Council in London. In a report for WVS headquarters the Scottish council "gave the impression of being practical and active – very willing to dispense with 'red tape' if this would help to get things done."[11] As the war progressed and its size and influence grew, WVS viewed the advisory council not so much as a sounding board for future activity, but as a means of telling the other organisations what it was doing.

Women's Voluntary Services for Air Raid Precautions, forerunner of today's WRVS, was announced to the public in a statement by Sir Samuel Hoare in the House of Commons on June 16 and in a broadcast by Lady Reading on the BBC the same evening. Within days of its role being further detailed "with the maximum blare of the Press, cinema and wireless publicity," thousands of letters had poured into Tothill Street from women saying they were anxious to be trained for ARP work. Thereafter Stella Reading embarked on a tour of Britain, arriving in Scotland in the autumn to explain her philosophy, rally support for her young organisation and to appoint more administrators.

Edinburgh headquarters controlled the evolving WVS structure north of the border and enjoyed considerable autonomy over membership affairs in Scotland. Indeed, Sir Charles Cunningham, secretary of the Scottish Home Department, recalled that it was "in outward appearance at least a very self governing part" of WVS.[12] Within Scotland Ruth Balfour agreed early on that a Glasgow centre should have considerable powers, not so much in terms of policy, but in how WVS activities were to be co-ordinated across the West of Scotland. Thus it was a pressing duty for her to open and staff a regional office in Glasgow. This was done with typical efficiency, and by the autumn of 1938 an office was established at 136 Renfield Street, under the administration of SWRI stalwart Griselda Tomory. It was the twelfth centre to open in Britain.

Ruth Balfour's achievement over subsequent weeks was to establish a network of women that helped to bring home to every household what air attacks would mean and one that could be mobilised in time of national emergency in support of the defence of the country. She began recruiting for the new organisation's hierarchy, persuading women to work a few hours, which became years. Her instinct told her that much of Scotland's civil defence infrastructure was dislocated and its effectiveness hampered by divergent local authority policies and boundary constraints. Leadership duties would typically be entrusted to establishment figures with influential contacts. Thus she followed Lady Reading's approach to recruit titled women or the wives of public figures for the leading appointments – the lady of the 'big house' in the countryside, in towns the wives of Lord Provosts, bailies or major industrialists. They included, for example, Lady Elphinstone to lead Midlothian and Lady Cadogan for Perthshire. Mary Elphinstone could certainly pull strings – she was the Queen's sister. When Griselda Tomory wrote to Lady Steel-Maitland of Sauchieburn, Stirling to ask her to become county representative for Stirlingshire, her potential duties were described rather less onerously than they would actually become: "To represent the WVS on the National Committee, to collect reports from each Centre for the monthly meeting, to handle instructions/literature from HQ to branches, giving advice re centres or people ..." In reality, county or burgh organiser was a full-time job, one of constant worry, heavy commitment and permanent responsibility.[13]

Volunteers between the ages of 17 and 65 were sought. What was required was "calmness, reliability and good local knowledge," but especially women with common sense and tact. Pre printed application forms bearing the addresses of the London, Edinburgh and Glasgow centres, were widely circulated in Scotland. These were headed 'WVS for ARP' and opened with the words, "I am interested in ARP work and should like to receive further information as to how I can be of use." Below was a long list of activities for which the applicant could volunteer. It included nursing, cooking, driving, typing, and even "the ability to provide and ride a pedal cycle." The net was cast wide and thousands joined WVS over the closing months of 1938, keen to shoulder the burden of an integrated women's service – one which the Home Secretary warned would have to "be prepared" for war. Such was the uptake that training courses run by WVS in Dundee "had to be doubled up," while after enrolment began in Edinburgh City Chambers, "many additional administrators had to be hastily collected to deal with the overwhelming numbers. In spite of this no woman was turned away."[14]

From the outset WVS assisted national government in close co-operation with, and under the instructions of, local authorities. This clever positioning of the organisation under county and burgh councils ensured that local government became responsible for providing branch premises, heating, lighting and telephone. WVS had no central funds of its own, relying on womanly powers of persuasion for many running costs. Only on the eve of war did the Home Office instruct councils that reasonable additional expenses borne by the women could be paid to them from their ARP grant.

Lady Reading also pointed out that the arrangement with councils had its practical side. The associational link to local authorities ensured, she said, that "a nationwide coverage of Great Britain was obtained, instead of the springing up of WVS groups wherever enthusiasm happened to be very strong."[15]

As war threatened, volunteers who joined WVS were distributed in large numbers to nursing, first aid, evacuation and air raid warden duties, such as fire-watching. Members also became telephonists, storekeepers, planners, messengers, stenographers and laundry assistants. Work was always available for those who could cook, knit and sew for large numbers. Transport was also identified as an area where women were under-represented. Thus not only were more women taught how to drive, a special WVS course instructed them on driving without lights in black-out conditions, zigzagging between straw-filled pillow-cases representing casualties. Owner-drivers were also taught to drive in convoy under black-out while wearing gas masks. Drivers – all volunteers – learned never to question their assignment – whether it involved taking a minister to a meeting, a sick person to hospital or, as happened on one occasion, a goat to Victoria Station! From the very beginning, WVS organised lectures and training for women across a range of activities, including first aid, anti-gas and fire-fighting. By the time war was declared Tothill Street had organised 850 training lectures in London alone, covering 19 different jobs that voluntary workers could do. At an early stage the slogan 'WVS never says No' was adopted. It was one the organisation lived up to as the nation's needs were met wherever they arose. As one centre leader put it, "It was the habit to say 'yes' first and wonder how afterwards."

The political situation across Europe deteriorated and WVS began to plan independently for war. Its principal remit remained enrolling women volunteers for local authority Air Raid Precautions departments, still staffed mostly by men. But the first important task of WVS was to covertly prepare for a mass evacuation of civilians from potential target areas, as predicted by Sir John Anderson. To this end Lady Reading arranged a secret meeting of Girl Guide commissioners at which names of adult Girl Guide leaders who could take charge of evacuation arrangements locally were passed over. Further meetings to discuss emergency preparations took place with the National Federation of Women's Institutes. The three organisations subsequently dispatched telegrams to suitable women across Britain asking them to take charge of important work for the government, "the nature of which would be explained to them at a meeting at WVS headquarters." At this stage, WVS could not say what the work involved. Despite the vague request and secrecy, 42 women accepted and only five declined to help, two through illness.[16]

Neville Chamberlain's 'peace for our time' pledge came and went and WVS worked on. In the harsh winter bridging 1938 and 1939 women volunteers took the initiative to survey rural families to act as hosts for evacuees, appealing to the patriotism of the reticent and unpersuaded. Nearly two thirds of 1,760 UK local government areas were thus discreetly surveyed. Within two days of the government creating an Evacuation Department, it had the assurance from Tothill Street that, "If bombing started, a quarter of a million women up and down the country, geared to carry out official orders, would know under what local leader to rally." It was an astonishing promise, and it was upon WVS and its guarantee of nationwide support that the Government eventually based its complex plans for evacuation.[17]

Who were these founding WRVS pioneers who helped expand WVS from five members to 300,000 by the end of its first year? Early records indicate that many single women between the ages of 30 and 40 enrolled with WVS for air raid precaution and civil defence work, while younger women volunteered for nursing or transport roles. Older women in their thousands offered their services to centre administration, canteen work, evacuation preparation, knitting and clothing groups, while many teachers came forward for evacuation duties. Ambulance drivers were often young married women. Of the 420 women who enrolled at the WVS Dundee centre in February 1939, 80 volunteered for transport duties, 89 for the centre (which included clerical staff), 36 for warden duties, 77 for first aid, 27 as auxiliary nurses, 24 for hospital supply work, 54 in canteens and 33 for evacuation services.[18]

Senior positions were initially filled by well-to-do and professional women. County and burgh organisers in Scotland were typically upper middle-class or the wives of the emerging managerial classes or from the still-limited ranks of graduate women. "Everyone on the committee seems to have such a lot of money," volunteer Nella Last noted. But women drawn from across society became involved as the political crisis deepened. Stella Reading proudly told an audience that the WVS membership comprised "the wives of labourers, railway men, cabinet ministers, farmers, parsons, all kinds of women of every political colour." And a circular from Ruth Balfour urged Scottish centres to cast the recruitment net as widely as possible: "Women who are over 50 need not consider themselves ineligible as volunteers, for there are many useful functions they could fulfil." Thus the elderly, the young and the housebound and mothers with children at home felt they could usefully contribute by enrolling for the few hours' commitment asked of them by WVS. As for an upward age, it was said "so long as you can hold your knitting needles" WVS welcomed you.[19]

It is also evident that Women's Voluntary Services attracted women unable to join the uniformed women's services or to do essential work, which contributed to its 'mature' age profile. Several organisations already recruited women for duties in support of the armed services. These included the Auxiliary Territorial Service (ATS), Women's Auxiliary Air Force (WAAF), and Women's Royal Naval Service (WRNS). And, from 1939, women in Scotland could also join the Women's Land Army to provide help on farms in the absence of called-up men. Thus although women were not permitted to fight in battle, they eventually worked in every branch of the Services, helping to man searchlights, directing anti-aircraft fire, plotting enemy raids, driving and maintaining military vehicles, operating barrage balloons and serving as radio operators and ambulance drivers – a contribution often neglected in military histories or dismissed in a meagre quota of words.

The role of WVS was always intended to be different. From the start it was concerned with all aspects of air raid precautions work, including casualty services, evacuation services, hospital services, ambulance services, home safety services and communication services. It was mostly voluntary and almost entirely unpaid. Neither was it full-time work for most members. It was a motivational mix of care, compassion and patriotism, but no doubt foremost in many women's minds was the urge to play a direct and useful part in the impending war with Germany.

Before 1938 was out WVS had also launched its Housewives' Service, accommodating those women who were confined to homes with children, or older women, who could be trained to help with welfare or casualty work in the event of incidents in their neighbourhood. Such women were issued with identifying armbands and provided with blue cards for their windows to act as beacons at times of emergency. At first many working-class housewives had difficulty in overcoming their "innate modesty," as Stella Reading put it, and hovered near doorways as enrolment for training took place. Yet the service would eventually involve one in five WVS members across Britain and had 10,000 members in Scotland in its first year. In the troubled times ahead the Housewives' Service would prove its usefulness, quietly and heroically, as a focal point for community co-ordination and co-operation.

Above all, WVS was the flexible link between government, councils and the public. It placed women where they were required and, by its first birthday in May 1939, by which time its diversifying role had seen its name changed to Women's Voluntary Services for Civil Defence, it could offer volunteers 39 types of jobs, from working with sewing machines, to concocting a meal out of nothing, to shameless begging for wool for knitting groups. At the heart of all of it was the gloomy prospect of war. Lady Reading told members, "You must keep in the forefront of your minds that your main purpose in WVS life is to serve local authorities and help them in a gigantic task such as they have never before been called to carry out." And addressing women's groups in Glasgow City Chambers, Ruth Balfour recalled how unprepared Britain was for air attack in the previous war. It was the "one thing that was demonstrated to us" she told her audience, adding, "Let us never think that will happen again so long as there is any danger of war breaking out."[20]

In the spring of 1939 Stella Reading decided that a uniform would raise the profile of the organisation and she went about the process in her matchless manner. Mary Smieton, her general secretary at Tothill Street, recalled: "I went away for a few days' holiday some months after the start of WVS. When I got back I found that the Chairman was half-way through some very skillful negotiations to put the WVS into uniform without incurring any public expense at all. I asked if she had got the approval of the Home Office, who might be startled to find that they had created a new uniformed corps. No she hadn't, but she and I would go round at once to see Sir Wilfred Eady, the Under-Secretary in charge (and of course an old friend), and seek his approval. We got it."[21]

Various services by then had adopted colours, including khaki by the Auxiliary Territorial Service, blue by the WAAF and brown by the Women's Land Army. The Red Cross wore blue and St John's Ambulance black. A Headquarters committee eventually approved London fashion designer Digby Morton's proposals of a green uniform with a grey thread running through it, and commissioned designs for a greatcoat, a felt hat with a maroon band, a jacket and skirt, a maroon cardigan and blouse, a woollen green, grey and maroon striped scarf and a dark green wrap-over overall. The clever pragmatism of the grey-green and beetroot red clothing – unveiled to the public in London in July 1939 – was self-evident: "The greatcoats were designed in such a way that even if women slept in them all night they would not look too dishevelled. The skirts were without pleats and therefore did not need ironing . . . the schoolgirl felt hat was deliberately selected so that it could be worn at any angle and in any shape." Not only did the grey-flecked thread conceal dirt and grime, the artificial silk blouse had no sleeves to roll up – "reinforcing the impression that WVS members were always ready for work."[22]

Badges to be worn on duty were also commissioned but not entirely with success. One of Lady Reading's Tothill Street staff recalled: "We consulted the Royal Mint, who suggested names of badge makers who would submit designs . . . I remember the despair with which we went through sheet after sheet of those beautifully hand-painted badges, all of which we turned down because they looked too regimental. Eventually we roughed out the WVS badge ourselves."[23] A square white metal badge bearing the inscription in red 'ARP Women's Voluntary Services' (later 'WVS Civil Defence') and surmounted by the Royal Crown, was issued free to all members who had completed 60 hours' work on behalf of the organisation and who had undertaken basic training. Similar cloth badges were to be worn on the sleeves of the uniform. Upward curved area name tabs were also sewn on to coats and jackets. Eventually a variety of embroidered armbands bearing the initials 'WVS' were adopted for types of work where no uniform was provided. The exteriors of centres were also equipped with white enamel signs bearing the WVS crest, and car badges were eventually available. Even gas mask 'handbags' in WVS colours were advertised as fashionable accessories.

Several Scottish outfitters were authorised retailers of the new uniform. They included Binns of Dumfries, Draffen's of Dundee, Beveridges of Kirkcaldy and George Watson of Stirling – though Orkney WVS were complaining as late as November 1939 that "no uniforms were available" there. A memo from Tothill Street set out the recommended prices for the various items:

> Green felt hat with maroon band 6/6d.
> Grey-green coat and skirt 57/6d.
> Grey-green tweed overcoat 57/6d.
> Green overall with red monogram 7/6d.
> Red artificial silk blouse 6/11d.[24]

Stella Reading had always expected her organisation to be classless and non-judgemental, one created for work essentially of a peaceful nature and concerned with educating the public so that they would never be taken by surprise under conditions of war. When it adopted a uniform she was determined to have no signs of rank on it. The chairman wore the WVS badge as did her newest member. Those who were group leaders for a specific task could simply be part of a team with another leader the following week.

And as war began, from the Dowager Marchioness of Reading to the youngest volunteer, all WVS members had to use their clothing coupons to obtain uniforms. That they were not provided except in exceptional cases of hardship ensured they were worn with pride. Often, however, volunteers went about duties simply wearing the WVS metal badge on the lapels of their everyday clothes.

By the tense summer of 1939 the Department of Health for Scotland had made public the plan to evacuate in the event of war schoolchildren, pre-school children, teachers and helpers as necessary, expectant mothers and adult blind people. It had based its recommendations on the advice of the Scottish Advisory Committee on Evacuation whose members comprised representatives from local authorities, the Educational Institute of Scotland and WVS.[25]

Vulnerable groups were to be evacuated initially from five strategically-important areas – Clydebank, Dundee, Edinburgh, Glasgow and Rosyth – and taken to a number of rural destinations. Edinburgh evacuees were to go to the Lothians and the Borders area, but also as far distant as Banff and Inverness. Glasgow's children and mothers with pre-school children would be billeted across a great swathe of Scotland, ranging from Wigtown to Perthshire, while evacuees from Clydebank, Rosyth and Dundee were to be housed in neighbouring rural areas; respectively, Dunbartonshire and Argyll, Fife, and Angus and Kincardine. In October 1939 Inverkeithing, North Queensferry and South Queensferry were added to the sending areas.

The size of the task was enormous. The predicted total of priority evacuees in Scotland was 247,000 and an appeal was made for 5,000 women to help with the exodus if it came. The prominence given to WVS in the *National Service Handbook* of January 1939 ensured "a stream of woman-power pouring in at the rate of 10,000 a week" across Britain. Few recruits knew what they could do to help, but in Scotland they were told, "The work ranks in importance with any other work in the national interest."[26] Trial evacuations took place across Scotland, firstly in Fife, where 200 children acted as 'Edinburgh' evacuees at Cupar in June 1939, then at a country-wide practice in August involving schools located in danger areas. In the run-up to this exercise, WVS volunteers helped with the distribution of gas masks to virtually every Scottish citizen over the age of four and visited homes to pass on information on how to fit the masks. The threat of gas poisoning was everyone's basic fear.

The tense pre-war period also accelerated air raid planning and preparation. In Perth an air raid precautions display staffed by WVS and others, intended to provide a realistic impression of wartime conditions, had exactly that effect for some and the opposite for others. Fifteen thousand people watched as wailing sirens warned of the impending 'approach' of enemy aircraft, 'residents' in the arena ran to two temporary Anderson shelters and 'incendiary bombs' were dropped on to wooden structures. The event proved too realistic for some, however. When anti-aircraft guns opened up on their imaginary targets, one woman collapsed, others screamed and children ran away in tears. On the other hand, the audience reaction to sloppy efforts at fire-fighting and rescue by the 700 ARP personnel on parade led Perth's Lord Provost to write angrily to the local newspaper to complain of "the levity with which some of the operations were treated by the public." Another exercise, involving waves of imaginary bombers crossing the East Coast, reportedly resulted in a haphazard response with "gas casualties lying in streets forlornly waiting for ambulances." And after a mock ARP exercise in Dundee letters of complaint poured into local newspapers. One said: "The staff work was lamentable . . . and showed a miserable lack of co-ordination." Another commented, "The muddle that ensued was alarming . . . where we had eight gas casualties no services arrived." Such incidents led to renewed criticism of the reluctance of local authorities to take ARP work seriously – precisely the ambivalence which had contributed to the creation of Women's Voluntary Services a year earlier.[27]

To emphasise the urgency of the situation, cinemas across Scotland showed the WVS film *The Warning,* which encouraged the population to prepare for conflict and women to contribute to the defence of the country. But the release of the H. G. Wells film *Things to Come*, which predicted a decades-long world war ending with plague and anarchy, served only to jangle frayed nerves. A momentary escape from the gloom was the eve-of-war announcement that Queen Elizabeth and Mary, the Queen Mother, had agreed to become joint Patrons of WVS, Buckingham Palace writing to Lady Reading that, "The Queen knows well the magnificent work which is being taken up by the Women's Voluntary Services for Civil Defence." It was an association the Queen – later Elizabeth, the Queen Mother – would proudly maintain until her death over 60 years later.

Away from public gaze, the Scottish Health department quietly began the unhappy task of preparing for mass casualties by asking local authorities in threatened areas to arrange "additional mortuary accommodation." In Dundee provision was secretly made for the use of playground shelters in the city's primary schools to accommodate 350 bodies. In Edinburgh it was decided to use, of all things, a slaughterhouse. Meanwhile, WVS members busied themselves with the distribution of leaflets advising on how sandbags could be stacked to protect against bomb blast and how a cellar or basement could be converted into a refuge room. Seventy thousand women had enrolled in WVS across Scotland – but Ruth Balfour wanted more, warning that their country was only "an hour's flight from Europe."

WVS had been promised 24 hours' notice of the intended evacuation, and on 31 August 1939, one day before Germany invaded Poland, headquarters in Tothill Street received an urgent government message warning them of the impending exodus. Twelve telegrams were immediately dispatched to regional administrators, who in turn contacted their county and urban organisers. Within 14 hours, 120,000 WVS women across Britain had been alerted, 17,000 of them for escort duties on the first evacuation.

WVS was mobilised.

2

THE ARMY THAT HITLER FORGOT

War was declared on 3 September 1939 as dark political clouds gathered and a thunderstorm lashed rain across much of Scotland. On that day, WVS chairman Stella Reading sent a sombre telegram to King George VI to pledge the support to the country of Women's Voluntary Services. She told the King: "WVS came into being as an expression of the desire of women to preserve peace. Now that war is upon us, we wish to assure Your Majesty of the determination to work unceasingly, and with steadfast loyalty, to play our part in the Civil Defence of our country." The King's reply, signed 'George RI', read: "Please express to all members of the Women's Voluntary Services my sincere thanks for their message. I know very well that they will continue to serve their country in the present grave emergency with the same efficiency and determination that has characterised their work hitherto."[1]

The declaration led to a rush to join WVS. Edinburgh headquarters was described as "a beehive" as hundreds queued to enrol. "Volunteers for all kinds of services have been coming in splendidly," reported *The Scotsman*. Young clerical workers, occupied in offices throughout the city, eagerly volunteered for similar duties in the evening. Older women signed up at the rate of 350 a day. By the end of the first week of war Edinburgh WVS alone had recruited 11,000 new members.[2] Yet, despite the rapid mobilisation of women volunteers, Scotland still did not have a fully developed defence to respond adequately to enemy attacks from the air. Public buildings were sandbagged. ARP wardens patrolled the streets at night. A black-out had been imposed. But urban Scotland had emerged from the 1930s' economic stagnation with a socialist hope that conflict could be avoided. City councils were pacifist by nature and reluctant to commit resources to air raid precautions planning – or anything else to do with war. Glasgow Corporation refused the ARP free use of the city's halls for lectures until compelled to do so by the Scottish Office. In 1936, Clydebank Town Council declined to send representatives to an ARP conference. The local MP stated that he would not send a Clydebank boy to war on any consideration and that there would be "no war for me under any circumstances."[3] A feeling prevailed that something would turn up to prevent war. It was partly to overcome passivity that the Home Secretary created the quasi-governmental WVS with the direction to councils that they were under obligation to involve its motivated volunteers.

As Scotland braced itself, children packed their belongings into little suitcases, hung gas masks around their necks, attached identification labels to their coats and embarked upon an evacuation scheme described later as the "greatest sociological experiment of all time."[4] In Glasgow, Edinburgh and Dundee, railway stations were filled with long lines of little passengers boarding trains for the countryside. They were permitted only one change of under-clothes and stockings, handkerchiefs, night clothes and toothbrush, a comb, towel, face-cloth, one tin cup and just one day's supply of food. In support of parents and teachers, thousands of WVS personnel helped and escorted mothers and children on outward journeys to 'clearing house' centres in reception areas. The first had been opened at West Linton in Peeblesshire, Abington in Lanarkshire, Aberfoyle and Meigle in Perthshire and Gorebridge in Midlothian and acted as shock absorbers between sending and receiving areas. There evacuees found their feet before being taken to their rural billets or camps. Volunteers also staffed canteens at railway stations and distribution points across the country. Those women who were drivers took the invalid or poorly, others helped with clothing or set up information points. Members also worked at temporary hostels, nurseries for children and communal feeding centres. Some young evacuees had their heads washed and were given extra clothes before being passed to another volunteer for the next stage of their adventure.

The scale of the task facing WVS women and their local authority partners was formidable. By the end of September 1939, nearly

175,000 people had been evacuated in Scotland, 120,000 of them leaving Glasgow in three days, all to be billeted with strangers in receiving areas up and down the country. Sir John Anderson had warned of the probability of antagonism: "There may here and there be considerable friction, especially at first, between the inhabitants of those areas and the incomers who are billeted upon them." Anderson's misgivings were not misplaced. The clash of cultures and social gulf between ill-shod, ill-clothed tenement dwellers from poorer city districts and the middle-class rural householder was stark. When seven thousand evacuated Glasgow children arrived en masse in Perth, for example, accents as well as standards of cleanliness were met with considerable bewilderment. In the first week of war 10 of the children had to be admitted to hospital with diphtheria. The local paper noted that from "practically all districts complaints have been received concerning the verminous and filthy condition of the children."[5] When the 2,542 children and mothers from Dundee arrived in Forfar as part of the 17,200 tranche which left the city in the first two days of war, Provost Hill of the Angus town expressed his shock to find "a very large number were filthy and diseased." In a letter to Dundee town council he complained, "Really, to expect us to billet these people in decent houses, or houses at all occupied by country people, who are not used to that kind of thing, is disgraceful." Another letter, to the *Inverness Courier*, labelled the billeting arrangements in that town "a rotten bad scheme" and claimed that the authorities had expected people "to fall for what is little less than sentimental blackmail."[6]

One wartime history described the cultural upheaval in Scotland: "On arrival there were 'pick your evacuee' sessions where hosts haggled over the most presentable children while the sicklier and grubbier were left until last. Complaints of thieving, swearing, bed-wetting and general smelliness were made time and time again against the 'townie' children who came in disproportionate numbers from the slums and backstreets of Britain's big cities." A contemporary account by Helen Jackson noted the arrival of Glasgow schoolchildren in rural Perthshire in September, 1939: "There were no chip shops. There was no cinema. They were appalled at what they found in the country, and they thought we were primitive. And we thought they were . . . oh dear! It was a complete clash of cultures."[7]

The misery was not confined to well-to-do householders terrified of working-class mothers and uncontrollable children invading their homes. Before the first week of war was out, several bus-loads of homesick women and children had endured enough of country life and had beaten a path back to the cities. They, too, had been met with strange dialects. They had endured loneliness and boredom. The quiet was intimidating. Food was cooked in a different way. Rural schools were overwhelmed. To the young evacuated the countryside was full of terrors. By the end of 1939, nearly 80% of all uprooted mothers across Scotland had drifted back to their homes taking their evacuated children with them.

Why was evacuation in Scotland not as successful as it was in England, where WVS received praise for its leadership and participation in the exodus there? A post mortem carried out by Lady Reading's regional administrator Mrs Lindsay Huxley concluded that there were two principal causes of disenchantment with the scheme north of the border. Firstly, whole family units were not adopted for evacuation in Scotland, and parents baulked at the prospect of separation. When mothers of evacuees in Lanarkshire discovered that individual families were to be split up, police had to quell a near riot. Secondly, Mrs Huxley determined that there was "undoubtedly high feeling between the rural and urban populations in Scotland," which had resulted in "definite pressure being brought to bear on the evacuated to return to the towns." Or, in the words of Dunoon and Cowal WVS, rural householders "were glad to get rid of them." More explicitly, testimonies Mrs Huxley had received from the Scottish membership suggested that a number of unaccompanied evacuated children had been treated "with hardship" by the "country people." This, though, is not corroborated in official accounts. Likewise, she also cited reports of ill feeling among Catholic families sent to Protestant receiving areas, though she added that "broadly speaking, the Catholic families have not returned to the towns, as the priests have forbidden them to do so."[8]

Clearly there was a lack of communication, co-ordination and at times co-operation between sending and receiving areas which placed a considerable strain on WVS volunteers. Members required patience and diplomacy and, mindful of the sensitivities involved, Lady Ruth Balfour attempted to calm the deteriorating situation. In a letter to the WVS evacuation assistant for Denny, who had complained over the sanitary habits of incomers, the Scottish chairman admitted that the evacuation had led to problems "in a good many areas." She added, however, that she believed WVS could have a tremendous effect in making evacuation a success "in spite of all the difficulties," and in doing so "being the cause of a wonderful social reform." Lady Balfour added sensitively, "I know that some of the mothers and their children have been dirty, that some have been ungrateful, that others have not wished to take their share of work in a house, but I believe that the great generosity of the country hosts could be appealed to if it could be pointed out that these mothers often come from very bad homes where they have not had much of a chance." She also told the exasperated Denny organiser, "You may reply that all the mothers in your area have returned to Glasgow. Even if this is so, I feel it probable that they will come out once more if there are raids, so I want everyone to be prepared." Ruth Balfour's concerns were justified. Of the 3,400 schoolchildren evacuated from Clydebank in late 1939, all but 300 had returned by the time air raids killed around 500 of the town's inhabitants in March 1941 – many first-phase evacuees among them.[9]

What should not be lost to history is that thousands of evacuees settled well and secured warm relationships with their adoptive families. The report from Arrochar and Tarbet WVS was typical of that received from many centres. It said: "The evacuees are well and happy and in good homes." Neither should the contribution of WVS, parents, teachers and members of other voluntary organisations be overlooked in smoothing out the difficulties of the scheme. In total, 175,812 persons were safely evacuated in Scotland in September 1939 – 62,059 unaccompanied children, 97,575 mothers and accompanied children, together with teachers and helpers. Across Britain, WVS helped local authorities to evacuate 800,000 schoolchildren,

500,000 mothers and young children, 12,000 pregnant women, 7,000 disabled persons and over 100,000 teachers – a total of one and a half million people from major cities to rural safety in just three days. Altogether, 210,000 WVS members were engaged on evacuation work. As one internal WVS report pointed out, if the heavily criticised evacuation scheme had been effected under aerial bombardment, it would have been "hailed as a triumph of foresight."[10]

Indeed, myriad ways in which WVS supported evacuees are highlighted in monthly centre returns to Tothill Street – how one little boy in Fife put on a stone in six weeks thanks to a better diet; how the sick bay in Garelochhead was empty because the health of evacuees was so good; how Ayr and St Andrews centres developed a card index of all evacuees and made regular checks on their progress; how WVS social clubs in Selkirk, Galashiels, Kilmacolm, Bridge of Weir, Helensburgh and Moffat proved popular with mothers and became known as Penny Clubs because that was the going rate for tea and a bun; and how North Berwick clinic, which had previously dealt with impetigo and dirty hands, "now only heals cuts and bruises." Helensburgh centre staged a Hallow'een party, Kinross borrowed skates for the children during a cold spell, Gifford WVS provided free cinema films for evacuees, Bridge of Allan put on concerts for bored mothers and Glasgow ran communal singsongs to keep evacuated children amused. In December 1939 uproarious Christmas parties were held across Scotland and the WVS was asked, at short notice, to distribute 1,000 toys to child evacuees. Boys were piped to a Christmas service in St Andrews, every evacuee was presented with a book at Larkhall and in Penicuik the children sang carols. Thus, while recent historical overviews have concluded that Scotland's evacuation scheme was flawed, on the ground much hard work was carried out by women volunteers in attempting to meet the difficult challenge of reconciling sending and receiving areas and to make the scheme a success.

Being wise after the event or not, once evacuation had taken place appropriate clothing and footwear for evacuees for the harsh winter ahead became a priority across Scotland. WVS clothing depots were hastily improvised to hold garments collected by the Service, or made by elderly volunteers from wool donated by Scotland's knitting shops. In order to cope with the request for patterns from the 377 work parties established in Scotland by the end of 1939, mostly by WVS members, Scottish headquarters organised a postal pattern service. Fifteen sets of knitting instructions were issued, covering articles for evacuees, hospital supplies and troops. Fifteen other leaflets were issued for cut-out patterns.

On the eve of war Lord Woolton had broadcast a radio appeal for blankets, naming WVS as the agents who would deal with donations. Contributions were to be handed into the Post Office, whose vans would carry them to the depots set up by WVS. Many thousands of blankets were collected across the country in this way, with the first 5,000 sent out from Edinburgh clothing headquarters at City Chambers in the week following the Scottish evacuation. "Ladies knitted squares from scraps of wool and sewed them together; tailors gave up their pattern books at the request of the WVS; every possible warm covering was begged, borrowed, almost stolen, to meet the emergency." *The Scotsman* reported how one couple called with their car at 7 Coates Gardens to deliver a pair of blankets, but soon found their vehicle piled up with bedding "and themselves off to a reception area to deliver the same, almost before they realised it."[11] Lady Reading also broadcast to countries overseas about the urgent need for emergency clothing in Britain. By the end of 1939, members of the Imperial Order of the Daughters of the Empire in Canada had sent the first of many batches to WVS headquarters in London. Bundles reached Scotland in the early days of January 1940; dresses with little hankies placed carefully in their pockets, mittens in different colours, even zip-up lumber jackets in batches of 100 per bundle. Every centre was encouraged to write in thanks to its Canadian benefactor. The broadcast also led to the arrival of the first 'Bundles for Britain' clothing consignments from the American Red Cross, to be distributed by WVS as the sole agents for relief in Britain from their 5,000 chapters across the United States. Scottish head-quarters staff noted in a Region 11 report: "If only the donors could see the pleasure their presents gave they would be more than repaid for their kindness." It told how one old lady, who had received a new jumper after she had lost all her clothes, kept examining the label inside it, which read, 'The Gift of the American Red Cross'. "She felt it was a personal gift from America and insisted on diving down her back to fetch it up and show it to all visitors in her rest centre."[12]

Any complacency over the threat posed by the war to Scotland evaporated just two days into the conflict when the passenger liner *Athenia,* on route from the Clyde to Canada, was torpedoed and sunk by a German submarine. In considerable secrecy 50 survivors were landed on the quayside at Greenock by the Royal Navy and effectively left to themselves until someone realised that the local WVS organiser should be notified. Only then, "The women of Greenock rose to the occasion with a will, securing food and clothing for the survivors who were in an awful condition."[13] The sinking of the *Athenia* was the first test of local government emergency planning and it highlighted one of the problems WVS faced in the early months of the war; the tendency to overlap services with other well-meaning organisations. Where government instructed WVS to take a lead, for instance in the preparatory work for the September 1939 evacuation, co-ordination in many parts of the country ran smoothly. The first casualties at Greenock brought home not only the horrors of war, but the necessity to organise and train for unforeseen circumstances. The urgent need to review preparations was also demonstrated when German planes attacked naval shipping on the Forth estuary on 16 October 1939. The lack of proper preparation for air attack was highlighted in a Ministry of Home Security report: "No general warning was given and great indignation has been expressed by the populace which crowded into the streets to watch under the impression that a practice was in progress."[14]

Uncertainty often prevailed and in the early part of the war air raid alerts sometimes sounded impotently after raids had begun, or wailed half-heartedly, leaving people like Frieda Anderson of Edinburgh to recall, "The sirens went off and it was really comical. Everybody was running about knocking each other over because you didn't know what to do." Jim Lannan noted the attack on the Forth and how few believed that the war had reached the boundary of the capital. "I was quite excited and I said, 'I have just seen a

German aeroplane shot down.' 'Oh, rubbish. It would be a practice do,' everybody said, even my dad at five o'clock at teatime when he came in and I told him. Nobody would believe me." *The Press & Journal* in Aberdeen added, "The first stage of the raid was over before people began to understand that a raid was on at all." It was not as if Edinburgh was ill prepared in the practical sense. The city could boast over 19,000 trench shelters, 6,190 concrete shelters, 768 closes had been provided with blast walls and 13,538 Anderson domestic shelters had been delivered. Moreover, leaflets warning of the consequences of air raids had been pushed through every letterbox in Scotland. What was lacking was effective education and organisation and, as it became evident that people needed clarification, so WVS was increasingly called upon to disseminate advice and information.[15]

The 'Phoney War' continued as 1939 turned into 1940. The winter had come but the bombers had not and more and more evacuees returned home. During the lull, WVS had become an effective civilian reserve and it was invariably turned to by government to take on new commitments. Edinburgh HQ had 30 staff and the development of its work was described as "remarkable." By the end of 1939 it had recruited 12,000 women for various roles in the city. Tothill Street headquarters now boasted 300 experienced workers, around 50 of them in paid posts. It had street-level windows in WVS colours displaying leaflets and photographs of the membership's activities. By the end of 1939, its 12 regions comprised dozens of organisers and administrators and upwards of half a million members. The *Daily Sketch* was impressed: "Originally the aim was to enrol and conserve ARP resources, but its scope has so widened that at Tothill Street the departments include transport, evacuation (with nine sub sections on health, feeding, infant welfare, maternity care, transport, leisure, management of buildings, clothing and general information), technical (all matters connected with ARP training of auxiliary nurses) and all questions of staffing for hospitals." Stella Reading summed up the progress of the organisation in January 1940: "When I toured the country in 1938 I was asked what to do. Now I'm told what to do. That means that instead of 5,000 subordinate officers, I have 5,000 administrators."[16]

The Germans' advance into Scandinavia, the Low Countries and then France in the spring of 1940 prompted WVS work parties in Scotland to launch a remarkable flow of knitted 'comforts', initially for men fighting the war at sea. These included Balaclavas (helmets), gloves, scarves and special mittens for sailors. Prestonpans sent 400 comforts in one month, Gullane over 500, Ayr nearly 1,000, Kinross over 2,000 and Dundee an impressive 8,000. One Scottish headline enthused, "They Knit For Victory." But the simplicity of the statement did not capture the extraordinary effort of the women and the additional toll on their time in collecting, storing, packing and distributing the colossal mountains of clothing which the Home Front and the war overseas required. To help with the costs of materials, work parties staged a succession of fund-raising whist drives, flag days and concerts and sought donations from businesses and philanthropic individuals. One member noted how she was "shameless at bringing raffle books out to sell 3d tickets" and marvelled at the "woman of today" who "coaxes pennies where once she would have died rather than ask favours."[17] Blankets gathered coins for WVS thrown by spectators at New Year's Day football matches in Scotland in 1940. In Aberdeen a War Comforts Fair raised over £2,000, around £75,000 at today's values. WVS manned the pay booths in two-hourly shifts and took £300 in sixpences – 12,000 of them!

Neither were the needy closer to home neglected by WVS clothing specialists. In addition to thousands of bundles distributed to evacuees and sent to military units, parcels packed with blankets, quilts and pyjamas were delivered to civilian hospitals across Scotland. Cardigans were knitted and distributed to women in the Auxiliary Territorial Service. Bundles of warm woollies were sent to Wrens serving at hush-hush coastal installations. Meanwhile, the WVS Hospital Supply Section redoubled efforts to produce dressings and lint, theatre gowns and towels. Its work parties in Scotland had received a boost in 1939 when women members of the League of Remembrance, all specialists in making bandages and dressings, became affiliated to WVS. By 1940, the Hospital Supply Section had opened sub-centres in Edinburgh, Colinton and Musselburgh.

Material received at the section's headquarters at Rothesay Terrace in Edinburgh, where over 50 women in white caps and overalls worked, was distributed to these centres, from where the finished dressings, gowns and aprons were returned. The day after the first air raid on the Forth estuary 200 yards of gauze were cut and folded ready for use in two hours after an SOS from a first aid post. When the Northern Isles came under attack Sutherland WVS made 12,500 swabs in three months. The normal output of dressings supplied by the section averaged 3,500 a day, which included one order from Scottish hospitals for 500 surgeons' caps, 600 theatre gowns and 3,000 towels, and another for 900 nurses' dresses when manufacturers could not cope. And as political tensions mounted, a great number of women enrolled in WVS to become hospital drivers. Some helped with the emergency movement of patients to and from hospitals, still more collected and delivered blankets, sheeting, even beds. They took doctors and nurses to their patients, transported urgently-needed blood supplies, and ran a hundred and one errands on government service. In nearly every case they provided their own petrol. Stella Jackson, a young ambulance driver, with four empty stretchers in the back of her modified vehicle, admitted being "scared to death" as she set out to a bombed area in the black-out, but she never for one moment regretted volunteering.[18]

In spite of the tremendous volume of WVS activities, the organisation's original purpose of helping ARP services was never overlooked or abandoned. During the spring, enemy offensive shelters in vulnerable areas were readied for those who might be temporarily rendered homeless. Under ARP direction, community houses stocked against an emergency were established in Edinburgh, Dundee, Dunoon, Kilbarchan, Kirkcaldy and in Midlothian. Kinross WVS designed a package of support for scattered anti-aircraft and searchlight units in the Ochil Hills. Their six-point plan consisted of the distribution of books, papers and games; the washing and darning of socks and repairing of uniforms; the distribution of cigarettes and food; hospitality in members' homes; the offer of baths and the supply of comforts. Melrose supplied 90 volunteers for ARP telephone duty at Loanhead. WVS in Dunoon formed a committee to help ARP to keep up the morale of the community. Wishaw set up an office for the registration of cats and dogs under a national ARP scheme for animals. And across Scotland members helped ARP with the sterilisation of gas masks. This involved taking them to pieces and reassembling them, intricate work which had to be carried out every month or so.

The government knew that only WVS extended street by street, house by house across Britain, and when the call went out for bones, empty bottles, waste paper and scrap metals to be collected for the war effort, "Who better to organise the salvage drive than the WVS?" Everyone was encouraged to economise – to save money and materials that could be used for the war effort. WVS members pushed prams and barrows around villages making door-to-door collections of paper, cardboard, rags, rope, string, bones, bottles and tins. Scottish farmyards gave up tons of scrap metal. People cut off garden railings. A co-operative venture in Edinburgh involving the city's cleansing department and Edinburgh WVS created an exhibition lorry to display the scrap materials wanted and the uses to which they could be put. This toured the city, and when WVS speakers addressed salvage meetings, the van was positioned outside each location. At a cleansing department exhibition at *The Scotsman* buildings in North Bridge, Mary, Princess Royal, the daughter of King George V, was said to be astonished by an Anderson shelter which had been constructed from re-melted tins.

Another major responsibility handed to WVS further expanded its role to include welfare for men on active service. This involved the launch of mobile canteens to feed soldiers on exercise or in transition – or to be rushed to areas where emergency feeding was required. WVS received the first improvised mobile canteens in the autumn of 1939. These were initially snack-bar trailers towed behind private cars. More manoeuvrable mobile canteens built on to the chassis of lorries or vans were gradually introduced. These were designed to serve light meals with two or three WVS members doing the driving and catering. In the months afterwards, mobile canteens became symbols of WVS emergency work, providing lunches to essential dockyard workers on the Clyde, feeding troops on the move in remote northern parts of Scotland – even distributing cosmetics for detachments of Wrens, WAAF and ATS. By January 1940 over 30 canteens and communal kitchens had been established across Scotland, including static units at Perth, Stirling, Dingwall and Inverness railway stations. Some catered for evacuees only, others for troops, and one, at Aberfeldy, for evacuees by day and troops at night. Helensburgh WVS imaginatively established a self-service canteen, where a kettle, tea, coffee and soup cubes were provided and users put coins in an honesty box according to the printed tariff displayed. At this time, the usual charge made for a midday meal was 3d.

WVS canteens were not only ready to meet any emergency – staff became adept at peeling potatoes while wearing gas masks – they proved popular and were well supported by the communities in which they worked. Teviothead, for example, reported that Borders farmers gave them presents of potatoes and rabbits. Dunfermline landward WVS were gifted linoleum for their canteens and Torryburn promised first-aid assistance by local miners. When a unit of English servicemen arrived in Helensburgh late one night and were served with supper and an early breakfast by a WVS canteen, a note was afterwards found reading: "To the villagers of Helensburgh . . . words cannot express our immense gratitude for the way in which we were greeted and made to feel at home. We also wish to thank the members of the WVS who very kindly stayed at their posts to help us after a trying day." The note was signed 'From the New Arrivals' and it was placed beside the men's sugar and tea rations, gifted in appreciation. When the time came for a regiment stationed in Arbroath to leave the area, the men went out of their way to march past the town's canteen. As WVS helpers came to the windows to watch, the CO gave the order "Eyes Left" as a mark of acknowledgement for the hospitality provided. It is not known if staff curtsied in reply!

As with evacuation and knitting work parties, the operation of canteens demonstrated friendly co-operation between WVS and its sister women's organisations in Scotland – a feature not always evident in activity south of the border. A Region 11 report to Tothill

Street in February 1940 must have been read by envious eyes. In Scotland, they learned, there was "happy co-operation between the WVS, YMCA, Church of Scotland, and other groups, in the running of canteens." Another report praised the work of the bodies on the WVS-led Scottish Advisory Council and stated: "In all cases there appears to be great friendliness existing between them, and all give each other mutual assistance." One WVS centre communicated that local organisations had agreed to carry out any wartime task asked of them. Another described various organisations as working together like one "happy family." Yet another reported that the women's groups were "intertwined." In Angus, Mabell, Countess of Airlie quickly aligned the Angus branch of the Red Cross to WVS activity, and the two organisations worked hand in hand throughout the war. She recalled: "We were gratified by many members of the WVS also becoming members of the Red Cross. The County of Angus speedily became a busy hive of industry."[19] It was possible for women to work unselfishly and harmoniously together, but it was a Scottish phenomenon that frequently did not extend to English branches, where stories emerged of the Women's Institutes, in particular, resenting WVS's semi-official status and its access to Home Office funding and patronage.

The Phoney War ended for Scotland in March 1940 when the Luftwaffe attacked the naval base at the deep water harbour at Scapa Flow in Orkney, scattering bombs across the main island and causing the earliest civilian casualties of the Second World War. The first WVS centre to "engage" the enemy was thus Orkney where, following the raid, centre leader Mary Work confirmed modestly in her monthly return to Tothill Street that "owing to air raids and sea battles Orkney has become very active, with casualties in hospitals." Mrs Work reported that she was co-ordinating the island's civil defence from Kirkwall and that 25 householders had volunteered to look after convalescents sent from Balfour Hospital, while other members had started to co-ordinate blood donors. Additionally, Orkney members had secured accommodation for an RAF sick bay, which they had cleaned out, scrubbed and painted ready for use in three days. A list of names was also made up of houses where members of the Services could obtain hot baths. But time and time again WVS activities on the island had been "interrupted by the shrieking of sirens."

Mary Work scarcely mentioned that her own home, Craigiefield at St Ola, was damaged in the attack while she was inside with her husband tending to a wounded soldier. Fourteen bomb craters were found close to the house and 20 incendiary devices exploded in the garden and adjacent field. Her windows were broken and fires had started around the house. Even with this terrifying cacophony around her, and the telephone down, Mrs Work nursed the badly wounded man. In her report to London she noted modestly, "The experience of that evening is unforgettable, but I was so busy attending to a casualty and to people who came into the house for shelter that I did not have time to realise the extent of the damage . . . I shall miss my greenhouse which was a joy in this northern climate, but let us hope that the war will soon be over, and that we shall be able to cultivate in peace once more." In a timely reminder to the membership of the demoralising effect of bombardment, she added, "Sometimes we feel as if we cannot stand the strain any longer and would go away and leave our homes to the wind and rain." She also told her sister Ida a few days after the raid that she could no longer sleep at night: "I was so strained I couldn't shut my eyes, couldn't bear to put out the light." Mrs Work received the MBE for her selfless service under enemy fire.[20]

In the light of the Orkney bombing and the likelihood of a wider offensive against Scotland, the Scottish Office instructed a second phase of evacuations from potential target areas in the Central Belt, including this time vulnerable residents in Greenock, Port Glasgow and Dumbarton. It soon became clear, however, that the authorities had miscalculated the mood of Scottish mothers. Mindful of the social horrors of the initial exodus, parents simply refused to register – an internal WVS assessment stating that "about 70% of the parents appear to be against the scheme." The Sunday Post carried a headline proclaiming "Glasgow Mothers Say No" and revealed that a survey of 60 Glasgow parents showed a 60–0 score against the new evacuation. Family separation was the principal cause of refusal given according to the paper. It concluded: "The idea of forcing children on unwilling householders is repugnant to parents." Ominously, it also quoted an official saying, "The first bomb to drop in a British town will make them change their minds."[21]

WVS felt it necessary and wise to press ahead with evacuation arrangements whether the uptake would be met or not. Dundee, for example, enrolled 60 extra women to help with the scheme, and Edinburgh nearly 100. New meeting places and transit routes were surveyed, children registered were medically examined, gas mask drills regularly carried out and teachers and parents better informed. And with the strong objections of householders in reception areas in mind, WVS-staffed hostels were established across swathes of the Lothians, Fife, Perthshire and Inverness-shire to provide parents and hosts with reassurance. Members redoubled efforts to try to make the second evacuation a success. Galashiels WVS assisted with a new Borders survey of priority cases. Helensburgh provided a communal kitchen able to cater for 1,000 people. Lochwinnoch prepared a "panic" evacuation scheme. Balfron members offered cars. Dunkeld made ready three hostels for the reception of 85 children. There was a spirited response to an appeal in Perth for equipment. Practically-minded Dunfermline WVS issued pamphlets on bed-wetting. The activities were thus varied, but considered prudent by the women involved.

After the collapse of the Allied Armies in Europe in May 1940 the membership at large stood ready to respond. Enrolments had climbed to 700,000 across Britain, and many others had been passed on to sister services. Nearly 200,000 volunteers were carrying out ARP work, 12,000 distributed across 700 static and mobile canteens, 40,000 in transport, 65,000 in nursing auxiliary work, 150,000 dealing with the government's evacuation scheme and 100,000 helping hospitals. Scotland's contribution by then embraced 70,000 volunteers spread over 200 city, town and village centres.[22]

Local committees prepared for the defence of their district and spoke of resistance in the event of invasion. Wailing sirens and fire-fighting procedures became reality. A new leaflet distributed by WVS called for more women to volunteer for air raid work, first aid posts, decontamination centres, hospital supply, communication work and as emergency drivers. Demonstrations of respirators took place and teams of WVS were trained in first aid for gas casualties and in assisting mothers to fit the baby protective helmet. More barrage balloons appeared in the sky and aeroplane trapping poles on the ground. The ringing of church bells was to be the warning that parachutists were landing and people everywhere were urged to report suspicious movements. Everyone had a role to play in protecting the country from the feared arrival of German troops and a civilian war. WVS member Clemency Greatorex recalled, "It was a panicky time . . . we fully expected to be invaded . . . all the time. Whatever was happening, we were nervous about invasion."[23]

With the country at high alert, War Minister Anthony Eden established the Local Defence Volunteers, later to be re-named the Home Guard, to keep watch on coasts, roads, railways and public buildings. Scotland was divided into LDV zones and regional administrators appointed to run each one. A quarter of a million men joined the Home Guard within a week, but women were not included in the appeals and WVS members were told that under no circumstances were they to carry arms or take part in fighting. Still, a WVS centre organiser in rural Yorkshire was able to capture one of the first German parachutists. Eveline Cardwell was at home when she saw an airman baling out over farmland. She emerged with a pitchfork and challenged the German, who had sprained his ankle on landing and was not able to resist. After disarming him, Mrs Cardwell's first words passed into WRVS folklore: "Remember now, you are my prisoner. In the meantime I'm going to make you a cup of tea." King George awarded her the MBE for her "coolness and gallantry" – but made no comment on her arresting hospitality!

On 31 May 1940, at the height of the evacuation of 337,000 men from Dunkirk, Lady Reading sent a letter to every county and town organiser in which she wrote: "There is no need for me to tell you how serious things are, nor that you will be called upon to undertake many and difficult tasks during the coming weeks and months. It may well be that on the measure of calm shown in your district, on the strength of the background to life you can provide – might provide the local resistance to attack, the local domination of the situation."[24] The story of how the Army, surrounded and under fire, was snatched from disaster by every available small boat at Dunkirk is part of Britain's history, but the drama did not end with the heroic rescue. It was only then the work of WVS began. Mobile canteens rushed down to the receiving ports, one feeding 15,000 exhausted men in a week. Across the south of England WVS members fed and watered troop trains sometimes at the rate of six an hour. Regions quickly despatched parcels of clothing and food to besieged coastal centres. A handful of Scottish volunteers upped and travelled south to take part in the dramatic scenes unfolding at Channel ports. In Scotland, WVS volunteers staffed canteens on station platforms at Perth, Stirling and Inverness to meet troops evacuated to bases in northern areas. Up to 500 soldiers arrived on each train and it took half an hour to feed them. "Buns were buttered and cakes prepared at the house of one member, placed in washing baskets and conveyed to the waiting train amid cheers." At Aberlady station an elderly woman who had lost her son in the previous war did the washing up for hours on end. On a lighter note, while intrepid stories of Dunkirk were being told at one WVS gathering, the small daughter of the householder muddled her medals and innocently asked, "Mummy, don't you think they deserve the WVS?"[25]

At this time Edinburgh WVS pioneered an information service which would prove indispensable to visiting and displaced servicemen and refugees who knew little English and who, often, had lost everything except their courage. The story of the Allied Information Bureau began with a train journey in which a convalescent Polish soldier, a member of the French mountain infantry and a British sergeant were sharing a carriage to Edinburgh after the Dunkirk evacuation. The men were to spend the day in Edinburgh, knowing no one and unable to speak to each other. On hearing this tale, a group of linguists approached WVS to offer their services. Among friends they found people speaking French, Russian, Polish, Norwegian, Dutch and Czech who were then enrolled in WVS. What was initially called a foreign bureau was opened at 45 Princes Street with funds raised privately. By July 1940, posters in five languages advertising the re-named Allied Information Bureau were placed in trams and buses, while in readiness its staff's "pencils were sharpened and our equipment of Woolworth's notebooks put in place." The nervous interpreters did not have to wait long for their first clients. "Two Polish soldiers came in with an untidy brown paper parcel. This was undone and a garment shaken out before us, as they said in a chorus, 'la chemise du colonel, must be beautiful wash'."[26]

After Dunkirk, Edinburgh's streets were thronged with thousands of foreign soldiers and the busy bureau provided information on trains, trams and buses, arranged visits to doctors and dentists, took men shopping, arranged a Norwegian wedding and even corrected an inscription for a tombstone in Polish. Interpreters gave lessons, translated letters, offered advice on hotels, lodgings and canteens and took visiting troops sightseeing. One letter from a group of 50 Czech soldiers read: "Dear Madam, we beg beseech one pretty command lady to show us the castles and palaces of Edinburgh."[27]

Edinburgh's Allied Information Bureau was unique and set the pattern for others around WVS regions. During the war it dealt with inquiries in 33 languages and could call on interpreters in 22 tongues. Perhaps its greatest challenge came when it was asked to procure vestments for a Polish priest, refreshments and musical instruments for a gathering of Polish soldiers after the celebration of Orthodox Easter Midnight Mass. A church hall adjoining St Mary's Cathedral was loaned to WVS and all the equipment painstakingly collected, including instruments from the Edinburgh Police Band. A Russian-born WVS member knew what an Easter pudding ought to be, but the ingredients were not easy to find in wartime. However, a private donor sent the curds and the Polish NAAFI helped with sugar and raisins. A Polish unit had saved 50 eggs from their rations, and WVS dyed these in brilliant colours. As the men came out of the dark cathedral into the light, there were spontaneous cries of joy and the outpouring of traditional folk songs. Afterwards, the WVS women were solemnly promised that Poland would do everything possible to prevent any invasion of Edinburgh by German forces![28]

Another 'first' for the Scottish capital also came about through the post-Dunkirk demand to provide immediate information to transient troops. This was the Station Guide scheme, which began in Edinburgh's Waverley Station and extended to four stations in Glasgow, where it grew into a major WVS commitment. The Station Guides took up duties on platforms day and night to answer questions about times of trains, fares, where to sleep, local amusements and long-lost relatives. In particular they met incoming trains and gave information to first-time visitors, including workers moving to war work in Scotland's industrial cities. In the first three months of its operation in Glasgow over 6,000 people were helped by the guides of the 'midnight service' at Central Station, which operated from 11 at night until two in the morning. The chief station guide, a Mrs R. A. Young, described how she cared for an RAF wireless operator who was recovering from breaking his back. "We ordered a taxi-cab to convey him in the morning to St Enoch Station. After we had helped him into the cab, I produced cash to pay the fare in advance to the taxi driver. I felt a thrill of pride when the driver flatly refused to accept the money. 'Surely,' was his explanation, 'after what he has come through for us, I can do that much for him.'"[29]

July 1940 brought the Battle of Britain. Here at last was the emergency for which WVS was originally formed, and Ruth Balfour wrote to every centre in Scotland asking members to stand resolutely together as aerial preliminaries to the expected invasion of Britain began. Day after day the Luftwaffe took off to attempt to destroy the Royal Air Force and its airfields. Day after day, and often four or five times a day, the RAF scrambled pilots to engage them. The dramatic events in the sky were matched by the heroism of WVS volunteers as they responded to calls to attend to bailed-out airmen, to those landed at ports, at shot-up airfields and at damaged anti-aircraft positions. Charles Graves recalled, "One canteen was passing an aerodrome when the attack on it began, and for half an hour the WVS canteen crew lay under their vehicle until the bombing was over. Then they emerged, dusty but undaunted, to serve hot drinks and snacks."[30]

With the country's future hanging in the balance, the government's introduction of compulsory collection of waste in the summer of 1940 galvanised the entire membership once again. WVS in Scotland assisted the renewed drive for salvage in three ways – by impressing on the public the importance of salvage, by instructing on the best way to save scraps, and by conducting propaganda campaigns, particularly through doorstep pamphleting. Every WVS centre in Scotland was involved along with other organisations and council cleansing departments. In Balfron the WVS had the assistance of the Boys' Brigade to collect waste paper. In Cowal the Guides and Scouts helped WVS women to gather rags. In Dundee a WVS appeal for 1,000 women to co-ordinate salvage collection reached its target in just three weeks. Elsewhere – locations in reports were often censored – visits to individual householders were carried out, supported by notes on salvage sent by Headquarters. Everywhere, WVS encouraged people to accept the food shortages, to 'dig for victory' by planting vegetables and to save for the nation.

A new priority was the collection of aluminium. Stella Reading was told by the Air Minister Lord Beaverbrook that WVS "would be doing a national service if they could collect every kind of aluminium pot and pan in the country" as they contained one of the main components of Spitfires. Receiving depots were quickly set up across Scotland and as pavements became blocked with ever-growing dumps Ruth Balfour noted proudly, "A tidal wave of pots, pans, hot water bottles and kettles has swept across the country."[31] As the hunt for aluminium continued, Mea Allan wrote a poignant account of what happened to her frying pan when she responded to Beaverbrook's appeal and took it to Tothill Street . . .

"When I got to the WVS headquarters the place was already besieged by people dumping equally beloved frying pans and kettles and shoe-trees, meat covers, trays and teapots. The lorry came and hundreds of kettles, cake moulds, vacuum cleaners, coat hangers, pots and pans, coffee percolators and hot water bottles were shovelled up into it. The following day my frying pan went for another ride in another army lorry. It went to a London railway terminus and was there unloaded. That night a queer train slid out of the station. It was the first aluminium train, consisting of eight trucks full of pots and pans. My frying pan was bound for a place, which must be nameless, there to be turned into an ingot . . . it was at this stage that I said goodbye to my frying pan as a frying pan and began to think of it in terms of a Spitfire."[32]

Scotland, as always, responded wholeheartedly to the appeal. WVS, Girl Guides, Boys' Brigade and other volunteers formed heaps of precious aluminium before carting it away to depots, often in requisitioned prams and barrows. The false legs of war veterans and pieces of an airship brought down in the Great War were among donations. By the end of September Scotland's contribution was 150 tons, sufficient material, said Scottish headquarters, to make twelve squadrons of "Flying Kettles." Meanwhile, WVS started a Fighter Aircraft Fund, and within a year three Spitfires had been paid for and were in commission, a report adding: "WVS has fitted out their pilots with a complete set of knitted comforts."[33]

Elsewhere, the troubled summer of 1940 brought an expansion of the WVS Hospital Supply Section at the behest of the Department of Health. In most cases the hospital involved requested assistance with supplies and provided materials, and WVS work parties carried out the necessary labour. For the month of July 1940 Motherwell WVS reported making 600 pillow slips for its local medical officer, the women of Meigle in Perthshire cut out and made up 238 laundry bags for the evacuation camp at Belmont Castle, patients' clothes were mended in Selkirk and Stornoway women were loaned Harris tweed machines for making scarves and socks. Dundee work parties supplied an astonishing 24,000 articles to hospitals that month, while women at Bridge of Allan collected sphagnum moss for Stirling's war wounded. Other contributions included the party of volunteers from Selkirkshire who scrubbed the floors of Peel Hospital every week, and the women of Wishaw WVS who recruited 19 men to act as emergency stretcher-bearers after knocking on doors and badgering occupants to become involved.

As more towns had their first experience of tip-and-run air attacks, both Lady Reading and Lady Balfour redoubled efforts to remind the membership of its core duty of air raid defence work. Remarkably, the more bombs fell, the more women wanted to become involved. Following the attack on Scapa Flow and the start of the Battle of Britain, recruitment levels across Scotland rose sharply. July 1940 saw 223 women enrol for ARP duties in Ayr and another 204 apply in Dumbarton. Kirkcaldy reported that the emergency had "brought hitherto timid women out to learn about ARP." Wishaw attracted 100 women to its weekly lectures while 500 turned up in Hawick for a fire-fighting talk that month. Indeed, recruitment generally went well in 1940, with the total membership of WVS in Scotland exceeding 80,000 for the first time. Two impressive examples – Dunfermline burgh centre had 732 members and nearby Kinross 500 volunteers.

Another dramatic turn in the conflict came in June 1940 when secret arrangements were made to arrest enemy aliens. Covert Home Office instructions had told WVS centre leaders that they might be asked to help police in a confidential matter, details of which could only be given when the request was made. At the same time WVS headquarters in London sent to Chief Constables throughout the country letters of authorisation which were to be handed by them to local WVS organisers when their help was needed. When Italy entered the war, thousands of nationals among Scotland's large Italian community were rounded up. Many were taken from their beds, their homes searched, and cameras and other potentially suspicious belongings removed. It was a measure partly aimed at their security. Benito Mussolini's declaration of war had sparked waves of anti-Italian suspicion, and angry mobs had attacked Italian-owned shops and restaurants. The responsibility for the arrest of aliens lay with the police but to meet the unusual situation, the Department of Health for Scotland allowed WVS rest centres to be used as assembly points for the families of internees, most of whom initially were male. WVS centre staff were entrusted with helping wives and children of Italians who had been left to fend for themselves and whose movements were restricted. Later in the process, WVS volunteers accompanied police officers making the arrests of female aliens and, in some cases, they provided escorts on trains to internment camps.

As 1940 progressed, the numbers of outgoing aliens was offset by the arrival in Scotland of refugees from the Channel Islands, after Winston Churchill had deemed them indefensible. Next came a small number of the 12,000 civilians evacuated from Gibraltar, when it was feared Hitler would launch an attack on the colony. Short-term rooms had to be found for them, help with their food, schools for their children and books and toys provided. Clothing was always required and in August 1940 a donation of £100,000 from the American Red Cross allowed WVS to purchase a quarter of a million sweaters, 100,000 pairs of trousers, 60,000 overcoats, 60,000 dresses and 50,000 pairs of boots for children. The WVS network responded by arranging and distributing the clothing across the country in vast bundles. In the last quarter of 1940 alone, the London clothing depot in Eaton Square sent out over 25,000 garments weekly to bombed areas and regions where refugees had been billeted.

Luftwaffe attacks on London in the closing months of 1940 tested Women's Voluntary Services to the full. Over the weekend of 7-8 September over 1,000 people lost their lives. WVS worked on, though many centres were badly damaged. One clothing depot was hit by bombs twice in eight hours, but its staff "went on issuing just the same in a rubble of plaster and broken glass." Several volunteers were killed at their posts, however, as London suffered raids on 82 out of 87 consecutive nights and the word 'Blitz' passed into our language.[34]

It is difficult to imagine the terror of aerial bombardment. Nella Last's diary for the Mass Observation study, a series of 500 personal diaries collated as a national writing project from 1937, complains indignantly of no given warnings at the start of bombing raids in 1940, to resignation towards the end of the war when life almost went on normally as bombs fell. As the Blitz took its terrible toll she speaks of jumping "at the least bump or slam of a door," of how, at times, she felt "useless" and that her efforts were "feeble." She is often too tired to sleep and constantly thinks of WVS mothers whose boys have gone off to fight – those "sad, withdrawn faces." One of the volunteers commits suicide, another speaks of keeping a razor-blade in her bag in case of invasion and she fell into German hands. Despite the inner fears, the permanent anxiety, the dread of the nights before a full moon when the bombers would reappear, the WVS centre gives Nella inner strength and the hours spent there offer release from the suffocating confines of domesticity. "I thank God that I work at the Centre and keep back bogeys waiting to pounce on mothers." Amid flying ambulances and the scream of sirens, we capture a glimpse of what women of the WVS endured, their disturbed nights, the frights and fears and their stoic resistance. "I am not alone," Nella writes, "Just one in a group of mothers strained and anxious." And when her own house is bombed and she is "about to die" she records laconically: "I'll never forget my odd sensations, one a calm acceptance of 'the end', the other a feeling of regret that I'd not opened a tin of fruit salad for tea – and now it was too late."[35]

Determined now to help the British war effort, and contrary to its country's continued neutrality, the American Red Cross next provided a dozen mobile canteen units, each consisting of eight snack bar trailers, two large trailers, one small tea van and one large van. Initially they were in demand in central London, which continued to endure enemy attacks from the air as 1940 closed. Five mobile canteens were stationed near WVS headquarters and rushed to any hard-hit borough. This unit fed 120,727 civil defence personnel and householders in three months. In response to the raids on London a further contribution from the American Red Cross of £78,000 helped to equip 100 nurseries for younger children from bombed areas.

The Luftwaffe bared its teeth further north. The first bombs to drop on western Scotland had hit Mull on 11 July 1940. On 13 July raiders bombed the Clyde Valley, and the first raid in Glasgow took place on 19 July. This was followed by a more serious attack on 18 September in which HMS Sussex, berthed at Yorkshill, was badly damaged with the loss of 16 sailors. The danger of her magazine exploding led to the evacuation of adjacent housing and the mobilisation of Glasgow WVS. Pondering the lessons of London, some 400 people were taken to Govan Town Hall and a further 300 to another hall in Langlands Road. Volunteer teams provided clothing and hot drinks, while sweet drinking-chocolate sent by the American Red Cross was distributed and eagerly accepted. Further raids in Glasgow and Greenock in October 1940 cajoled the Scottish population out of any remaining complacency and led to WVS rest centres being established to comfort the bombed-out from the after-effects of their shattering experience. To casualties who had lost almost everything the mugs of tea and words of comfort provided by the women of WVS must have seemed a godsend.

It was during the aerial attacks of 1940 that the Housewives' Service of WVS came into its own as a street organisation. Its duty was to assist ARP wardens before, during and after raids. Members kept records of the numbers of people living in each house in their street or area, or temporary absences, or the arrival and departure of visitors. They learned by rote the position of shelters, ladders and stirrup pumps that might be of use in fire-fighting or locating casualties. With this knowledge they often saved rescue squads from digging unnecessarily for absent householders. Participating housewives were trained by WVS in providing hot water bottles, blankets and drinks for the treatment of shock. They undertook to provide shelter for passers-by during air raids, and to help mothers with young children. Many showed quiet initiative and common sense under the hail of incendiary bombs. Mary Work's experience after bombs fell on Orkney was typical. The Kirkwall centre organiser described how two men brought a badly injured soldier to her house. As the attack continued there was . . . "another knock at the door . . . two more people, an airman and his girl, who had been sheltering under the dyke." Moments later "two other men" came in seeking refuge. After the worst raids in London in late 1940, members of the Housewives' Service went from house to house, sweeping up glass and debris and helping householders to salvage property with tender cheerfulness. One WVS volunteer recalled, "The first thing that the housewives had to learn was 'immediate aid.' Not first aid, mark you, not as far advanced as that, but immediate aid." Many members of the Housewives' Service were themselves casualties, one of them found dead still holding a suitcase containing the properly arranged items of rescue advised by WVS – candles, matches, tin openers, hot-water bottles wrapped in towels and feeding bottles. But for every sad outcome there were many acts of heroism – one London housewife served 1,200 civilians from her tiny kitchen "after one grim night of bombs."[36]

The role of WVS women on the Home Front is often missing from wartime histories, their day-by-day bravery excluded from gender-prejudiced accounts of the Blitz – the comfort and compassion, the making, the providing, the scrimping and saving, the salvage sacrifices, the years of being sick with worry and conjecture. Seldom does history record that their contribution to Britain's war effort was in addition to running homes without menfolk, losing their children to evacuation, losing their houses in enemy action, or queuing for hours every day for food. Left unstated is that such roles were carried out unselfishly and, all the time, working on with "aching hearts" awaiting news of their husbands and sons, hoping that someone somewhere was looking after them, too.

By the end of 1940 Women's Voluntary Services for Civil Defence was already 800,000 strong – considerably more than the Wrens, ATS, WAAF and Women's Land Army put together. It was filled with the belief that if people could be organised, trained and provided with protection then they would not panic. Its efforts had helped Britain endure and survive the evacuation, Dunkirk, the Battle of Britain and a massive influx of refugees. And as 1940 ended, it was not only the awards of DBE to Lady Reading and CBE to Lady Balfour which made WVS members proud, but five George Medals and a clutch of British Empire Medals had been awarded to volunteers for outstanding bravery under enemy fire – a typical BEM going to a member who went "from house to house cheering people who were trapped, crawling through an aperture too small to admit a man and rescuing a baby and three other people."[37] But all were richly deserved, for no job was too difficult or too dangerous, too small or too dirty for the Women in Green.

If it had to be done, it was done.

3

SCOTLAND'S 'BLITZ' – ORDER FROM CHAOS

War left a terrible mark on Scotland in the spring of 1941.

Just before 10 p.m. on Thursday, 13 March, the Luftwaffe began a devastating attack on Clydebank. For the next nine hours, wave after wave of German bombers pounded the town. The inferno that began with dazzling incendiaries engulfed entire streets, schools, churches, factories and dockyards. The high explosive bombs and parachute mines which afterwards fell on the burning town rained down death and destruction. Whole families were wiped out, entire streets set alight. Eighty died in Second Avenue when a row of terraced houses was struck. Ten members of one family died at No 76. In a house in Jellicoe Street, 15 members of a family perished. In the worst incident a parachute mine landed between a tramcar and tenements in Nelson Street. Over 100 people lost their lives.[1]

On the morning of Friday, 14 March, Clydebank's dazed citizens emerged from their shelters into almost unrecognisable smashed and smouldering streets. A town of 50,000 people, swelled to 60,000 by an influx of war workers, had been reduced to rubble. Only seven houses out of a total stock of 12,000 remained undamaged. "All along the Dumbarton Road files of shocked and bewildered survivors shambled their way to safety. Their faces were caked with plaster dust and soot and many were still in their night-clothes."[2] Clydebank was still burning when German bombers returned the next evening to carry out a near seven-hour raid on the smoking ruin of the town. When the drone of the last plane had faded over 500 lay dead, all but 50 from that terrifying first night of bombing. Hundreds more were grievously wounded by exploding bombs, fires, falling masonry and shards of broken glass. Many others were killed and injured in Glasgow, seven miles upriver. The human toll was unparalleled in Scotland.

The Clydebank Blitz, as it became known, resulted in dreadful physical damage, too; 4,000 houses were completely destroyed, 4,500 were severely damaged and rendered uninhabitable and 3,500 suffered some damage. Some 35,000 people were left homeless. Many of the town's schools, churches, public buildings, retail and industrial properties were destroyed. Among major employers hit were John Brown's shipyard in Rothesay Dock, the Singer factory, which had converted to war work, the Royal Ordnance factory at Dalmuir and the Admiralty oil tanks at Dalnottar. A government report conveyed the horror of the aftermath: "It is difficult to find any house that is undamaged; some of the housing estates are completely wiped out . . . the numbers made homeless greater than that in Coventry."[3]

Rescue work began as soon as the first incendiary flares had landed. Workers toiled until they dropped and the medals for heroic actions awarded later are testament to determined attempts to save lives. Such was the intensity of the raid, however, that local emergency services were overwhelmed. Rescuers toiled against hopeless odds. Within an hour, gas, water, electricity and telephones were cut off. Huge craters and collapsing buildings disrupted road communications and the ability of the emergency services to reach burning buildings. Amid scenes of appalling horror, bombs fell indiscriminately on first aid and fire stations.

Remarkably, the WVS response is almost invisible in the written record of events at Clydebank on 14–15 March 1941. The Scottish historian Andrew Jeffrey claimed that the volunteer response simply "disintegrated." Rest centres, he reported, "collapsed completely" and they were invariably described in official reports, he said, as "very shaky" and "a most serious problem." Clydebank historian Iain MacPhail concluded that at the height of the bombing, "The pace of the control centre had dropped to almost nothing" and that emergency staff were left with "a feeling of helplessness." Such remarks are supported in a report by a government information team which arrived on the morning after the first raid: "The local machine had broken down . . . there was no administration centre and there was little or no staff for the rest centres." The dreary picture painted by such statements contrasts with Lady Reading's account of housewives during the earlier London Blitz: "Again and again, women who had lost their homes reported to the Incident Inquiry Points because they had undertaken to do so and were not deflected from the duty they had to undertake or their own hardship." Thus it appears that the shocking intensity of the attack on Clydebank had a dramatic impact on the local WVS response.[4]

Secondly, many children registered for evacuation had remained at their homes in Clydebank. At the height of the bombing 7,000 schoolchildren were still in the town; all but 300 of those evacuated in September 1939 had returned. Sadly, many of these vulnerable children became casualties during the bombardment. Had WVS failed them?

Thirdly, WVS was criticised over post-raid arrangements to accommodate bombed-out victims. Some 35,000 Clydesiders left their homes after the raids, by shuttle bus, cars, bicycles or by foot on the so-called 'trek to the hills' practised during air raid exercises. But the WVS rest centre at Vale of Leven, to which the majority of evacuees were taken or travelled to independently, was reportedly over-run and chaotic. More than 10 times the number of people it could accommodate attempted to find sanctuary there. Hundreds were turned away. Conditions inside were so bad that mutiny was feared.

WVS in Scotland was damaged by this apparent impotency and invisibility during the Clydebank raids and the subsequent abandonment of order at its rest centres. The evacuation scheme, meant to protect the town's children, had also failed. So what went wrong?

The first bombs on Clydebank fell shortly after 10 o'clock on the Thursday evening. By 4.30 a.m., just six hours later, Ruth Balfour was meeting the ARP Regional Commissioner for Scotland, Lord Rosebery, in Edinburgh. By 7.30 a.m. Lady Balfour was in Glasgow; within an hour of that, she was in Clydebank witnessing the extent of the devastation for herself and being served breakfast by a WVS canteen that had worked through the night. By that Friday morning 40 members from Glasgow and Giffnock WVS had entered the town. Others quickly arrived from centres such as Airdrie and Paisley. Catherine Scott, who was instrumental in forming WVS in Airdrie in 1940, recalled Airdrie WVS "swinging into action" immediately news of the bombings reached them. Kathleen Hanton Coffey, a current WRVS volunteer, recalled that her mother disappeared from Paisley for three days during the Blitz . . . "Nobody knew exactly where she was or how she was. She eventually reappeared completely healthy, except she couldn't use her hand because she had been cutting bread for those three days to help feed the Clydebank refugees."[5]

WVS, in co-operation with civil defence authorities and the Scottish Council for Social Services, quickly established an administration centre in the still-standing Pavilion Theatre in Kilbowie Road, before moving to the adjacent West Church Hall. By noon on the Friday, social services sent into the devastated town were quietly taking over and began to operate effectively, and these dealt with tasks like tracing relatives and improving communications. At 1 p.m. 4,000 lunches were sent into Clydebank to feed the remaining civilian population and rescuers. By 2.30 p.m. rest centres were beginning to function. Later in the afternoon, seven rest centres were opened. By this time WVS across the West of Scotland had rallied to Clydeside, sending help to bombed-out streets and giving hospitality as best they could in evacuee receiving areas. These included volunteers from Bishopton, Bridge of Weir, Elderslie, Gourock, Kilmacolm, Lochwinnoch, Barrhead, Johnstone, Kilbarchan and Renfrew. Airdrie WVS loaded a convoy of eight trucks with supplies of fresh water, bread, rolls and milk and set up a distribution centre on a bombsite where, amongst other activities, fires were lit to provide hot food and drinks. Glasgow centre's rescue and relief work continued "for 24 hours daily." Three clothing receiving depots were opened in the city centre, and 11 vans with roughly 250 parcels left for Clydebank after the second raid there. Glasgow WVS members on the ground also clothed 1,600 people in the devastated town, while the city's emergency WVS drivers covered 5,212 miles in the aftermath of the bombing. An Information and Casualty Centre staffed by WVS volunteers was opened at 72 John Street, and tribute was paid later to the compassion shown to victims seeking information on missing relatives. It was this team, led by centre organiser Annie Stevenson, soon to receive an MBE, which was presented to the King and Queen before March was out. A report by Glasgow WVS, severely bombed itself, mentions "momentous events" and days "full of incident" but it also refers to the "camaraderie and goodwill between all its members" and that "a team spirit prevails." The report added, "The horror of the Clydebank 'Blitz' shocked the city, but the WVS was ready for the inevitable SOS, despite the total disorganisation of the telephone service." In fact, centres across Scotland "worked around the clock" to provide emergency supplies to the town. Agnes Mair, later to give sterling service to WRVS in the capital, but in 1941 a schoolgirl in Bonnyrigg, recalled her mother shouting to her to quickly fill a suitcase of clothes for the Clydebank victims. "I rushed to my room and filled it with dresses that I had outgrown."[6]

What seems to have occurred during the bombing is that rest centres and ARP control posts still standing were abandoned as the volunteers supposed to be manning them desperately rushed to deep shelters or to tend their own loved ones. Given the ferocity of the attack this is completely understandable. Rather than WVS being entirely posted missing, however, there was "hardly anyone in the burgh who was not dependant on mobile canteens, army field kitchens, rest centres and the Town Hall feeding centre" in the aftermath of the raids. Indeed, on the Tuesday following the attack on Clydebank, no fewer than 42 mobile canteens were reported in the burgh, serving food to between 15,000 and 20,000 people.[7] The independent and co-ordinated action which lasted for several days undoubtedly helped the situation until formal arrangements were made by the authorities. It also took place in the immediate post-raid period when the presence of delayed or unexploded bombs was a constant danger. Moreover, we shall probably never know how individual members of the Housewives' Service of WVS coped at the height of the raids on Clydeside, how many incendiaries they extinguished with bin lids to prevent targets being illuminated, how many neighbours they coaxed to shelters or pulled from burning buildings, or comforted in their loss, or inspired to keep going when all seemed hopeless. We do not know how many of the Service unselfishly took responsibility for the care of old people, invalids and children during the raids, especially those who were alone, isolated or frightened at the time – enough surely to neutralise later histories which discount or omit the women's contribution and courage.

In any case, it was not only WVS who were hampered by the scale and intensity of the Luftwaffe attack on Clydebank. Roads and rail links were blocked, gas, water and electricity cut off. In the ARP control centre, 16 phone lines were down to one. Bombs put three of the four first aid stations out of action, and three fire stations were destroyed. Fire, police, ambulance, ARP and youth messenger services performed heroically, but were overwhelmed as fires burned unchecked and the casualty toll mounted. Even still, exhausted rescue workers were criticised for lack of effort and there were complaints about "negligent" demolition squads.[8] Fire appliances ran out of petrol and units from other brigades found their equipment incompatible. ARP personnel failed to turn up for duty. The police presence was too thinly spread. Offices of officials were disrupted or destroyed. Local government collapsed and councillors and officials were left dazed and bewildered. Thus at the height of the bombing it is probable that no service was functioning properly in Clydebank – and for good reason. Casualty services had become casualties themselves.

The response of rest centres also requires scrutiny. The centres in Clydebank itself were badly disrupted by the bombing. Three were destroyed and others were understandably avoided as bombs fell, or where there was unexploded ordnance or, indeed, where further raids were anticipated. It is also clear that the Vale of Leven centre on the road to Alexandria manned by a Mrs Beaton and WVS staff was inundated by the human exodus from Clydebank. The problem of overcrowding there was plainly much more visible than, say, the several thousands of bombed-out victims absorbed by relatives and friends in nearby Glasgow.

It seems that all routes led to Vale of Leven through word of mouth and that "the people settled like a hive of bees because they met their friends and were tired and miserable and so stopped." Rest centres, designed as self-contained units that could be opened up with the minimum of delay in an emergency, usually catered for around 300 people. Some 35,000 were driven out of Clydebank over the course of 12 hours and bus drivers, when asked about their destination, were told "to take them to the Vale of Leven or anywhere they could think of." Even days after the raids, the night-time population of Clydebank was estimated at 2,000 as compared with over 50,000 before the attacks, and it seems probable that many "trekkers" from the burgh who could not find accommodation had to sleep in farm buildings, public halls, churches, even under hedges in the open country. This undoubtedly fuelled criticism of rest centre provision.[9]

That there was insufficient food to give the Clydebank homeless, that supplies of clothing and blankets ran out, that washing facilities were inadequate and accommodation limited, must have been a demoralising blow to all concerned – not least WVS volunteers trained to cope with such shortages on a smaller scale. The problems, however, appear to have been exacerbated by government 'spin' which put out misleading information about the situation in Clydebank. While the town had been through a terrible time and many thousands were homeless and desperately seeking help, the country at large was informed officially about the raid in terms very far from suggesting that the attack was in fact a devastating blitz. Official communiqués stated that while an attack had taken place on Clydeside, the casualties "were not expected to be numerous."[10] Confidential papers reveal that it was not until the Scottish Secretary had been petitioned along with the regional APR Commissioner and the Censorship department in London that official statements were issued four days after the raids adjusting the perspective of the devastation to 500 deaths, about half the actual number in the Glasgow-Clydebank area. Even still, one Home Guard veteran in Clydebank greeted the report of 500 fatalities with the remark, "Which street?" It appears that the government, interpreting a civilian exodus on any significant scale as a symptom of lowered morale, was anxious that nothing should be done to publicise such movements. By doing so it limited the scope for help. This added to the concentration of people at rest centres. It caused friction and anxiety and probably contributed to stories about rest centre ineffi- ciency. The fact that Clydebank was not specifically identified in news reports as taking the brunt of the Luftwaffe attack also added to the frustration and anger that its people had suffered for nothing.[11]

In any case, the Scottish Secretary duly acknowledged the "invalu- able" work of the WVS at Clydebank, not only in the bombed-out areas, but also in the areas which had received people. He told Ruth Balfour, "In these tasks, where what is needed most of all is the immediate and sympathetic relief of distress with a minimum of formality, the help given by Women's Voluntary Services has been invaluable and on behalf of the Government I would ask you to accept our sincere thanks for all that the WVS has done, and our congratulations on the manner in which they have met their first severe test of this kind in Scotland."[12]

Lady Balfour, in turn, felt that the authorities had been compla- cent. She suggested that many civil defence officials believed they were "safe from attack in Scotland." This partly explained how public services were completely paralysed after the raids on the burgh, she said. Nella Last also noted how "I don't think our council ever thought we would get it." Her diary covered the bombing of the town of Barrow and revealed how people "rushed from the little box-like back street shelters into their houses, and then out in to the street again – frantic with fear not knowing where to go." The social historian Richard Titmuss has more recently suggested that it seemed as though "each local council, its officials, and the general public had first to live through a heavy raid before they could form any idea of the real nature of its consequences."[13]

In fact, in spite of the terrible experiences of London the previous year, it was rare for a provincial town to take adequate precautions before it was actually attacked. A post-raid post-mortem by Mrs Lindsay Huxley, the former Women's Institute treasurer who would hold the position of WVS chief regional administrator for nearly 30 years, showed that the department run by Scotland's

Commissioner for ARP, the soon-to-be Scottish Secretary Tom Johnston, was "to blame for (1) not having been better prepared, and (2) for not having diverted the stream of refugees from the Vale of Leven." Mrs Huxley had been telephoned by the pre-war Scottish Secretary Walter Elliot, then Health Minister at Westminster, to be told that he had been on Clydeside "immediately" following the raid and he had been enormously impressed with the work WVS was doing everywhere: that Glasgow was "full of busy WVS members in uniform steadily carrying out their work" and that he had talked to quite a number of them. In order to calm the situation, Mrs Huxley wrote immediately to Lady Balfour to say that she "must not be too depressed by the frightful difficulties that arose." She added, "It seems to me a monstrous thing that the WVS should be blamed and I think that Mrs Beaton and the other women at Vale of Leven behaved with great courage to stick it out in the way they did." As it transpired, when the contributions of various WVS centres were collated, Lady Balfour was able to tell the Scottish Advisory Committee that 57 shifts of women, comprising nearly 2,000 helpers, had been sent from outside areas to give assistance on Clydeside.[14]

As for evacuation, it was true that Clydebank's mothers and children had been left vulnerable to enemy action. Various reports, however, showed that the dispersal policy had been sound. For complex reasons, parents had drifted home during the Phoney War. Half of the Clydebank children evacuated in September 1939 had returned by the end of October, three-quarters by Christmas. The attacks came over a year later. Despite the efforts of WVS and others to organise safe passage, it is clear now that parents had under-standable misgivings about having their children committed for an indefinite period to the care of strangers whom they had never seen. Perhaps this is why when 3,400 children left Clydebank under the evacuation scheme in September 1939, 4,000 others had remained in the town. There was nothing WVS could have done in this situation to reduce risk.[15]

Lessons were learned from the response to the terrible bombing raids on Britain. WVS Headquarters staff went into emergency planning with the Food Ministry about the use of rapid response convoys which could go into badly-blitzed areas anywhere in the country and provide food until local services were re-established. WVS helped in the design of the convoys, which were to comprise 12 vehicles – two food storage lorries, two canteen equipment lorries, one water-tank truck, three mobile canteens and four motorcycles. After the Queen's inspection of the first two convoys, which were her gift in May 1941, the scheme was christened the Queen's Messenger Convoys. These were the prototypes of a wartime fleet of 18 convoys dispersed around the country, Scotland's pair being based eventually in Falkirk and Chapelhall, near Airdrie. Convoy staff had to be prepared to leave their homes at a moment's notice and stay away for days at a time. In situations where normal feeding arrangements were destroyed, the convoys provided facilities for cooking a hot meal for 3,000 people within a few hours. The need for permanent emergency feeding centres was also pressed home, and it was decided to expand the fledgling British Restaurant service, a chain of restaurants which had been opened in major centres of population to provide cheap communal feeding.

In the heavy raids on Greenock in early May 1941, the first of Scotland's two Queen's Messenger Convoys and its staff of WVS volunteers was put to severe test – ironically in the week of its intended debut training run. As at Clydebank, two nights of intensive bombing shook the town, destroying houses and damaging churches, schools, public buildings, shipyards and industrial concerns, such as a distillery, a sugar refinery and a foundry. Over two dreadful nights 280 people were killed and some 1,200 injured. From a total of 18,000 homes nearly 10,000 suffered damage and 1,000 were destroyed.

This time WVS and partner agencies were better prepared. The rumbling sound of the Queen's Messenger Convoy entering the blitzed town lifted the despondency of rescuers digging desperately in the debris. Arrangements had not yet been completed for communal feeding and the convoy's emergency rations were the only supplies available at the time. The 50-strong convoy staff, all WVS members, fed the homeless and serviced mobile canteens arriving from other centres. Thousands of people were provided with soup, tea, porridge, milk and sandwiches in a compassionate, humanising way. Lorry loads of hungry, dirty, injured and frightened men, women and children were fed in partnership with other voluntary organisations. Mary Denholm, daughter of Catherine Morton, who founded Airdrie WVS, recalled her mother receiving a medal from the Ministry of Food in appreciation for her work with the convoy in the aftermath of the bombings.[16]

A WVS Scotland report after the Greenock raids highlighted improvements made: "Large numbers of teams were brought from surrounding areas by bus, and returned on the arrival of further bus loads," it said. Closer liaison had taken place between the WVS in the area being helped and those coming to help, in order that teams knew exactly what action to take. Local centres had been better prepared to offer immediate assistance. Barrhead, Bishopton, Elderslie, Houston and Johnstone were among the Renfrewshire centres to send mobile canteens to Greenock to help with community feeding after the battering that the town took. Linwood, Lochwinnoch, Kilbarchan, Uplawmoor and Bridge of Weir opened rest centres. At Port Glasgow five centres were manned at the time of the raids and the homeless who arrived there were provided with bedding and given four meals a day. One rest centre there dealt with 21 stretcher cases until they could be moved to hospital. So many evacuees attended the Kilmacolm centre that a fully-equipped emergency kitchen was established to feed them. Gourock members tended to casualties and their families at Smithston Hospital. Johnstone members took charge of Renfrewshire's clothing store. WVS drivers also contributed by transporting officials, rescuers and relatives and carrying food and clothing. Some 2,500 miles were covered during the blitz "under conditions of great difficulty."[17]

Thus although Greenock suffered terribly in the May raids, WVS appears to have made a significant difference to the lives of the homeless, dispossessed, injured and bereaved. A report told how its emergency teams "worked under high pressure and continuously for many days" and how the tasks they faced "would have overcome the faint-hearted."[18] In one instance, a bombed-out family arrived late at night in a west coast village. The mother and her brood of children were given a room in an old building. One WVS volunteer swept the chimney and lit a fire. Another scrubbed the floor and borrowed a large double bed from the mother of 13 children, whose sons were mostly away on active service. They contacted the nearest WVS rest centre whose members were holding a committee meeting. The meeting was adjourned, the members seized blankets and clothes and went immediately to the house, while others scurried round the village in search of food. Thus one Greenock family who had lost everything was safely settled.

Mrs Nan MacLaren, supervising a WVS work party in Glasgow during the raids, recalled a woman walking into her office carrying a new-born baby which had not been bathed or changed for over a day. The woman had been bombed out of Clydebank. She had then suffered a similar fate at Greenock and was at the end of her tether. "None of our kind donors had thought of sending us a tin of baby power, but one of my team came to the rescue with a box of face powder, which was quite a good substitute . . . when we started on that infant it was like a lump of ice, but once we had it in the bath before our electric radiator, its whimpering ceased, and soon after its mother had fed it the baby was sleeping soundly. That night our guides saw them aboard a northbound train. They were on their way to find refuge with their only living relative in a Highland town." Again, "it was the volunteers of the WVS who brought some order to the chaos."[19]

Another important lesson from the bombings was that more evacuees would inevitably descend on reception areas than were anticipated or catered for, and that they would stay longer than expected. The unexpected mass arrival at the Vale of Leven rest centre after the raids on Clydeside and the subsequent chaotic scenes of overcrowding had proved a steep learning curve for WVS in Scotland. A week after the double raid on Clydebank there were still 3,500 townspeople in the centre and a further 4,400 people billeted with householders nearby. No one, it was reported, "had considered, even as a remote possibility, that large numbers of evacuees would sleep, eat, and live there for a few days, far less weeks." One harassed rest centre leader had "apologised to her 300 'guests' who had arrived in the early hours of the morning that she was only able to give them a cup of tea until food arrived. 'Dinna worry', one of the women who had lost everything assured her, 'We had no time to send you a telegram to let you know we were comin'.'[20] Great efforts were made, therefore, to co-ordinate rest centre activities. It was no simple task. Across Scotland there were 2,700 centres, staffed by 60,000 volunteers to provide safe accommodation for 300,000 people at times of emergency. Edinburgh had 100, with another 70 in landward Midlothian, Dundee had 61 and smaller towns, like Kirkcaldy, Perth and Paisley had around two dozen each. But by the summer of 1941 all centres had been restocked with adequate supplies of clothing and improved equipment. Many had enrolled additional staff – 579 volunteers coming forward in Edinburgh during September 1941 alone. All of them took part in training exercises, and panels of so-called 'umpires', whose job it was to test responses at centres, were set up at Dundee, Edinburgh, Ayr and Glasgow. Various rest centre staff attended courses on emergency relief organisation arranged by the Department of Health in Glasgow and Edinburgh. Many centres were inspected personally by the Secretary of State for Scotland and the Regional Commissioner for ARP. Additionally, precautions such as the cutting of duplicate keys were taken, and staff given pre-arranged times for clocking in. The number of joint training opportunities for emergency relief also increased – in one of the exercises, involving Scotland's West and South-East WVS areas, tear gas was released and work had to be done while wearing gas masks. In other tests the public co-operated by arriving 'homeless' and taking cards with them on which were written the 'problems' to be solved or 'injuries' to be treated. Such exercises were usually followed by a crop of gloom-lightening anecdotes . . . like the incident in the autumn of 1941 in which two Scottish WVS organisers were conferring by telephone to the distress of one of them who kept shouting into the mouth-piece, "You can't talk to me. The phone's cut off!"[21]

WVS brought out its own report on precisely what work the Service should carry out after heavy air attack. This re-emphasised the need for co-operation. It called upon its county and large burgh centres to prepare a detailed, written plan of action for submission to civil defence authorities. It also requested each centre organiser to give particulars of her heads of departments and their duties, together with the local authority official whom they would contact at times of emergency. Out of several meetings arose the need for recruiting fast-response teams of WVS workers, the training of these teams, the formation of bodies of women willing to do emergency cooking, and the arrangement of instruction for these volunteers. Practice and training should be the immediate aim of WVS Blitz shifts, the report said, and it concluded: "The importance of constant rehearsals cannot be too greatly emphasised."[22]

The raids on the west coast and the difficulties of communication thereafter resulted in a movement away from centralised control by the WVS head office in Edinburgh. The Home Office had initially divided Scotland into two of the 12 British WVS regions along the lines of the 12 Civil Defence Regions already instituted. Region 11 was projected to cover from the Shetlands to the Borders, while Region 12 was to be the West of Scotland and the Western Islands. From the outset, however, Scotland was merged into a single WVS Region 11 under the authority of Coates Gardens. From September 1941, it was decided that the country could be best run under five districts with their own figurehead representatives and with autonomy for day-to-day decisions, though still formally under the control of the Scottish chairman and Edinburgh headquarters.

These districts were:

District 1 – South. Edinburgh and south to the Borders.
District 2 – East. Fife, Dundee and surrounding rural counties.
District 3 – North-East. Aberdeen and counties in the north-east of Scotland.
District 4 – North. Inverness, northern counties and the western Highlands.
District 5 – West. Glasgow, counties in the west and the Western Islands.

Following the London pattern, leading public figures continued to fill the positions of representatives for the five districts – Lady

Rosebery in District 1, Lady Elgin in District 2, Lady Lovat in District 3, SWRI stalwart Mary Gouch in District 4 and WVS Scottish vice-president Helen Shaw in District 5. Coates Gardens continued as the Scottish headquarters, joining the other 10 regional headquarters in London, Birmingham, Leeds, Liverpool, Newcastle, Nottingham, Reading, Cambridge, Bristol and Cardiff. Ruth Balfour carried on as chairman. Norah Ross was appointed administrator for Scotland and the two largest Scottish centres, at Renfield Street in Glasgow and Castle Terrace, Edinburgh, were run by Annie Stevenson and Mary McCall.

That autumn Scottish local authorities initiated Emergency Relief Personnel training and in many cases councils asked members of WVS to take the courses. At the first of them, in Edinburgh, the guest lecturer was Mrs Lindsay Huxley, the chief regional administrator from Tothill Street, who was visiting Scotland that week, and who gave the talk *Work in a Heavily Bombed Area*. The opening address was given by Tom Johnston MP, the new Secretary of State for Scotland, who had formed a Council of State to conduct the government in Scotland. In the course of his remarks, Johnston described WVS as "one of the discoveries of the war."[23] At another training course, the London lecturer ended the talk on WVS work by mentioning that probably the only thing that WVS had not been asked to do in connection with local authorities was to look after lunatic asylums. One member immediately intervened to point out that her centre in the Borders had helped mental health institutions for many months and had provided a rota to conduct patients to shelters when an alert sounded. As the London lecturer was reminded, WVS in Scotland never said no.

Another development during the worst raids was the WVS Incident Inquiry Point (IIP). These temporary centres were rapidly established on the request of local civil defence authorities. The job of IIP staff was primarily to give out authentic information to the public about air raid casualties, or to pass on as much reliable information as possible from a central position. From rest centres, hospitals and mortuaries, and from friends and neighbours, information was collected so that inquiries from anxious relatives could be properly answered. Courageous members involved in Blitz bombings sometimes established IIPs in the front room of the nearest undamaged house, even while raids were in progress. Pragmatically, WVS staff at Incident Inquiry Points also took interim charge of jewellery or personal items found by ARP personnel and other rescuers, indexed and stored them ready to hand over to local authorities after enemy action had subsided. They took care of family pets found wandering around bombsites until owners could reclaim them. The more harrowing duty of informing loved ones of fatalities often fell to WVS emergency workers, some of whom were instructed in this unhappy task. No training, however, could prepare helpers for the grim and heartbreaking task of taking parents to try to identify the little victims of bombing raids.

The strain on the WVS in the blitzed cities had been considerable. By the summer of 1941, 25 WVS offices had been destroyed by raids. Before the bombing ended, 241 members of Women's Voluntary Services had been killed and hundreds of others wounded. Nobody knew at that terrible time that an almost complete cessation of mass aerial bombardment would come through Hitler's decision to launch an extensive attack on Russia in June 1941. The great effort in Scotland to re-organise and co-ordinate civil defence after the Clydeside attacks would, mercifully, never be required to be put into practice.

4

"A MILLION MAGNIFICENT WOMEN"

By the end of 1941 WVS had 959,000 members in 1,700 centres, over 100,000 of them in Scotland dispersed across 250 offices. Membership had grown by 600,000 since the start of the war. It represented a formidable mobilisation. The organisation's role had grown exponentially. It was fulfilling functions for 20 government departments and extended to every corner of the country. It was co-ordinated into a "vast woman-power" and Lady Reading announced proudly, "Such an army of unpaid workers has probably never been equalled in history."[1]

A quarter of a million members were still engaged in ARP work, with nearly twice that number contributing some of their volunteering hours at clothing depots. A further 145,000 manned rest centres. Over 100,000 women were organised and trained as part of the Housewives' Service. Over 65,000 members worked in canteens – more than the entire enrolment of the Women's Land Army – and 20,000 in British Restaurants. But smaller groups also made vital contributions to the war effort. In rural England members distributed one million pies each week to agricultural workers in 2,750 villages. Elderly WVS darned 38,000 pairs of socks a week for British soldiers. In over 350 depots women made camouflage netting . . . "Crawling about on their nets with bruised knees and aching backs, women drove themselves on for that extra hour which meant so many more square feet of cover for the British Army."[2] These elderly members knew they were at last able to contribute practically to the war effort and it drove their fingers to weave scrim on to camouflage nets day after day in colours adapted to suit the terrain of the various countries in which fighting was taking place.

As German U-boats threatened to starve the country into defeat, salvage remained vital work. The WVS in Scotland spent many hours campaigning and promoting various schemes, using slogans such as "Feed Your Pigs and Save Your Bacon". They filled roles as street salvage stewards and bin supervisors, and duties included leaflet distribution and staffing salvage depots. An initiative known as the Cog Scheme enlisted schoolchildren to work with adult helpers to collect items like bottle tops, wool and paper but occasionally they had the opportunity to show independent initiative in organising local house-to-house salvage work. The Cog children had an anthem, *There'll always be a dustbin*, which was sung to the tune of *There'll always be an England*. Often Scotland's 12,000-strong Housewives' Service, where news travelled fast, was pivotal in salvage schemes, passing round word that it was almost a crime to put anything in a dustbin. Paper, string and scrap metal were hoarded and members carefully swept up nuts and bolts from aircraft factory floors and sorted them for re-use. In the small village of Sprouston in Roxburghshire, members salvaged 519 lb of rubber from a river bed. Dingwall WVS broke up packing cases to make coat hangers for the Army. Kirkcaldy remade worn sandbags into mats and rugs. As another slogan put it, "Raw Material means War Material".

Most centres also ran National Savings schemes – collecting from households, delivering leaflets, selling savings stamps at booths and special shops and organising street savings groups in support of the National Savings movement, which encouraged people to lend money for the war effort. The schemes gained in impetus and by 1941 there were 292 WVS-run savings groups across Scotland, members using local knowledge to act as group secretaries or collectors. Edinburgh's streets, for example, were divided into blocks of 20 or 30 houses and 3,000 collectors called weekly. Airdrie was told by the government savings agency: "I think the total of 34 affiliated groups in your town is magnificent." Hawick delivered leaflets to 5,000 houses in 155 streets in just three days. But the community which led the country was Selkirk which boasted a savings scheme in every street. Within two years of their launch in 1941, there were 1,250 savings groups in Scotland operated entirely by over 5,000 WVS personnel. Between them over that period they amassed £1.6 million, an astonishing £37 million at today's values. No wonder a little song became popular as the savings returns were noted in WVS ledgers:

> Britain never shall be slaves,
> While every street in Britain saves.

All WVS centres trained women to cook under the worst possible conditions. A report explained: "This training is being given so that when a raid puts out of action most of the facilities cooks take for granted – gas rings, running water and good ovens – they will not be caught unawares." Known among members as The Kitchen Front, women were expected to know how to manage a boiler, to fill an insulated urn, to build an emergency field cooker, to operate a hurricane lamp and to be adept with the different kinds of tin openers likely to be found in rest centres. Scottish Girl Guides helped by providing lecturers who were experts in wood and coal fires and the Guides later issued a penny leaflet on camp cooking procedures. This obviously found favour with members of Dumfries WVS who, during bad weather, were once discovered practising indoors by building a pretend fire with dominoes. Even the back garden of 7 Coates Gardens became home to a variety of emergency cookers for demonstration purposes. Other activities where networking was required included co-operation with the Army to provide WVS access to field kitchens, and links with education authorities to allow members to practise on disposable Soyer boilers – robust field cookers developed in the Crimean war – which were set up in school playgrounds. Food Weeks were declared and WVS demonstration vans took to the streets to educate housewives on how to eat economically and what to stock in their cupboards. Members drew attention to their message in Edinburgh by holding a 'potato party' outside Headquarters, where volunteers and guests gathered to eat potatoes "baked in their skins."[3] Food, as Lady Reading often remarked, was "something which we in WVS understand." But in Scotland where food stations were established "on the run" during manoeuvres in remote areas, it sometimes took more understanding than anticipated. On one Army exercise in the north, WVS cooks were in danger of capture by the 'invaders' and only managed to escape by climbing over a cemetery wall. A veteran of WVS among them, who felt her climbing days were over, abandoned the idea and instead held a frying pan in front of her to divert the enemy's 'fire'!

Well away from the sounds of sirens in the urban Central Belt, WVS members had emergencies of their own to attend to, as survivors from sunken and damaged ships were disembarked at ports as far distant as Ardrossan, Helmsdale, Peterhead and Dundee. Gourock provided food and clothing for 500 shipwrecked mariners in one day, receiving a letter of thanks from the Department of Health. Bereaved relatives of Merchant Navy victims were comforted at the WVS canteen in Campbeltown at the request of the British Sailors' Society, and when 69 men exposed to the Atlantic side of Lewis were safely landed, it took the Stornoway centre women just over an hour to gather sufficient garments for distribution to survivors. Rest centres in far-flung communities undertook the same pre-raid plans and post-raid procedures as centres in vulnerable industrial areas. Theirs, too, was the task to remain always prepared for call out . . . ready to receive survivors, to serve food, to provide clothing, to offer washing facilities and warm billets, to translate and to provide information.

Bombs or blizzards, a WVS priority throughout the war remained the provision of warm clothing. Clothes rationing had been introduced in June 1941 when it had become almost impossible to import raw materials from abroad due to shipping losses and after UK manufacturers had geared production to the provision of military uniforms and other materials required in the war. A 'most secret' memorandum from the Prime Minister's War Cabinet spoke of shops running out and panic buying: "Stocks are now giving out and shortages are beginning to appear. These shortages will increase rapidly, and I fear that unless either supplies are increased, or the distribution of the existing supplies is equalized (which means rationing) some part of the population will have to go short of clothing in the autumn and winter. There will be panic buying and shop queues, prices will rise and the shops will be cleared . . . I need not dwell on the social consequences of such a condition of affairs."[4] The government response was to issue clothing ration books of tear-out coupons to every man, woman and child in Britain to allow them to obtain a small number of items. The fact that the clothing rationing scheme depended on a points system – for example, a woman's raincoat was 15 points, a blouse 4 points, a man's jacket 12 points and a child's nightshirt 6 points – signalled major disruption to the work of Women's Voluntary Services. It meant members had to unpack almost £5 million worth of clothing held in depots. Each item, thereafter, had to be measured and labelled with its coupon value – every coat, jacket, blazer, cardigan, vest, sweater, waistcoat, shirt, blouse, shawl and skirt, every pair of trousers, pyjamas, shorts, socks, stockings and each item of underwear. This created an enormous amount of extra work for the organisation's hard-pressed clothing depot staff.[5]

The Make-do and Mend campaign launched by government in June 1941 in support of clothes rationing encouraged people to get as much wear as possible out of the clothes they already had. Naturally, much of the onus for this fell to WVS who were by nature inventive with ways of 'making do'. Training courses were held to show housewives how to make 'new' clothes from old and posters and information leaflets were circulated to provide advice on economising. Old blankets were converted into overcoats, trousers torn apart to make children's clothes, old knitwear unpicked and re-used, curtains transformed into dresses and flour bags made into tea cloths. It became fashionable to wear unfashionable clothes to show you were 'doing your bit' for the war effort. In Dundee, a Make-do and Mend exhibition in the city's art galleries was visited by 1,900 people on a single day, perhaps the attraction for some being WVS 'models' attired in scraps of clothes collected without a single clothing coupon being used! They had followed, they said, the example of Scarlett O'Hara, of *Gone With The Wind* fame, who had torn down curtains to make herself a frock.[6]

Towards the end of 1941 WVS cleverly initiated clothing exchanges, whereby people could bring outgrown clothing, but not outworn clothing, and swap it for second-hand garments they required, often larger sizes for growing children. As no coupons were required for second-hand clothing the 400 WVS exchanges created with the agreement of the Board of Trade became an integral part of life for many households. Doubtless the existence of the swapshops saved many poorer families from the impact of clothes rationing and the cost of expensive replacements – though one WVS stalwart noted wryly that "a good deal of diplomacy, and indeed, firmness was needed, the difference between what a mother brought in and what she wished to take away often being quite remarkable."[7] A charming oil painting by Evelyn Gibbs in the Imperial War Museum in London shows two clothing exchange volunteers in distinctive WVS uniforms helping to fit clothes on to two growing children as their mothers watch.

Alongside clothing exchanges, WVS continued to organise the nationwide distribution of donated garments. In the summer of 1941 300 cases of clothing from the British War Relief Society were given to the Association of Highland Societies in Edinburgh and thereafter sent all over the north by WVS. Several parcels were diverted to Clydeside for the many families of Highland origin who had moved there for work. Aberdeen WVS forwarded clothes to the Timber Corps, Land Girls and to rural hospitals. Members there also inspected and repaired 5,000 bundles of clothes for the Forces, and its 16 work parties darned a similar number of pairs of socks for the Army. Dundee responded to an urgent appeal for 200 gloves from a minesweeper commander. He was so desperate that he offered the Dundee depot 200 woollen scarves in return, for rattling down. And when Linwood members sent off woollen gifts to reach the men in time for Christmas that year they included five shillings with every parcel. It was as if women were using membership of WVS as a means of 'bonding' to missing loved ones. Enrolment also offered an outlet where practical support – through disciplined hard work – could go some way to releasing bottled-up feelings of uselessness among those left behind on the Home Front.

Everybody was encouraged to knit and WVS set up knitting circles for this purpose. Despite rationing and strict regulations regarding the sale of wool, WVS soon enrolled 35,000 knitters across

Scotland. These women were formed into work parties and drew supplies from the WVS wool depot at 32 Coates Gardens. By 1940 over 300 work parties were registered with the depot. Nan MacLaren, of Glasgow WVS, recalled how her coven of elderly ladies, valiant veterans who knitted quietly at their own firesides with a patriotic fervour the envy of younger workers, once received a warm tribute from the Royal Marines. "Those boys had numbered upwards of 3,000 and the job we undertook for them was the sewing of divisional signs and other distinguishing marks on their battle blouses . . . 'The men were very pleased,' wrote the major. 'They were able to go on leave or walk out with everything looking nice.'" WVS and other women contributed so many comforts that "wool was knitted into their dreams at night." The staggering contribution to troops' welfare not only included knitted donations and the three million items of clothing mended annually by WVS. In addition to the despatch of 140,000 garments in the space of a year, the North East district depot in Aberdeen sent out 201 wireless sets, 22,697 books, 9,176 magazines, 35 gramophones, 1,206 records and 128 musical instruments.[8]

When, in late 1941 the BBC asked Scottish WVS to provide a programme of activities for its *Life over Here* series for broadcast in North America and Australia, members from Glasgow, Edinburgh, the North and the Borders described how they threw nothing away in their salvage and make-do and mend efforts and how determined they were to contribute to home defence. Soon after, the Ministry of Information made its own film of WVS work and "caused an excited stir" in the five Scottish centres it visited. In Edinburgh, Poles and Norwegians were filmed being shown over Edinburgh Castle by staff of the Allied Information Bureau, kilted Scots and overseas soldiers were photographed with Station Guides at Waverley, and scenes were taken of vegetables being harvested on the city's outskirts for minesweeper crews. In Glasgow the vital canteen work for Clydeside dockers was filmed, as was the Queen's Messenger Convoy on exercise in Perth. A return to Perthshire was made to film evacuees in apparent blissful happiness among heather, hills and lochs near Dunkeld. The star of the show appeared in Dundee. There, a re-enactment of a recent North Sea rescue took place, where a lime-light-loving dog rushed on to the lifeboat to meet its shipwrecked master, ran at the head of his stretcher-bearing party, and finally jumped into the waiting ambulance with him!

The success of various clothing schemes inevitably led to WVS being asked to assist when full-scale ration books were introduced in 1941. Food rationing had begun the previous year over fears of increasing interruption to supplies by enemy action. The close relationship between WVS and the Ministry of Food meant that various leaflets were produced and talks given to advise the population. Items included under rationing legislation increased intermittently throughout 1941 and 1942 – firstly clothing, then coal, then soap, then gas and electricity, then sweets and chocolate. Britain's adult population was quickly issued with a ration book containing coupons that had to be handed in to shops every time rationed goods were bought. In a remarkable mobilisation, WVS members addressed and issued ration books in Airdrie, Coatbridge, Dundee, Edinburgh, Galashiels, throughout Clackmannanshire, in Kinross-shire, where the whole work was undertaken by just 28 members, in Dunfermline landward, where 19,000 cards were written, Kilmarnock, Selkirk and throughout Roxburgh, where 48,000 books were prepared and issued. In one Scottish burgh 60 members were on ration book duty every day for five weeks and still found time to marshal queues and to see that application forms were correctly filled in. No doubt they also provided tea. In late 1941, Ruth Balfour received a letter from the Minister for Food praising the "valuable help" of WVS in Scotland in helping to distribute its share of 45 million ration books across Britain.

How exhausted members must have been as 1941 became 1942. And yet, in her Christmas message as the fourth year of Women's Voluntary Services ended, Lady Balfour warned that "the hardest year" was before them. And she added, "In this season of goodwill let us resolve to be linked together as a band of sisters for mutual support and to meet all demands made upon our services with our whole minds and strength and with initiative for the better preservation of this dear land of ours against attack." Stella Reading, meanwhile, opted to look back and addressed her Christmas epistle directly to her members' achievements over a difficult year: "I want to stress to you, as your Chairman, how splendid a piece of work you have accomplished, and what a wonderful spirit you have achieved." She went on, however, to sound a sombre note of warning: "To win the war we shall all be called upon to pay a heavy price, it may be in health, it may be in other ways, it may be life itself . . . whatever we are called upon to do, I know that WVS will not be found wanting."[9]

With the Government encouraging communal feeding in order to save food and fuel, canteens across Britain were serving eight million meals each month by 1942, with 90% of them run by WVS volunteers on two- or three-hour shifts. During 1942, the purchasing department at Tothill Street used Treasury funds and money donated by the American Red Cross to equip a fleet of new WVS and civil defence static canteens. This involved a monthly expenditure of about £20,000 and covered every form of equipment from furniture to pots and pans. Former damp and dreary halls, public buildings and disused factories were transformed into cheery, warm and welcoming canteens where green-overalled women provided tea, sandwiches, cakes, biscuits and simple meals at a reasonable cost, seven days a week. Here men and women of the Services, and those in essential occupations, could talk about their experiences, wind down, write to loved ones, or play cards or darts with colleagues, families and friends. In canteens, too, gathered the concerned wives of Prisoners of War to seek solace in each other's company, or the lonely men whose wives and children had been evacuated. Often canteens were simply a place of refuge when gas or water had been cut off. Always they were stocked overnight in case of a sudden call. Stirling's canteen, open day and night, supplied 6,000 men in one month. Over the same period one static canteen in Glasgow served 10,000 dinners and 3,500 teas. The Stranraer canteen reported that its customers had conservative tastes – "preferring bacon, sausages and chips to all else." Wherever men were stationed, they were looked after.

Mobile canteens became 'shops-on-wheels' around Scotland. WVS in Kirkcaldy ran an American snack bar as a canteen for landward areas. Ayr and Uddingston used theirs to feed industrial workers, while two were used at Glasgow's docks, serving 2,500 meals a day and using a rota of 160 helpers and 20 drivers. East Lothian became the first centre to provide a canteen for mine workers, and WVS in Fort William helped to feed lumbermen at a timber camp. Kirkintilloch raised £1,000 for a canteen for East Dunbartonshire, and Bearsden collected £470 to buy one to serve the Home Guard. When Bridge of Weir's canteen was commandeered by soldiers during manoeuvres the staff left behind tea, scones and hot water for the men. Next day the women discovered the canteen in perfect working order, the washing done and two letters of thanks left for them. Even in remote areas, such as across Sutherland and Ross and Cromarty, mobile canteens were readied and fully stocked for emergencies. These vans were often owned by local authorities, the YMCA, the Scottish Churches or the British War Relief Fund, or supplied by companies such as Ford or by folk in the free world – one was even donated by the Scottish Football Association – but in many cases they were entirely staffed by WVS volunteers who often roped in their husbands as drivers or as labourers to lift heavy equipment.

Many canteens were painted in shining green and bore in scarlet the legend 'WVS' as well as the lettering of other contributing organisations. Equipment was generally coloured green and mugs had a green band around them. A calor gas stove, urns and stainless steel sink were neatly arranged, with trays for biscuits and cakes fitted into niches around the sides. Such canteens could keep food hot for several hours and called at small isolated groups of men serving on monotonous postings at searchlight stations, anti-aircraft batteries or radar posts. How delighted they must have been when a little WVS van trundled down the lane with its promise of tea, sandwiches, cigarettes, newspapers, toiletries – and occasionally the men's post. And in Scotland, as elsewhere, this service was gradually extended to the provision of mobile libraries for military personnel in outlying areas. During one period of six months Edinburgh WVS sent out 16,000 books on loan, the 'advance party' of the hugely-successful Books on Wheels projects of the modern-day WRVS.

Among canteens to see service was one which survives at Glamis Castle. This Austin three-ton van was presented to Angus emergency relief workers by the then Queen Elizabeth, the future Queen Mother, who had spent some of her childhood at Glamis. Capable of providing meals for 300, and one of 30 vans in District 2, its original wartime staff of three would have been expected to serve that number in under an hour. After the war the mobile unit continued in use with WRVS until the 1970s to provide refreshments at local functions, still with its original cups, plates and cutlery. After well-deserved retirement in a local yard, the van underwent a full restoration in the 1990s and was soon back on display at the castle.

Elsewhere in Scotland WVS undertook the improvisation of a vegetable service for the crews of minesweepers and other small naval craft. Ships tied up or lying off ports were anxious to receive fresh vegetables and fruit, and such produce was collected from people's gardens for delivery to the vessels and, along the east coast, put in sacks heaved on to lorries by women whose female forebears had lifted fishermen husbands from boats to the shore. Thousands of fresh vegetables grown on allotments, public parks, railway embankments and even on bomb sites were provided and, when winter came, mince pies and cakes were added to the boxes. At the Aberdeen naval base one woman donated the remarkable total of 4,700 lb of vegetables, while another dealt with a request by a minesweeper crew to provide a kitten. Gloves for minesweeper crews from donations of old mackintoshes and other waterproofs were also supplied, much of the work carried out by members of the Housewives' Service.

Another important area of activity was the provision of warm drinks and food to the thousands of men facing long train journeys to and from the north of Scotland training areas and sea bases. At railway junctions such as Perth, Stirling and Inverness WVS members hopped on and off trains with urns of tea to fill mugs held out by cold and hungry men. In Helmsdale alone, 105,000 teas were served during 1942. Stirling, that year, had an astonishing serving time of five minutes for 200 men. As a teenage volunteer at Perth Station, Flora Kirkland recalled the men who invariably sauntered in with the words, "Any tarts for sale?" She recalled, "Of course, they didn't have jam tarts in mind! Utter cheek! But the station was so full of sailors that we used to say the Admiralty didn't know what to do with them – so they were stuck on a train at Portsmouth to go up to Orkney, then turned round to travel south again!" Through the nights urns were washed and refilled in members' homes and army drivers cajoled into taking them to the stations the next day. To meet demand, the WVS Station Guides service, run from an office in Central Station in Glasgow was expanded to include satellites at St Enoch, Buchanan Street and Queen Street stations. Guides normally operated in pairs, and their duties included meeting arriving American and Canadian soldiers and locating their accommodation, welcoming visiting naval personnel, meeting Polish airmen and Czech personnel on leave and advising evacuees leaving Glasgow. During the Blitz on Glasgow three of the guides left their shelters to answer an emergency call for food, wearing steel helmets and dodging flying debris as they picked their way through burning buildings. The commanding officer wrote later that their arrival had "been like a breath of spring."[10]

Not all calls for assistance were genuine cases, and maybe the sight of young WVS volunteers at the end of a long stint of overseas service brought many a young man forward with a chat-up line. But as the organiser at Central Station, in charge of 96 such guides, pointed out: "Do not run away with the idea that we women of the WVS can be hoodwinked with any cock-and-bull story. We're not as simple as that." And yet often there were occasions when the poor women found their office at the station turned into a pets' corner as servicemen owners went to enjoy a meal or an hour or two at the pictures. And on one memorable occasion, "One of our guides came upon a merchant seaman at a loss to find a spot to leave a monkey."[11]

Elsewhere the WVS Allied Information Bureau in Edinburgh had opened a subsidiary office in Glasgow as the first trickle of what was to become a tide of American troops arrived on liners in 1942 to be welcomed by a full mobilisation of Gourock WVS. This was the pioneer centre for the 200 Welcome Clubs which would open across Britain to provide hospitality for North American servicemen. A report for September 1942 noted the arrival of the "white pork-pie hats of the American sailors and the unusual shades of khaki of the dough boys' uniform," but waywardly forecast that it was "not likely that American forces will be coming to Scotland in any great numbers." It was also reported that an American unit on exercise in Lanarkshire was so wonderfully entertained by WVS that its commanding officer claimed that his men had "purposefully tried to do badly in the weekly tests, thinking that if they failed they would be given the opportunity of having a further course in the same district."[12]

Two major developments impacted upon WVS in 1942 as the war's new complexion took effect. The first was the compulsory call-up of younger women to National Service. The second was the introduction of a formal WVS Basic Training Scheme which all members had to take.

Men between the ages of 18 and 40 had been called up at the start of the war in September 1939, with the upper age limit rising to 51 in 1941. In February 1941 emergency powers saw single mobile women between the ages of 16 and 49 registering for essential work. In December that year women between 20 and 30 were compulsorily conscripted for the women's Naval, Army or Air Force auxiliary services, unless they were employed on essential war work. Prior to that, the recruitment of women for both the auxiliary services and essential industry had been voluntary. The government's intention was to use the short working hours which women with homes to run could spare – and while WVS was adept at publicising the importance of this part-time work through its industrial liaison officers, centre organisers up and down the country knew that the call-up of younger women which gathered momentum in 1942 would also have repercussions for membership. Stella Reading was eventually successful in persuading the Ministry of Labour that essential WVS staff should not be directed into other employment but the sudden loss of thousands of its younger foot soldiers gave the organisation the middle-aged profile associated with WRVS in modern times.

Thereafter the increasing responsibility borne by remaining members was exacerbated by the "practical impossibility of obtaining domestic help." Members were told in an internal report that "an enormous number of women now have to do household chores and shopping as best they can, in odd intervals between cooking for the Home Guard, attending the Basic Training lectures, sorting clothing for Rest Centres and acting as drivers. Inevitably some members have had to resign and this has added to the strain of those who have managed to carry on." No doubt the burden was felt by many women who had lost housekeepers to the Services and it would be wrong to underestimate the impact such situations could have on domestic harmony. One Derbyshire WVS organiser reported that "nearly all the Centre Organisers are women with homes to run and are suffering from the lack of domestic help." The organiser in Bradford complained that she was losing members in a steady stream partly "because of home difficulties and the lack of maids." Nella Last, busily working on her comforts at the bomb-damaged WVS centre in Barrow, noted the ages of the women around her: "We were getting ready to go home early at the Centre and Miss Ledgerwood (64), Mrs Machin (66), Mrs Waite (73), Mrs Lord (66) and myself (59) were all in the committee room getting our coats on." Little wonder, then, that Tothill Street was keen to devise a streamlining approach to retaining membership morale and consolidating numbers.[13]

The Basic Training Scheme, introduced by WVS in the summer of 1942, was considered essential for the future relationship between members and air raid wardens during emergency work. It was also intended to increase members' commitment because of the strain on the WVS membership as more men and women were released for the Services and essential work. Launched in Scotland on 5 May, the scheme offered members courses in immediate aid, anti-gas, fire-fighting, elementary ARP and the role of WVS in civil defence. It was designed to enable members to have sufficient knowledge of what to do in an emergency – and importantly what not to do. Within six months a quarter of a million members had been trained. The scheme was particularly useful in readying the Housewives'

Service for future eventualities, as they played a vital role in street assistance and keeping communications open between housewives and wardens. In order to move it more snugly under the Tothill Street umbrella it was renamed the Housewives' Section of WVS in July 1942, and training was given to members to enable them to each look after blocks of 50 houses. Herbert Morrison, then Home Secretary, paid warm tribute to this formidable urban force of half a million women: "There are always people who say, 'we don't want to join an organisation, but we should be quite ready to help if anything happened.' The WVS Housewives go one better than this. They are not only ready to help – they are also organised and trained so that they can give the most efficient help possible. That is the spirit required among the population as a whole." Morrison, a vocal supporter of WVS, would not, however, have wished to diminish the role and enthusiasm of the organisation's half-million rural members. Country volunteers were often given their Basic Training ahead of their urban colleagues to enable it to be completed before "the haying started." A report commented, "This seems a typical WVS touch about women who, having learned to extinguish a phosphorous bomb, calmly go off to the work of getting in the harvest."[14]

It was also Herbert Morrison who paid the most telling tribute to WVS as its fifth birthday approached in the spring of 1943. At a well-attended press conference in London he commented: "If we try to sum up the achievement of the WVS I would say that they consist of a million magnificent women who are simply applying the principles of good housekeeping to the job of helping to run their country in its hour of need." There was, he said, "a touch of genius" about the way WVS went about its tasks, which it was doing relentlessly, unstintingly, indispensably, "and they are doing it under the problematic, sometimes heart-breaking, conditions of total war." Their role was not one that men could do and, he concluded, it was "something the whole nation will not forget."[15]

Other important work carried out included the formation of Invasion Committees, on which 80% of the women involved were also WVS members. Among duties here were the finding of premises for emergency feeding in the event of an invasion, and the proper stocktaking and distribution of foodstuffs. There was widespread talk of what would happen if the "worst came to the worst," and the women's role was to maintain the population in every way, from feeding them to taking in the homeless to looking after the wounded. Alert to Ruth Balfour's warning that "The WVS must be prepared," Beith WVS helped to organise the first invasion drill in Scotland, Bearsden undertook to maintain a supply chain for food, 30 members sorting and tabulating the information, and Renfrewshire investigated the running and staffing of food depots, made arrangements for secretarial work and formed plans for evacuation. The timing of the launch of these committees has drawn comment from post-war historians, as the threat from invasion had largely passed by 1942. But those involved carried out their duties earnestly and with typical efficiency. Katharine, Duchess of Atholl, Scotland's first woman MP in 1923, believed that blocking roads and digging trenches in the event of an invasion was a matter of "the greatest strategic importance" – though few on her vast Perthshire estate apparently thought so.[16]

By 1943 war was to impact on areas of Scotland hitherto unaffected by the attacks on the Northern Isles and Central Belt. On April 21, Aberdeen bore the brunt of severe German bombing. Sirens sounded at 10.15 in the evening and the first bombs hit the city shortly before midnight. Extensive damage was caused, and sadly over 90 people lost their lives. WVS staff reported for duty just half an hour after the raid began. Thirteen rest centres were opened and 967 people were looked after in them. The centre reported that "canteens and food vans were in constant use" and that members had received 102 requests for emergency transport in the hours following the attack. An Incident Inquiry Post was opened on the morning after the raid and was still operating a week later.[17] The Housewives' Section in the city was described as "invaluable" as its members picked their way through debris amid clouds of acrid plaster dust to bring people the latest information. Furniture salvage work also started as daylight broke. An inventory was made in damaged properties and furniture loaded into vans for delivery to five stores. Two members were placed on duty every afternoon in an office in Aberdeen Town House, a car standing by, and people wishing to see their furniture were taken to the place where it was stored. The centre's report to Tothill Street added, "Some just want to see their belongings, others want to get articles from drawers, clothing, linen, etc." It is from such poignant sources that 21st century observers can glimpse the terrifying upheaval bombardment caused to people's lives and be reminded again of the imperative which drove the creation of Women's Voluntary Services in 1938 as a means of preparing the country for such attacks.[18]

In the summer of the previous year, two small areas of the East Anglian coast had been selected as Battle Training Areas and all civilian residents evacuated for safety reasons. WVS was asked to help and its report was destined to be used as major evacuations of civilians from areas earmarked for training in Scotland were mapped out in 1943. Inverness had been a centre of intense military activity from the start of the war. Special passes had been required for movement north of the town, largely because of the presence of the fleet at Scapa Flow but also because of other secret schemes. In 1943, however, beaches at Nairn and at the Tarbatness Peninsula near Portmahomack were earmarked for covert training for the planned Normandy landings. WVS centres in the north were firstly requested to survey the population, and subsequently asked to distribute leaflets to householders in affected areas, advising of dates of removal. Residents had no idea when they would be able to return – some must have wondered if they would ever see their homes again.

For the Tarbat evacuation, which covered about 10 square miles and a rural population of around 800, a WVS information office was set up in Tain, where members provided information on journey routes and train times and "listened to the sad stories of the old folk and advised them to whom to go for help." Leaflets were distributed in advance of the evacuation, and five volunteers accompanied the officials who served the eviction notices among scattered crofts. Where transport was not available, members ferried residents to relatives or to train stations and made sure they had travel tickets. Adding to their difficulties was a shortage of daylight hours, bitterly cold weather and an influenza epidemic. It was no uncommon thing, one WVS organiser reported, "to drive across fields to reach a house. Several times the drivers had to seek help to get out of the mud." If people were travelling further south arrangements were made for WVS members at Inverness or Perth to meet them, help them with the change of trains and, of course, offer a welcoming cup of tea. A soup kitchen was established at Balmuchy, near Fearn, to supply meals as the resources of affected areas diminished, and mobile canteens were used for emergency workers toiling in the advancing winter to complete installations such as emergency airfields.[19]

Despite the upheaval and the realisation that Highland people "could not be hurried," WVS centres reported that the response was extraordinarily good . . . "All the people in the area had to find other accommodation. You can imagine what a job this was. However, it was readily accepted that by co-operating they were doing a service for the country." A WVS report concluded with considerable awe, "Even the farmers, to whom the order was a terrible blow, were all determined to play their part with goodwill." As one elderly lady confided quietly to a Tain member, "We won't let Hitler beat us."[20]

5

PEACE, BUT THE WORK CARRIES ON

Scotland had become a melting-pot of foreign nationals as the war reached its landmark year of 1944. The Polish army had been accommodated north of the border for several years. Remnants of Dutch, French and Belgian forces had been displaced to bases scattered across the country. A large number of Norwegians had landed in Scotland. Canadian airmen were based on the west coast. There had also been a tidal wave of refugees, from London, from Gibraltar and the Channel Islands, from Europe and, in 1943, from far-off Malaya. But then came the Yanks. Thousands of US troops poured into Scotland's western ports in readiness for the anticipated push into mainland Europe. Such was the secrecy surrounding their movements that Army authorities at first could not give adequate notice of their arrival. WVS had to improvise welfare arrangements, the women in green waiting to pounce on incoming trains and their unsuspecting passengers.

WVS worked closely with women of the American Red Cross who had come to Britain in an advance guard. After one night in which she served several trains and hundreds of men coffee and fresh doughnuts during a seven-hour shift, one experienced WVS volunteer recorded, "The impressions that remain uppermost in my mind after that night assignment are the sound of marching feet and sight of phantom Disney-like figures emerging from the fog. The depressing sound of rain dropping persistently on an iron roof. The pacing up and down, in the lull periods, of red-capped military police. The smiling, pictured face of Winston Churchill on the front page of the newspapers lying on the seats of the carriages; and above all, the delight of the country people on finding that this was not 'just an exercise' to which they had been summoned, but real work was waiting to be done." Women's desire to "be useful" was certainly facilitated by the massive build-up of North American forces. Two West of Scotland mobile canteens fed 1,000 Americans in one day, from 11 a.m. to 10 p.m., a culinary conveyor belt of pies, sausage rolls, cakes, jam cookies, chocolate and tea, though the WVS contingent had "to learn that the mysterious brew which is made from supplies of coffee essence does not comply with what the gallant allies from over the water refer to as a 'cupacawfee'."[1]

Eventually WVS staffed around 200 GI Welcome Clubs in an attempt to bridge the divide between the incoming troops and the civilian communities in which they found themselves. They visited American hospitals, such as the 57th Field Hospital at Prestwick, and provided flowers and friendship, books and magazines, cigarettes and clothes. They organised dances, provided partners, took soldiers on sightseeing tours – even loaned themselves out on Mother's Day. It would be difficult to quantify or, indeed, overstate the importance of women's unsung, unreported work in relation to visiting servicemen in the last years of war. When, for example, one member at Cupar WVS tentatively suggested that American soldiers might be able to contribute something towards the hitherto free accommodation provided by the centre's members, the branch monthly meeting "unanimously rejected this proposal."[2]

Another major commitment which reached a peak in 1944 was staffing the Volunteer Car Pools (VCP) established by the government after the introduction of petrol rationing. WVS provided many thousands of volunteer drivers, and over 20,000 cars were eventually registered for wartime purposes – about half to WVS members. By 1944, 40 car pools were operated throughout Scotland by WVS, with the exception of Perth, "where a man is in charge." The service, carried out under the control of ARP district commissioners, certainly had teething problems. At first the day-to-day work was not sufficient to keep the batteries of the cars fully charged. Drivers said there were not enough cars in the pool for emergencies. VCP organisers countered that drivers were not available at times promised. Yet the commitment of the women volunteers should not be understated as they carried out tasks "varied from deadly monotony to exhilarating excitement." A driver from the 'Get You

Home' scheme run by Ayr WVS was called out at 10.45 p.m. for a 44-mile trip, returned at 12.45 a.m. to find another call waiting for a short trip, and was called out again at 1.30 a.m. to a village 15 miles away where she was stuck in a snowdrift, was extricated with difficulty, and eventually completed her night's work at 3.15. One car belonged to volunteer driver Stella Jackson, who moved to Scotland in 1995 after over 40 years' service to WVS and WRVS. Trained to drive a civil defence ambulance, her skills were eventually used for a variety of purposes, on one occasion helping to deliver a baby en route to a rural maternity hospital. "What is generally forgotten about war-time driving is that the black-out made it very difficult for us to see where we were going," she recalled. "Added to that, there were regular roadblocks – and all the road signs had been removed. We really had no clue where we were at times." Indeed, Glasgow reported a rush of twisted ankles after the imposition of black-out restrictions, Edinburgh folk had bumps from walking into trees on the Meadows, while just about everywhere reported a rise in road accidents. Tragically, one WVS member was driving a mobile canteen through Bristol docks in the black-out when it toppled over the quayside into the water. She was trapped and drowned. She had been driving continuously for a week through nerve-racking raids on the city's port.[3]

Salvage remained a major concern in 1944. When the government made it compulsory for all 985 local authorities with a population over 10,000 to organise salvage collections, 10 million house-to-house visits were made in four months, three quarters of them by WVS volunteers. All told, 42,000 WVS members made salvage their chief duty during the war. "It was tiring and boring to reiterate the importance of salvage, yet day after day members of the WVS had to persuade every household to separate and save every little thing, from the four-page newspaper to the milk tops that Tommy had been asked to bring back from school."[4] The Ministry of Supply also promoted book drives and by 1944 had collected nearly 56 million volumes. The Edinburgh book drive, for example, involved house-to-house collections, and every shop in Princes Street carried a poster advertising the campaign. WVS commandeered two loud speaker vans to tour the city. On the 13th day of the appeal, 1,350,000 books had been collected and placed in stores across the capital. Of the 55,932,590 books gathered across Britain by 1944, five million went to the Forces, just over one million to libraries and the remaining 49 million to paper mills to be baled and reused, primarily for munitions. There was an in-house joke among centre salvage officers along the lines of "WVS always collected things, though it was not always certain why." 'Thrift' also remained a byword throughout the organisation, so a ringing 'three cheers for Lady Reading' can be imagined when Tothill Street circulated members with the news that owing to the need for economy, stockings need not be worn with WVS uniform "except on ceremonial or official occasions."[5]

While Scotland was a staging post for thousands of Allied troops, WVS volunteers along the south coast of England were rushed off their feet feeding the great army awaiting D-Day, often driving mobile canteens on to beaches to serve files of marching troops at embarkation points. Regions across Britain also flooded the south with clothes to facilitate a covert plan drawn up between WVS and the War Office for consignments of surplus clothing to follow the Army into liberated countries immediately after the beach landings. Any thoughts that the war was going one way quickly evaporated, however. Soon after D-Day Germany unleashed wave after wave of flying bombs on southern England. During a two-week onslaught in June 1944, 600 people were killed and 9,500 injured. As usual, those left homeless vastly outnumbered the casualties. Scotland was on call during the crisis. Its 360 clothing depots rapidly parcelled up emergency bundles for despatch south. Its hospital service sent huge quantities of dressings and swabs. At the height of the bombings, WVS members from Scotland hurried to London to serve in the civilian front line – the first team of seven travelling south at less than 12 hours' notice. Several centres participated and Scottish headquarters noted with considerable pride that the response to the appeal to help bomb-damaged London was "overwhelming, and hundreds from the region came forward."

The Scottish contingent was housed in Stepney and doubled up on shifts – rising at 5 a.m. and remaining at their posts until 10.30 a.m. At 6 p.m. they resumed work and their day ended at 10.30 p.m. Teams were despatched in relays to work in canteens, rest centres and clothing depots. It was difficult and dirty work among the shattered streets, often for seven days a week, and often by women whose own families were at risk at home, or whose husbands and sons were serving abroad. Later, Lady Reading was to tell how Stepney people would ask her, "How can people who do not know us and have not been through this be so generous?" Reinforcements from the regions also helped with yet another evacuation of children from London, took part in work parties in bombed-out areas and carried out distressing bereavement counselling with relatives of victims. They also worked at Incident Inquiry Points where people came to find out about their loved ones. None of these brave women knew when the next doodlebug would appear above them . . . but they were determined to help. "Bearing in mind the peculiarly terrifying effect of Flying Bombs, many of these volunteers had never been under fire before, and many were from areas where the sound of sirens was unknown. But they faced their ordeal bravely, whatever their inward qualms." WVS/WRVS veteran Isabella McKay of Brora, who lived in Hornchurch, Essex with her young family during the war, recalled that she just "got on" with duties as the buzz bombs rained down – though on one occasion she threw her baby's pram under a hedge when a doodlebug flew overhead. On another occasion she woke up one morning "to find the fin of a flying bomb embedded in the air raid shelter in the garden." She added: "I don't know if it was just because we were young, but we just seemed to accept the risks of what we had to do, and got on with the work required. That's what volunteering was all about."[6]

By the autumn of 1944 a WVS 'adoption' project called the Rehoming Scheme was proposed under which unscathed regions could formally 'adopt' the worst affected London boroughs. Ruth Balfour immediately arranged for WVS in Scotland to adopt four London boroughs which had suffered badly from bombing and to provide residents there with a range of replacement household goods.

West of Scotland district adopted Ilford and Walthamstow, the South district East Mitcham, and the North, North-East and East districts the battered borough of Stepney which had been the most severely damaged and whose bombed-out population numbered a quarter of a million. Appeals for donations were made across Scotland and by Christmas consignments of goods were on the way to the stricken boroughs. These included items of furniture, floor coverings, bedding, kitchen utensils, curtains, pictures and ornaments for those who had lost personal possessions and could not afford to replace them. WVS is credited with helping over 100,000 families across southern England through the scheme, with Scotland sending 300 tons of goods. The five districts north of the border also collected £2,500 to be forwarded to the besieged London communities, equivalent to around £80,000 today.

Proper clothing was also a concern for those who had lost everything but their lives. By the time of the flying bomb blitz, WVS clothing stores had 12,000 staff scattered from Land's End to the Orkneys. Six new clothing exchanges opened in Scotland between April and June 1944, with one of them reporting 615 registered customers who visited regularly. Stella Reading paid her unsung army of helpers this heartfelt tribute after the last bombs had fallen: "Yours has not been one of the spectacular jobs of this war. You have unpacked, sorted, sized, listed, fulfilled requisitions, turned over and cared for these millions of articles of clothing. You have rescued them from wrecked clothing stores, you have fitted them on to bombed people, you have cheered homesick evacuees with them. By your energy WVS has become one of the largest war-time clothing relief organisations in the world, and now the end of all the work is in sight for you . . . "[7]

The war was drawing to an end, but the work of WVS remained difficult and dangerous. Each month brought new demands upon them, and as 1944 crossed into the momentous year of 1945, the government asked Lady Reading if volunteers who had developed expertise in rest centres and canteens could now deploy their skills where they were needed in other theatres of war. An Overseas Department had opened at Tothill Street as far back as 1940 to co-ordinate gifts and donations from abroad. With the department's help several countries eventually launched their own versions of WVS – including Australia, Canada, India, Nigeria and the United States. Thus the green uniform became known in many parts of the world, not least in the Sub-Continent where WVS India soon enrolled 10,000 members. But early in 1944 the first WVS volunteers went to combat zones overseas – two to Algeria and four to Italy. After the D-Day landings, WVS set foot in France. By the end of 1944, over 100 WVS were serving abroad, among them a Miss Lawson from Ayr, one of three women reportedly "in the thick of the fighting" in Athens where British forces had been cut off from the outside world. "From their windows the women could see fighting, falling wounded and dead being rolled into a gutter." By early 1945, Scots women were also among WVS volunteers who from their base in Holland, in just eight weeks, forwarded over 3,000 orders for flowers to be delivered to wives, mothers and sweethearts in Britain. Many wore down their fingers writing letters home. One of these volunteers, Margaret MacDougall of Glasgow, recalled: "An interesting sidelight on Breda is the way the Polish troops on leave make a bee-line for the Scots girls here. Many of them regard Scotland, rather than Poland, as their home now." A WVS welfare officer was told by the Poles that wherever they were stationed "they make for those three little letters – WVS." Hundreds of WVS members eventually followed the Army to Burma, Malaya, Singapore, Hong Kong, Indo-China and Japan, where survivors of Hiroshima were helped. In Burma, for example, they greeted the first prisoners of war returning from the notorious Burma Road and travelled home with them. It was difficult to get the men to talk at first, but what really over-whelmed the men were the piles of food that awaited them. In her description of wartime Calcutta, Eugenie Fraser spoke of the work of the women volunteers who ran a camp for Allied soldiers in Barrackpore: "Tea and cool lime drinks were provided free and for a few annas; sandwiches, cookies, fish and chips were offered to the men. It was quite hard work for us especially during the hot season, but much appreciated by the soldiers who flocked to the club in large numbers."[8]

Members at home, meanwhile, turned to welfare for returning troops and those lying injured in hospitals. Dances, theatre nights and social events were organised, and hospitality provided as far as rationing would allow. The provision of health foods was also undertaken across Scotland. The Cowdenbeath centre, for example, reported in August 1944 that volunteers had collected 1,229 bottles of fruit juice for wounded soldiers. Glasgow's Station Guides, reaching the end of their six years of service, were re-enrolled to distribute vitamins. The good ladies of Inverkeithing's herb garden worked so hard for local chemists that "their skirts show an alarming tendency to become too slack." Again, clothing was in demand, and surplus stocks were despatched to Europe for refugees fleeing the fighting there. Edinburgh members contributed by collecting redundant black-out material for sending abroad and the Clothing Exchange in the city reported that it had 360 customers in a month, with 750 garments in and 730 out. Repatriation of prisoners of war was another major commitment. Leith WVS, for example, boarded ships lying off the Forth estuary to ascertain needs of passengers. On one occasion WVS and Red Cross canteen teams were stationed at Leith dock for 13 hours to provide refreshments to hundreds of PoW and civilian repatriates landed at the port. On one day this work involved the washing up of 3,000 mugs. Nonetheless, it was reported that the reception of the men from long service or incarceration abroad "gave everyone concerned great satisfaction."[9]

On Good Friday 1945, the final incident of the Home Front war was reported in London, and on 8 May 1945 the war in Europe was over. As its relieved canteen staff dispensed free meals to a joyous public celebrating VE Day, WVS could reflect on coping with difficulties unimaginable when it was formed in 1938. It had met every commitment with outstanding courage and success. It had won the public's confidence and admiration. It had become an indispensable arm of government, a trusted partner of local authorities and befriended Britain's people. And just a week after VE Day, WVS celebrated its seventh birthday with a peacetime thanksgiving service attended by the Queen in Westminster Abbey. There Lady Reading told her heroic but exhausted membership, "We have done work we never thought to approach and we have carried burdens heavier than we knew we could; we have learned that those things we voiced with our lips long ago are in verity truths with which we cannot live. We know now that in life no obstacle can block, it can only impede; that tiredness is an incident, not a finality; that faith and hope will dominate all."[10]

Peace had come – but at a heavy cost. Over 200 members of Women's Voluntary Services had died whilst on duty. Their names would later fill a remarkable illuminated Roll of Honour – its pages proudly recording the Scottish members who fell at their posts during enemy action. In Greenock, Mary McCartney was a WVS worker assigned to ARP duties and was on duty in her own house when a bomb hit it. She was killed outright. Paisley woman Isabella Hunter was on duty at a first aid post in May 1941, where she was in charge of drugs. A parachute mine destroyed the post. Agnes Lochhead, also of Paisley, was on duty at a first aid post when a bomb destroyed it in May 1941. No trace of her was ever found. Another WVS member, Elizabeth Sutton, not recorded in the Roll of Honour, died in the Aberdeen raid in April 1943.

Today, wreaths are laid by WRVS for the volunteers killed during the Second World War, marking the sacrifice of the heroic women who remained on duty while bombs fell and whose only thoughts were to tend others.

For all intents and purposes, WVS had enlisted for the duration of the war.

6

SOLDIERING ON

She was the woman in green who offered tea when your house was bombed. She met you with a smile at the rest centre. She was on duty every other day at the canteen. She called collecting salvage. She gave you ideas to make ends meet. She collected rosehips for vitamins. She met evacuees from trains and took old ladies to hospital. She tended to the graves of fallen servicemen . . . "Not a remarkable woman. Not so young and not so old. Not well-dressed; in fact a little war-shabby, distinguished only by that grey and red badge in the lapel of her coat."[1]

That badge was the proud symbol of Women's Voluntary Services, the million-strong ministering angels of wartime who suddenly, alarmingly, found themselves surplus to requirements when war was over. WVS had spectacularly fulfilled its initial responsibility to recruit women for evacuation schemes and air raid precaution work and had evolved into a disciplined auxiliary service during the fighting years. Lady Reading's directorate had become an integral cog of national and local civil defence and was engaged in activity with 20 different government departments. In its brilliant handling of women volunteers there was no part of daily life that it did not touch, recruiting, allocating and supervising its members through a nationwide network of industrious centres.

As peace dawned in 1945, however, members hung up green overalls, took off beetroot red sweaters and laid down felt hats to return to civilian life, some reluctantly, many determinedly. They had offered unpaid time and energies to a country in crisis and felt it an appropriate moment to embrace peacetime lives and returning husbands and sons. In soldiering terms they had done their bit. Never in history had women mobilised in such numbers. Nor had they faced such dangers. Under the wail of sirens, under a hail of bombs, in the misery and havoc of war, never had so many died as a result of enemy action. But the transition to peace was to prove complex and uncomfortable for a recruiting agency whose entire function had been to endow volunteer women with wartime responsibilities.

Country-wide appreciation for WVS war work in Scotland was expressed in a letter to Lady Ruth Balfour from the Scottish Office a week after VE Day. "We have called upon WVS on many occasions – often in circumstances of great urgency and difficulty – and not once have you failed us. The work of WVS and the spirit in which it was performed has immeasurably lightened the task of the department, and we are deeply grateful."[2] Indeed, never once had WVS failed Britain. It was considered precious – almost magical in the manner in which it had overcome so many challenges. Yet a circular from Lady Reading to members on the eve of VE Day had an astonishing effect. In it she described how she expected WVS to continue as a post-war "national service" and she asked the membership to reaffirm its commitment to the organisation. She could provide neither indication of what sort of work the women would be asked to do, nor how long it would take.[3] Rather than encouraging the movement to march together towards a Britain at peace, Lady Reading's letter seems to have had the opposite effect of demoralising her exhausted troops, fracturing the bond between grassroots workers and the WVS hierarchy in London. In effect, volunteers had expected WVS to close down after VE Day and began to resign in large numbers when it failed to do so. That members were not guided by the government one way or the other – some had been invited to civil defence 'Stand-Down' parades – loosened the ties further and added to the belief that WVS's job was done.

Ruth Balfour was in no doubt. She had been asked to run an emergency wartime organisation in Scotland and felt it had served its purpose. Indeed, it had performed magnificently. She saw no peacetime role for a service with air raid defence work at its core, and in any case she could ask no more of her Scottish volunteers and noted in a confidential report "the increasing tendency of members to consider that WVS work has, or should, come to an end."[4] Lady Balfour was not alone in her reluctance to continue.

Tothill Street correspondence is peppered with letters from regional representatives warning of a dramatic fall in membership and urging the WVS executive to formally wind up the organisation. In August 1945 the Scottish chairman set out her thoughts to the new Secretary of State for Scotland, Joseph Westwood. At this point, Lady Reading was still awaiting a statement from the incoming Labour government on the future of the organisation, firm in her belief that a convalescent country was in need of national nursing by a post-war WVS. Regarding Scotland, Lady Balfour was blunt: "If he [the Home Secretary] decides the WVS should close down, no problem arises in Scotland. WVS will close down everywhere." She cautioned Westwood over the large number of resignations expected among those who had enrolled to carry out ARP duties, and queried whether funding would continue in peacetime to allow commitments to be met. "Whatever happens," she added, "I hope to have sufficient personnel to carry on our responsibility with regard to clothing, services welfare, hospital car service, distribution of welfare food, national savings and salvage, until the need for these duties is concluded – although I could still count on the WVS to be available for emergencies."[5]

Ironically, in listing end-of-war WVS activities – particularly its integration with the government – the chairman served to remind Westwood of the women's indispensable contribution, aligning him against withdrawing government support for the organisation. Nonetheless, Ruth Balfour requested a private meeting with him "that week" to discuss the closure of WVS in Scotland. This brought the reply from Westwood: "I am extremely pressed just now." In delaying a meeting, he added, "I have not had an opportunity to consider what should be the future of the WVS. From inquiries I have made I do not think that anything will be coming up from the Home Office for a little while." Westwood was deliberately evasive. A confidential Home Office document, dated one day before his stalling reply to Lady Balfour and copied to the Scottish Office, revealed that Stella Reading was tenaciously "pressing" the Home Secretary for "the continuation of the WVS on something like its present basis." The memo hinted that it was thought WVS could "continue to be helpful" in the post-war era but warned, "This information should not be used in any approach to the WVS."[6] Lady Balfour, who had conferred with Lady Reading every fortnight during the war, pressed Westwood again, suggesting that several WVS welfare commitments were being jeopardised by the seemingly unstoppable run-down of the organisation. "I do not think that we shall be able to maintain the service to carry out day to day work, unless this is of such a nature that it makes a very obvious appeal to their patriotism." She was apparently unaware that Lady Reading was lobbying the government so vigorously to secure a post-emergency service.[7]

The future of WVS was a passionate issue within the movement. As post-war Britain faced unstoppable change so WVS commitments were transformed. Child evacuation was in reverse, rest centres mothballed, clothing depots closed, canteens returned to benefactors, knitting parties disbanded, salvage collection falling off and emergency feeding staff dispersed. The country – and WVS – now had to deal with the aftermath of the world war. Labour had swept into government and had embarked upon radical reforms, in part based upon the cradle-to-the-grave social security axiom contained in the 1942 report by Sir William Beveridge. The government believed peacetime welfare work could be achieved by the plethora of organisations which had been involved in such work before the emergency, including the Women's Institutes, the Red Cross, Women's Guilds, The Mothers' Union, Guides and nursing associations. Moreover, the Atlee Government was accelerating professionalism in the social services, notably in the provision of local authority staff as home helps for the housebound – a duty frequently undertaken by WVS during the war. Talk of the government assuming responsibility for dealing with the welfare state and of the launch of a national health service served only to instil fears of 'redundancy' among many WVS volunteers.

WVS work went on, of course. The practically minded Ladies in Green were still there at Glasgow's stations, as they had been on the same day at the same hour for the previous five years, but new commitments had emerged. They included, for example, the

Rehoming Department, whose duties including helping with donations of furniture for returning troops. Between January and December 1945, 97,000 London families were helped by a total of 1,581 consignments of goods from centres across the country. While it is a simple thing to state statistics, each load gifted by WVS regions had to be collected, packed and transported, and then unpacked, sorted and distributed. It was an enormous undertaking. A parallel project instigated in April 1945 and called the Garden Gifts Scheme saw hundreds of gardens and window boxes revived by donations of plants and vegetables to people rehoused in the first "prefab" properties. Get-togethers were now being organised for the elderly, the forerunners of Darby & Joan clubs, where "old people could meet over a cup of tea, and where someone could help with filling in forms and other problems of post-war life." Other initiatives included the creation of four WVS hostels for mothers of illegitimate children who had nowhere to go on leaving hospital, and the WVS Godmother Scheme, whereby children in institutions were visited and befriended by individual members. WVS-run Mother and Baby clubs were being established in many areas, and members continued to distribute welfare foods, such as cod-liver oil, orange juice, national dried milk and vitamin tablets. WVS was also helping in resettlement camps for repatriated prisoners of war, serving tea, sewing on medal ribbons and darning socks, as the men passed the first 24 hours of their return . . . often leaving little notes of gratitude as they made their way out of camp and homewards. Another new commitment in Scotland was the transitory care of thousands of American and Canadian troops, for whom accommodation and entertainment was organised to make their home-going more pleasant.

Several of these activities were temporary in nature, but they led Tothill Street to see a future for the organisation, although how it might develop in post-war Britain still remained uncertain. Stella Reading herself was unclear: "Whether we help the teachers in the schools with their extraneous duties or the re-housing officer with his re-homing problems; whether we conserve raw materials or assist with pie schemes, or the Under Fives, the objective is just the same – to do the most we can to lighten the burden of where it is heaviest." She knew WVS could play a role at times of emergency – but she was not fully certain how it could be positioned in relation to the restoration of normal conditions.[8]

Lady Balfour and the 30,000-strong remaining membership in Scotland did not have long to wait for the fate of Women's Voluntary Services to be decided. In a discussion paper marked 'secret' and titled *The Future of the WVS*, presented to Clement Attlee's month-old Cabinet on 28 August 1945, the new Home Secretary, James Chuter Ede, outlined the government's position. The problem, as Chuter Ede saw it, was twofold. The running cost of the service, he told ministers, was £125,000 per annum – equivalent to around £4 million today – met entirely by the Home Office under wartime emergency powers. How a post-war WVS could be funded presented a problem, and he wondered in his paper to Cabinet whether its revenue could be provided by government departments as and when they used the reservoir of WVS talents. He also raised the notion that WVS could continue "in a purely voluntary basis without government aid," but sensibly added that such a future "seems impossible."[9]

Secondly, the question of the role and relevancy of a post-war WVS had to be addressed. Lady Reading had previously submitted a paper to the Home Office which provided an impressive list of her organisation's activities. Beyond its Home Office responsibilities, she was able to list 114 services provided to 17 different government departments. It included canteens, libraries, clothes and food for the Admiralty; re-evacuation, refugee reception, rest centres, home help schemes, blood transfusion assistance and diphtheria immunisation for the Ministry of Health; while the War Office continued to be assisted by mobile and static canteens, information bureaux, ex-PoW work and mending schemes – including that of being official darner of socks to the Army. The Ministry of Food had benefited from WVS-run communal feeding centres, agricultural pie schemes, cooking and nutrition lectures and the distribution of food. The Ministry of Education could call on WVS help with school meals, transport, clothing and salvage schemes.

And so on. Lady Reading also had her supporters, among them the influential former Home Secretary Herbert Morrison, and in her submission she told government ministers that a "surprising number" of her members wanted to go on. The surprise might have been how few.[10]

Presented with activities and achievements from such a powerful figure as the Dowager, Marchioness of Reading, who numbered leading politicians among close friends, Chuter Ede advised the Cabinet, "On balance, if the fundamental difficulties can be overcome, I should be inclined to recommend that the WVS should be asked to continue in being." Over the next two to three days the Home Secretary's view was supported by departments making most use of WVS. For example, a confidential Health Ministry memo on August 30, pointed out: "While the need for WVS in some services has practically ended (eg evacuation), the withdrawal of their help either immediately or in the near future in other directions would be an embarrassment."[11]

When Cabinet met again just over a week later, on 9 September 1945, it was presented with conclusions from a ministerial sub-committee in a 'secret' paper titled *Future of Voluntary Services*. It concluded: "There was general agreement that Women's Voluntary Services could provide valuable help in dealing with many of the problems of transition from war to peace, and that any immediate discontinuance of the organisation would create awkward situations in Departments." And so, after what seemed an interminably uncomfortable analysis of the value of WVS, the decision of the committee was that: "Lady Reading should be informed that the service of the organisation would be required for a period of about two years" – though it added that "for Civil Defence" should be dropped from its title.[12]

So a public announcement was made, both by the Home Secretary and Lady Reading, that WVS would continue to operate at least until September 1947 when a further review would take place. It was also revealed that the general responsibility for funding the Service would remain with the Home Office, in consultation with other departments. Less widely publicised was that the Cabinet

committee expressed a wish that, with the return to Party government following the end of the wartime coalition, it "would be essential
to avoid any suggestion that a voluntary organisation of this kind
was being subsidised for political purposes." WVS, after all, had
thrived during the wartime political truce and noses would be out
of joint if it were seen as an arm of government rather than as an
arms-length agency of it. Mindful of the new government's left-
leaning orientation, the committee also found it desirable that "the
organisation should be encouraged to recruit its helpers from all
social classes." This comment somewhat unambiguously referred to
the lofty social status of the WVS hierarchy, it being so publicly led
by aristocratic women with many of its headquarters staff and
regional and district representatives unashamedly autocratic well-
to-do women. The post-war historian Rosalind Chambers reminded
readers of her study of contemporary voluntary organisations that
WVS was orchestrated by what she bravely termed "the potentates"
of Tothill Street: "The heads of departments at headquarters
are chiefly drawn from the middle and some from the upper
ranks of society, as are the principal regional officers . . . and the
whole service from top to bottom is strongly influenced by the very
remarkable personality of the chairman, Lady Reading."[13] It was this
perception of top-tier domination that the Cabinet committee sought
to dissolve – though we do not know Stella Reading's reaction to
Chambers' observation.

If the reinvention of WVS was a personal triumph for the
charismatic Stella Reading, it was a solution neither sought, nor
expected, nor welcomed by her Scottish counterpart. Ruth Balfour
had met the Secretary for State for Scotland at her very "under-
staffed" Edinburgh headquarters on the same day as the private
presentation to Cabinet in London. The record from the meeting
revealed: "Lady Ruth Balfour stated that the WVS in Scotland were
in most places being kept together with considerable difficulty . . .
At present the members were extremely tired and many were anxious
to quit, but above all they wanted to know their fate." Whether WVS
was to be kept on or not, it was essential, according to Ruth Balfour,
that "sooner or later there should be a definite stand down."[14]

Once informed of the Cabinet's decision to prolong the life of the Service by at least two years, Lady Balfour wrote again to Joseph Westwood. This time she expanded her views in emotive language on why she felt the time was appropriate for WVS to be wound up. She maintained that WVS members in Scotland were "nowhere prepared to work for the long hours they worked during the war." She added, "That applies to myself. I was on the job for six days a week, but many of the other WVS worked all through the war on Sunday. These long hours have meant that members have neglected their homes. They are not prepared to do so any longer." She told the Scottish Secretary that in many areas WVS had virtually ceased to exist. In the east of Scotland, for example, Dundee, Dunfermline and Arbroath WVS centres had closed, as had the county centre in Angus. There was only a skeleton service at Kirkcaldy and in the county centres in Aberdeenshire, Kincardine and West Lothian. She expressed fears for the organisation's commitments and urged the Scottish Secretary to make a case for a six-month review in Scotland rather than an open-ended commitment. She added, "If the Government wish us to continue they should in making such an announcement, also make it clear that a day would come when we would be definitely asked to stand down."[15]

With no closure timetable forthcoming by Christmas 1945, Ruth Balfour felt no honourable alternative other than to intimate her desire to resign as founding chairman of WVS in Scotland. In London, by contrast, Lady Reading's annual festive message to centre organisers was robust and buoyant. "If we can hold, for the months ahead, the tenacious and valiant spirit of the years just gone by, we shall be able to make a worthwhile contribution to the life of the nation in her anxious times."[16]

It would be doing Ruth Balfour a disservice to criticise her reluctance to lead the post-war organisation north of the border. She regarded WVS as an emergency service and believed its work was done. In letters to the government she repeated her view that ongoing work should be carried out by peacetime organisations. She knew resignations were piling up on her desk – 500 in December 1945 alone – and that offices were closing. Work was winding down

– two dozen of Scotland's mobile canteens had been driven south for use by the Ministry of Supply and rest centres across the country had been stripped of their equipment and stock. Women were being drawn back to the home by the return of service personnel and the re-establishment of the family unit. Ruth Balfour, who numbered among her aunts the feisty suffragist luminaries Lady Constance Lytton and Lady Frances Balfour, also alluded to the danger of WVS overstaying its welcome, telling the Scottish Secretary: "You are probably aware that in places there has been jealousy of the WVS." There was a "feeling" amongst other women's groups, she told him, "that if the WVS continued, it may be overlapping with such organisations." Lady Balfour's anticipation of friction was shrewdly perceptive. Mary Smieton, WVS general secretary, noted how Lady Reading "dreaded" meetings with other women's organisations . . . who were "likely to be critical of this upstart body with its Government backing, its wartime appeals and its dictator chairman." She recalled how relationships with these groups were "not always smooth" and that there was resentment over a service which disadvantaged them by being able to concentrate on any new national need "without being tied in any way by a constitution, by the need to pass resolutions at an AGM or by the need to raise funds."[17] Moreover, there was still antagonism from civil service unions who, at the start of the war, had advised their members that it would be "wise" not to have anything to do with WVS. So Ruth Balfour saw no need for WVS to become a permanent social service organisation where others already existed and where post-war government policies seemed set to rapidly expand the professional welfare state. This view was shared by other voluntary organisations who believed that WVS had outlived its maternalistic purpose and should not be funded as a privileged peacetime service. In any case they made the point, too, that WVS had taken many of their best members at the start of the war. Issues over its lack of democracy, its centralised hierarchy, its forceful personalities and, indeed, Lady Reading's autocratic leadership, were also raised at this time. At one point she was reminded by a courageous centre leader that WVS had "no monopoly on patriotism."[18]

The difference of opinion over the organisation's future meant it was inevitable that Stella Reading would not block the resignation of her Scottish chairman. So it transpired. A confidential Department of Health memo in January 1946 matter-of-factly noted: "Lady Reading's opinion was that it was desirable that a change should now be made and that Lady Balfour's resignation should be accepted."[19] Commendably, Ruth Balfour offered to stay on until her successor was found. This process produced new concerns. Stella Reading felt that another woman from one of Scotland's "top" families would be ideal to lead the organisation north of the border. When Lady Balfour suggested Mary Wilson, who had been in charge of the Glasgow centre towards the end of the war, Lady Reading circulated that she did not think Mrs Wilson would be a suitable candidate and would "not be well enough known." The implication was that the absence of a "title" would be a hindrance. Instead, Lady Reading's candidate list eventually included a trio of titled women as well as Florence Horsbrugh, who had held ministerial office in the wartime coalition government but had just been ousted in Labour's landslide victory and was thus "out of work." As the selection process dragged on into the early weeks of 1946, Ruth Balfour called Joseph Westwood in Edinburgh to update the Scottish Secretary on the health of the organisation under her caretaker administration. She told him how centres were closing across the five WVS districts in Scotland and how: "There seems no prospect of a check in the gradual dwindling of our Service. It is possible that within six months there may not be sufficient centres left for any day-to-day demands to be made upon them with success." With post-war work falling to other organisations, she appealed again for the closure of WVS Scotland "at a date not longer than two years from September 1946" at which time "there should be some ceremony in the principal towns."[20]

Stella Reading raced north to steady the ship. In Edinburgh she persuaded her outgoing chairman to remain in post until a successor could be found. Lady Reading clearly had a hand in an upbeat circular issued to Scottish centres in May 1946, but signed by Ruth Balfour: "Is this the moment for WVS to slacken? Should we not redouble our efforts . . . the battle against the enemy is over. The battle against want is on." Joseph Westwood, the politician ultimately holding WVS purse-strings north of the border, faced the dilemma of whether the organisation should or should not move into a new era. In June 1946 he asked civil servants representing the four Scottish government departments to review the Service from a Scottish perspective. This committee reported on 5 July. Firstly it expressed deep gratitude for the wartime work of WVS which "under stress of emergency" had responded "energetically and effectively to all the demands made upon them." But it concluded "that the time has come when, so far as the interests of Government departments are concerned, a definite term can be put to the existence of the organisation in Scotland in its present form." The committee was aware of Stella Reading's view, but argued: "The circumstances in the two countries appear to be so different as to justify separate and earlier stand-down action in Scotland." Its recommendation was therefore: "To stand down WVS in Scotland at the end of 1946."[21]

That was it. The end of WVS north of the border. Ruth Balfour's view had prevailed. There was to be no peacetime role in Scotland for the government's women volunteers. Then the committee added a curious clause – one which effectively stood its conclusion on its head: "We consider, however, that it would be in the national interest if some kind of shadow organisation took its place to be used as an instrument for rapidly mobilising women's voluntary help, either to cope with a national emergency, or to initiate and organise services in a particular locality." This "shadow" organisation, said the committee, would revolve around "a prominent woman as a central contact or organiser to whom the government might turn in case of need, and that there should be a small corps of local organisers who would have the necessary influence to make an effective appeal for the mobilisation of women's voluntary help."[22] If the Scottish Secretary scratched his head at such a recommendation he could be forgiven. It sounded familiar. This was precisely how the WVS was created and what it was tasked to carry out.

Confusion seeped through the Scottish WVS structure. By the spring of 1946 around a quarter of Scotland's 450 wartime centres and depots had closed – though admittedly some premises loaned in the emergency by the Ministry of Works were re-requisitioned for other purposes. In Scotland's District 1, which covered Edinburgh and the Borders, 19 of 59 centres had closed. District 2, which covered Angus, Dundee, Fife, Perth and Kinross, had seen 25 of its original 83 WVS centres end operations. In the heavily populated District 5, which took in Glasgow and much of central Scotland, 41 of 215 offices had closed. But across the north-eastern swathes of District 3, which included Aberdeen and the Moray estuary communities, as well as the Orkneys and Shetlands, 35 of 40 centres remained open. There had been little effect, too, in District 4, which covered the far north of Scotland's mainland, including Inverness. There, only three of 30 centres had ceased operations. Ruth Balfour, however, made the point forcibly that many others had "wanted to close."

The choice of a successor for Lady Balfour, who finally stepped down as chairman in August 1946, fell upon May Campbell of Dolphinston, coincidentally the sister of Florence Horsbrugh. Mrs Campbell had joined WVS on its formation in 1938 and had risen from evacuation officer in Peeblesshire to become vice-chairman of WVS in Scotland. She had previously sat on the central councils of both the Red Cross and SWRI. In an internal government memo Mrs Campbell is noted as being "very capable" and possessing "great tact, discretion, and judgement." Appointed to be her deputy was the Hon Mrs Hamilton, daughter of Lord Maclay. Hamilton was a qualified doctor, a former medical missionary in China and chair-woman of the Edinburgh Child Adoption Association. So ended eight remarkable years of chairmanship by Lady Ruth Balfour, who, despite the upheaval in her life, elected to remain an active WVS volunteer. As a parting gift, members across Scotland raised funds to present her with her portrait, painted by Sir William Oliphant Hutchinson, president of the Royal Scottish Academy.

At Tothill Street headquarters, meantime, Lady Reading's ambition to steer WVS from war to welfare was boosted by support from various influential departments. The Board of Trade, for one, announced in July 1946 that it wanted WVS to continue to run shoe and clothing exchanges, circulating other departments, including the Scottish Office, to that effect. And when another memorandum marked 'Secret' landed on the Scottish Secretary's desk, this time from the Home Office, revealing that Lady Reading had asked for the future of WVS beyond September 1947 to be set out, Joseph Westwood was told by an aide, "I gather that the idea of a 'stand down' is not likely to commend itself to Lady Reading."[23] So heads were knocked together again as the future of this once million-strong corps of volunteers was thrashed out. Meanwhile, remaining members got on with the job in a year that saw the expansion of two landmark projects regarded as the bread-and-butter work of today's WRVS.

Modern-day WRVS volunteers deliver around seven million mainly hot meals a year to people who have difficulty with shopping, carrying food home or cooking for themselves. In doing so, today's members provide friendly social contact for those who may have been confined to their house, and offer a regular check that they are safe and well. Back in 1946, Meals on Wheels had developed from a wartime scheme in Welwyn Garden City by housewives belonging to Britain's 24,000 wartime Food Leaders, most of whom were also members of WVS. This food education scheme involved women – many from the Housewives' Section – undertaking training courses in disseminating advice on nutrition and the distribution of welfare foods. As the British Restaurant in Welwyn Garden City sent out its first meals on four wheels in the winter of 1943, the pioneering WVS centre organiser noted, "The service is being tremendously appreciated and is working well, despite a certain amount of difficulty the staff are experiencing in serving the meals from a small car." Meals on Wheels, as they were apparently christened by Lady Reading's driver over lunch, were introduced to Scotland in Glasgow towards the end of 1947. Further trials took place in Edinburgh and Aberdeen before the service developed rapidly to extend to every major town. Today, Meals on Wheels remain synonymous with the world and work of WRVS.[24]

An equally important development in 1946 was the introduction of Darby & Joan clubs as gathering points to help the elderly cope with shortages caused by the war years. Especially for pensioners with limited means or in difficult circumstances, the clubs provided a warm and comfortable place to meet friends, hold dances and to take part in activities. Darby & Joan clubs proved to be so successful that their numbers grew rapidly after the war. Clubs varied from those open one day a week, to others where activities, entertainment and instruction were staged on five or six days. Ancillary amenities, such as chiropody services, gradually evolved at larger centres. No one in 1946–47 could have foreseen that some 2,000 Darby & Joan clubs would eventually open across the country, catering for a membership of 150,000 vulnerable elderly.

In respect of the organisation's future, it was proposed by the government in November 1946 that WVS be merged with the National Council of Social Services, while WVS Scotland would be placed under the umbrella of the Scottish Council for Social Services. An inter-departmental meeting in London on December 5 – to which the Scottish Office was not invited – agreed to arrange for the NCSS to recruit volunteers and to find someone with the courage to tell Lady Reading that the Home Office grant to WVS would stop at the end of 1948. And yet, even as a move into the NCSS framework was negotiated, it was becoming more evident that no group had organised on the basis of WVS and none had been so successful in expertly responding to requests for emergency or welfare assistance. Thus, in another government somersault, Home Office mandarins wrote to the befuddled Scottish Office in December 1946 that: "The particular brand of voluntary service given by the WVS is the kind of assistance the public services of the future will need."[25]

Thus the future of WVS became further confused. In London Stella Reading, who once joked to an Edinburgh audience that she had "not a single drop of Scottish blood in her," was lobbying hard for continuation through her charismatic powers while pointing to the Service's achievements and potential usefulness. While there was considerable sympathy in government for her ambitions, it is also clear that by 1946 Lady Reading had lost the confidence of many English centre organisers. Meanwhile, in Scotland, the organisation's founding chairman and other influential representatives had argued for closure, which had been supported by the Scottish departmental committee. This position, however, had not entirely found favour with the Secretary of State for Scotland. And, perhaps in an official huff at being left out of the loop, the Scottish Office responded to a request for comments on the London meeting by writing to the Home Office: "So far as the proposed merger with the NCofSS is concerned, the Secretary of State thinks that it would be a pity if the WVS were to lose its identity."[26]

Speculation over the Service's future had to wait a further six months to be brought to an end. In April 1947, James Chuter Ede announced to the House of Commons that Women's Voluntary Services would continue as a government-supported organisation without termination date. In explaining the decision the Home Secretary told MPs: "There is still much valuable work being done by this Service and there will, I think, be general agreement as to the desirability of keeping alive the spirit of a Service which has proved so successful in mobilising voluntary help for numerous forms of public work."[27] Mr Chuter Ede believed that whatever the future held, there would be a need for voluntary helpers to augment public services, both on occasions of emergency and at other times. Buoyed by the decision to continue WVS indefinitely, Lady Reading entreated her wavering troops to new goals: "Serious thinking people know that the days and months and even years ahead will demand of every member of this country the greatest contribution he or she can give, mentally, physically and spiritually . . . "[28]

The survival of her cherished service was a massive personal triumph for Stella Reading, but the cost was considerable. Her once million-strong organisation was just a rump of its former self. Barely 200,000 members remained, of which Scotland could muster only 20,000 from a wartime high in excess of 100,000. Entire areas of Britain were without centres and leaderless. Politically, her decision to engage with the Labour Government's austerity programme alienated many of her staunchest supporters, notably in rural Tory heartlands. Work that had previously fallen to her members had been absorbed by Labour's rapidly expanding welfare state. It was no surprise that many women quietly returned to Women's Institutes and other peacetime groups. Yet WVS had survived – and with it the flame of voluntary service still burned brightly in the hearts and minds of legions of caring women.

Amid the emerging news of survival, a more practical move was taking place in Scotland where WVS gave up its Coates Place headquarters to move to 4 Castle Terrace, formerly the home of the Edinburgh city branch. There, on 13 June, Lady Reading and May Campbell discussed the proposed merger with the Scottish Council for Social Services with the Secretary of State. The record from that meeting makes it clear that Lady Reading had not given up the prospect of retaining her organisation's autonomy and reassurance had to be given by a Scottish Office representative that "WVS would not be submerged, but would retain its name and continue to attract its special tasks on behalf of Government departments and local authorities." As matters transpired, the proposed merger of WVS Scotland and the SCSS was "not making much headway" as the 1940s drew to a close and appears thereafter to have been swallowed up as WVS found its post-war feet.[29]

By 1947 in any case WVS was being reinvigorated by substantial numbers of new and active recruits from redundant female factory workers and returning Services personnel, many of them newly self-confident of their skills and abilities. Records show, for instance, women volunteering in Aberdeen, Dundee, Edinburgh and Glasgow from local branches of the Association of Wrens to offset losses of experienced members. Enrolment was also boosted by a return to the Service of wartime members who had, understandably, resigned in 1945. As month succeeded month there was a growing realisation that there could be no normality as yet in a country so impoverished by war and short of basic needs, and gradually many of those who had dropped out after VE Day re-enrolled. One Scottish member, familiar with this phenomenon, commented: "Most of them began to miss all the public-spirited activities in which they had taken part during the war."[30]

War or peace, people still turned instinctively for help to WVS. Members, for instance, organised an information bureau at the first

Edinburgh Festival in 1947, where they found that the "fame" of WVS had spread amongst overseas visitors. This service quickly became a festival fixture. At the opposite end of the welfare scale, members re-enrolled to help with the government's immunisation campaign in an attempt to reduce the 18,000 cases of diphtheria recorded that year. In the autumn of 1947 WVS also launched an exports initiative called Women's Home Industries Ltd, to allow British housewives unable to leave their homes to produce items, such as woollens, to be sold in the USA, Canada and Australia. Gradually, as membership increased, WVS enhanced its links to NAAFI – the Navy, Army and Air Force Institutes – which ran recreational establishments needed by the forces. And some familiar activities continued into the late 1940s and beyond – among them the Volunteer Car Pool, hostels for the elderly, maternity homes for unmarried mothers and children's clothing exchanges. Meanwhile, on a visit to Scotland, Lady Reading spoke of those WVS still serving overseas: "The men are asking for the women in green – not because we look nice in it, some of us don't! The women were going out at the request of the commanding officers, and it was women with the spirit of WVS who were wanted."[31]

Like other department heads, the post-war Secretary of State for Health Aneurin Bevan knew that a body like Women's Voluntary Services was needed to fill gaps in public services until a peacetime welfare service could be fully restored and new services established. The winter of 1946–47 had been dreadful, with record snowfalls in Scotland and floods in England. Coal was in desperately short supply. There were power cuts. Shops and factories went on short time. National morale was low. As the worst fuel crisis of the twentieth century hit Britain, Lady Reading was inspired to take on nearly 100 public speaking engagements on fuel economy. Her high-profile, physically exhausting but symbolically patriotic effort on behalf of the country helped to swing the odds in favour of rebuilding the WVS network – not least because other women's groups, such as the WIs, had distanced themselves from Labour's policies. Meanwhile, members in Scotland responded rapidly to the worst snow for a century and the widespread flooding that followed by delivering meals on foot and staffing centres in isolated communities. After further bad weather in October 1947, WVS headquarters in Edinburgh heard over the radio that WVS emergency support was needed for 160 people left homeless by floods in Duns, Berwickshire. Headquarters immediately despatched two van-loads of clothing and one car, and helped to set up an evacuation centre at an empty school. Thereafter members in gumboots assisted householders by wading through clinging mud to reclaim possessions. In the same month Ayrshire members dashed to Prestwick Airport when a KLM airliner crashed, taking with them food and clothing to offer – in WVS tradition – to those in need, whether casualties, rescuers, relatives or ancillary personnel such as accident investigators or press. In May 1949 Glasgow volunteers rushed from their St Vincent Street centre to the terrifying fire which struck Grafton's four-storey gown store in Argyle Street. Thirteen women and girls died as a result of the blaze, Glasgow's worst in 30 years. Women WVS, conscious of the dreadful scenes unfolding as they worked, also faced a pressing surge of onlookers which required mounted police to control.

That year, an influential report by Sir William Beveridge drew attention to the continued use of WVS over far more fields than emergency response. In establishing evidence for the continuance of voluntary action within the welfare state, but at the same time attempting to give it an appropriate role, Beveridge hammered home the value of WVS and pointed out: "All voluntary work of a specialised nature should continue to be done by the specialist organisations, but there should be more co-ordination and less overlapping and waste of effort, and this could be supplied through WVS or by some co-ordinating Board of which WVS was the spearhead."[32]

The government listened. Civil defence, as such, had been disbanded at the end of the war. But in November 1949, partly in response to the threat of nuclear proliferation, the Home Office announced the formation of a Civil Defence Corps of Volunteers. WVS was asked to give whatever help it could to local authorities – and to join the corps as members, particularly in its welfare section. Later, the Home Secretary announced that WVS would become the women's auxiliary service to the Civil Defence Corps. What this meant for WVS was that in addition to all its other activities, it would be under obligation as the women's arm of the new organisation to encourage members to join the corps, to give assistance to local authorities in civil defence training and to build up its own membership so that it could help in an emergency as auxiliaries to the main services of civil defence. Members of WVS who enrolled in the corps retained their membership of WVS, however. From 1952, it was common to see women wearing WVS uniform with a new 'Civil Defence' armband. From 1955 a 'Welfare' arm flash was provided with WVS uniforms and members wore the 'CD Corps' badge on their berets.

As the 1950s beckoned, it was as if the social conscience of many Scotswomen had been re-awakened. They had become communally active again, perhaps not with the urgency and patriotic fervour of the war years, but with a public-spirited sense of duty which the emergency had engendered; as the Scottish chairman May Campbell put it at the time, "service beyond self" once more, but now adapted to the changing needs of society. Although new government legislation – including the introduction of the NHS in 1948 – was gradually replacing many of the original commitments of Women's Voluntary Services, a desire to increase the comfort and happiness of those in need was the lasting legacy of wartime voluntary work.

On a trip to Edinburgh in May 1949 a member of the London headquarters staff visited the Scottish War Memorial overlooking the city. She noted poignantly: "Standing there it was brought home to us more vividly than ever what great sacrifices had been made so that we might live, and we walked down the hill even more convinced that each one of us must play our part in creating a pattern of lasting peace."[33]

7

THROUGH STORM AND FLOOD

Women's Voluntary Services would face new challenges as the second half of the twentieth century began. There would be emergencies – floods, fires and accidents – which would draw upon the compassionate skills of its membership at times of great anguish and hardship. There would come the end of traditional roles and the launch of challenging new ventures. Stella Reading would go to the House of Lords, while her cherished WVS would change its name by royal appointment. And there would be a new war – a Cold War.

Before all of that, Scotland had the chance to remember the war heroines of WVS. In letters of gold inscribed on pages of the finest vellum and bound in red leather, the names of the 241 WVS members killed in action between 1939 and 1945 were listed for all time in a Roll of Honour created in 1951, which recorded the manner of each member's sacrifice alongside their names . . .

" . . . Killed returning from duty with a mobile canteen."

" . . . Killed by a direct hit on the Clothing Depot."

" . . . Remained sewing instead of taking shelter, as the work in hand was urgently needed in the hospital."

" . . . Received a direct hit while she was delivering wool to a knitting party. She was not killed outright, but with many others of the party, she was trapped by falling masonry. She tried to direct the rescuers, one of whom received the George Cross. But no one was rescued alive . . . "

The memorial to the fallen sisters of WVS told the story of civilian heroism and how the ordinary women of the country had risked their lives to help their communities. The Roll of Honour was the work of Claire Evans, who had joined WVS three days after war broke out. On its illuminated panels she painted scenes showing a clothing depot; women garnishing camouflage nets; a rest centre; a bombed-out family being taken to a rest centre; salvage workers; a mobile canteen; members evacuating under-fives, and an incident inquiry point. She then added in careful script name after name of the women who had died on duty in the grey-green uniform of Women's Voluntary Services.

In June 1951 the Roll was brought to Scotland. It was put on display at the memorial chapel in St Cuthbert's Church, Edinburgh, in the shadow of the castle wall bombed by zeppelins in 1916. Thereafter it was taken to Glasgow City Chambers, where it was placed under the Lamp of Remembrance, and finally and fittingly exhibited at Paisley Abbey, where relatives left flowers on the book in memory of the three members who had lost their lives in the bombing of Clydeside and who were recorded on its pages. Now resting in St Nicholas Chapel, Westminster Abbey, the WVS Roll of Honour ends with a poignant prayer: "Everlasting Father, we commend to Thee all those for whom the end of the war is not the end of suffering, the wounded, the homeless, the hungry, the bereaved." Today this special memorial is visited by past and present WRVS from across the world.

For the Queen, who had dedicated the Roll of Honour in the Abbey in front of 2,000 WVS volunteers, personal grief came the following February when her husband King George VI died. Uniformed lines of WVS members provided hot drinks for the thousands of people who stood in the winter air to see his lying-in-state. The queue on the first day reached such proportions that some had to wait in a bitter wind and pouring rain for up to five hours, many of them still in a state of shock and loss. On the second day, Tothill Street sent a mobile canteen to provide hot drinks. Although it served 374 gallons of tea during the next 12 hours, it still proved inadequate. WVS then had to seek permission from the

Ministry of Works to set up Soyer boilers on the Victoria Embankment, and kept them going day and night for the next 48 hours. Tea was served to 35,500 people who passed on the way to pay their respects to the popular monarch. Many WVS stalwarts who lined the funeral route wore a special badge issued by Headquarters to commemorate wartime duty.

The doldrums of the immediate post-war era over, WVS began to expand once more. Thousands of new members were placed into the Civil Defence Corps' welfare section, each taking eight hours of general training, nine hours of first aid and 12 hours of specialist training. Soon, WVS was able to supply local authorities with its own qualified instructors, their certificates signed by the Director General of Civil Defence on behalf of the Home Office, and by the head of the WVS Civil Defence department at Tothill Street. Scotland was part of this considerable revival in activity. During March and April 1951 alone, a new office was opened in Perth, two offices were allotted to WVS in the County Buildings in Hawick, and Aberdeen moved into new premises, large enough to accommodate a clothing exchange. Edinburgh HQ opened a clothing depot in Granton. Dundee, Dunfermline and Ayr centres began services in local hospitals. New recruits for civil defence work were recorded at Glasgow, Forres, Carluke and Elgin.

Caught up perhaps in the revival awakened by the Festival of Britain in 1951, Lady Reading enthused over the future of WVS at a mass meeting of women in Glasgow. The gathering was organised to discuss women's voluntary work in the post-war period and the rapid expansion of female roles and activities can be gauged by the delegates in attendance – representatives from the government and from across the spectrum of autonomous women's organisations, women welfare officers from industry and the Scottish universities, Lady Provosts from Scotland's cities and members of the women's military auxiliaries. And, of course, WVS was there in force – contributing to one of the largest conferences of women ever held in Britain. Another high-profile engagement followed that year when the Queen reviewed cadets and veterans in Edinburgh, which resulted in the mobilisation of volunteers from

Glasgow, Dunfermline, Midlothian and Edinburgh to provide refreshments and emergency cover. Among other things, 50 members were tasked with providing a supper for 1,000 boy cadets. This daunting assignment consisted of tables being set for 1,000, flowers arranged, 1,000 plates of meats and salads set out, followed by 1,000 glasses filled with sponge cake, ice cream and strawberries. One cadet captured the boys' appreciation: "It's easy seein' the WVS did this. The Army widna' have gaen us flooers."[1]

Other activities contracted, however, including the collection of clothing. Ruth Balfour had at one point mentioned to the Scottish Secretary that one million items of clothing remained in Scottish depots at the end of the war, from a peak of two million during the emergency. WVS stood by a long-standing arrangement with the American Red Cross that at the end of hostilities three quarters of their undistributed clothing gifts would be handed back to them for distribution in liberated Europe. Thus across Britain a major task facing staff was packing up millions of items for return. Quantities of Scottish clothing were also earmarked for direct deliveries to countries abroad, and some went to camps for Dutch children, who had come to Scotland to recuperate after the war. The care of children remained central to WVS activities and in 1951 the WVS Holiday Scheme was launched to provide holidays for city children who had special need for them or who would not otherwise have had a holiday. WVS ensured that a child was properly clothed for the holiday, and was responsible for travel arrangements and escorts to receiving households. Camps were organised for older children. Over the next decade, 3,000 younger people were given a holiday with the support of many external sponsors – work WVS volunteers often regarded as the most satisfying of all duties.

Another landmark was reached in the autumn of 1952 with the retirement of May Campbell as Scottish chairman. Mrs Campbell had led the Service through a difficult period and had witnessed its revival in the latter months of her six years at the helm. She was awarded a CBE for her unstinting contribution – and a new-fangled television set from her farsighted colleagues in WVS. Mrs Campbell's replacement was Lady MacColl of Dumbarton, the widow of the former Hydro-Electric chief Sir Edward MacColl, who had died in 1951 after pioneering much of Scotland's modern electricity provision. Tom Johnston, the wartime Scottish Secretary, was a close personal friend of the MacColls and probably influenced the offer to Margaret MacColl to lead WVS. There must have been chuckles when one of her first initiatives as chairman was to "evolve wonderful plans for electrically heated conveyors to assist Meals on Wheels delivery."[2]

Alas, emergency work was again to occupy the energies of the membership before the 1950s had much time to progress. In January 1953 a major seawater surge coincided with a high spring tide and winds of a force unknown for 90 years to send floodwaters crashing over defences along the east coast of England. Sea levels rose up to three metres above the normal high water mark and devastating flooding occurred in Essex, Norfolk, Suffolk, Kent and the outer Thames Estuary. Over 300 people were drowned, 24,000 homes were damaged or destroyed and 32,000 people were made homeless. It was one of Britain's worst peacetime disasters. To the relief of victims went, as usual, Women's Voluntary Services. Members from all over the country were called upon to help on a scale not known since the worst wartime crises. As the floods broke through in Harwich, the local WVS organiser was phoned at 3 a.m. At 3.30 a.m. her emergency rest centre was open. When the River Tees burst its banks and poured water into 300 houses, the Billingham WVS organiser was phoned by police and calmly swung her emergency plan into action. At Herne Bay rest centre food was prepared by the light of two candles and was served an hour after the call-out. WVS in inland centres, such as at Ipswich, immediately drafted in trained emergency workers to the worst hit areas, helping with evacuation among scenes of terrible devastation. Ten Hertfordshire WVS members took a transportable kitchen unit to a flooded margarine factory and fed 2,000 workers. Teams working at Canvey Island served 60,000 snack meals and 60,000 main meals from improvised canteens. One WVS organiser rescued from a marooned house worked continuously in a centre for 14 days because she had no home to return to.

Help from across the country poured into Eastern England. Food Flying Squads, the name given to the wartime Queen's Messenger Service when the Civil Defence Corps was re-formed in 1949 and now the Ministry of Food's 'front line troops', thundered along country roads to reach the stricken area. Each consisted of four canteens, one food stores van, one water tanker, one motor-cycle and one utility van, and was staffed by 30 to 40 WVS volunteers. Eight convoys were in action for three weeks during the East Coast emergency, each squad on average serving 6,000 meals daily to police, firemen, civil defence workers, lorry drivers, flood defence contractors and civilians. Later, WVS volunteers in the Civil Defence Corps' welfare section, wearing old clothes and wellingtons, and carrying mops and buckets, waded into deserted, evacuated streets to help scrub out and clean the houses. Everything had been soaked. Furniture was peeling, upholstery was rotting away and some items had been washed out to sea. One team cleaned 40 houses in four days – each house five feet deep in sand and slime. Other members went by boat to take hot food to men working to re-construct sea walls. People all over Britain gave magnificently to the stricken areas and it was later estimated that WVS members handled 12 million items of clothing in the disaster's aftermath. Lady Reading thanked her exhausted troops and spoke later of how the emergency had "made great demands on us, and strained us, as a service, to the full." But it was during such dreadful tragedies that the instinctive – almost mechanical – response of WVS to calls for help endeared it to the public and anchored its proud position as the nation's fourth emergency service.

If high-profile incidents turned the clock back in terms of mass-membership effort, it is also true that much of the contribution of members went largely unsung in the early 1950s. The Scottish WVS commitment to troops serving during the Korean emergency is an example. The Korean War began as a civil war when North Korea attacked South Korea in June 1950. It expanded across the peninsula when the United States, and later China, entered the conflict. The war also involved hundreds of British troops in support of a UN mandate. Among the first units to arrive in August 1950 were men from the 1st Battalion The Argyll and Sutherland Highlanders,

The WVS recruiting bus, Cannock in 1939

A WVS volunteer at Butterstone, Perthshire, with evacuee children from Glasgow, 1939

Evacuation from Dundee, September 1939

The WVS canteen at Perth Railway Station, November 1940

WVS organised salvage in towns across Scotland

Glasgow WVS provide replacement clothing for an appreciative shipwreck survivor

WVS volunteers load bundles at the WVS Wool Depot in Coates Gardens, Edinburgh, 1941

The WVS Allied Information Bureau, Edinburgh, May 1942

1940s

A WVS mobile canteen feeds rescue workers at Deptford in January 1943. Hundreds of Scots volunteers offered to help in London during the Blitz

West Kilbride WVS collect clothing aid to Russia, January 1943

1940s

Aberdeen WVS clothing exchange volunteers help a discerning young customer, 1944

Volunteers garnish camouflage nets

1940s

Aberdeen WVS volunteers prepare one of the first Meals on Wheels delivery runs in Scotland, in September 1947 (courtesy of Aberdeen Journals)

Lady Ruth Balfour
(courtesy of Fife Council)

1950s

May Campbell – WVS chairman in Scotland, pictured in 1954 (courtesy of Scotsman Publications Ltd)

WVS emergency feeding of rail crash rescue workers in 1957

WVS volunteers look on as Dundee Lord Provost William Hughes presents the visitors' book for Princess Margaret's signature during her visit to the Darby & Joan club at King George VI Memorial Club, Dundee, December 1957

Meat and potatoes are prepared in a rest home kitchen for a Meals on Wheels delivery run, 1959

NOT WHY WE CAN'T BUT HOW WE CAN

The coat of arms adopted by Lady Stella
Reading on taking her seat in the House of
Lords as Baroness Swanborough, 1959

1960s

Lady Reading, left, founder of WVS, lends a hand with washing up during a visit to Aberdeen centre in October 1963 (courtesy of Aberdeen Journals)

Dundee WVS centre organiser Eleanor Morgan hands out oranges at the King George VI Memorial Club in the city, which incorporated a Darby & Joan club. 1964

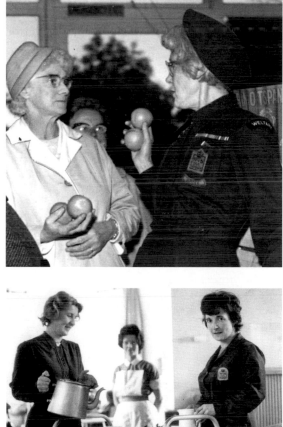

Soup for a grateful 'customer' in 1965

Some two months before they changed to WRVS, Aberdeen WVS hand out tea in one of the wards at Kingseat Hospital, 1966 (courtesy of Aberdeen Journals)

1970s

Sheila Heaney, Chairman, pictured in 1977 in her office at WRVS Scottish headquarters at 19 Grosvenor Crescent, Edinburgh

WRVS women collect blankets for the refugees of the India-Pakistan conflict at Grosvenor Crescent, Edinburgh in November 1971 (courtesy of Scotsman Publications Ltd)

Emergency Services exercise, Dumfries & Galloway, 1987

Mary Corsar, Scottish chairman, in her
Edinburgh office, 1987

Lemonade and treats and two WRVS 'trolley
dollies' on this hospital service in 1984

Princess Alexandra visits WRVS emergency workers during the flooding crisis in Perth in February 1993

Loading up for a Meals on Wheels run in 1994

Perth volunteers pose with mannequins in a range of uniforms during a WRVS exhibition in 1995. (courtesy of *Perthshire Advertiser*)

2000s

The Queen Elizabeth Canteen, gifted by the Queen Mother in 1943, seen on duty at Glamis Castle in June 2000, with volunteers Ann Nicoll, Mary Downie and Debbie Duncan

Members of WRVS serving hot drinks to evacuees at Montrose sports centre in January 2001 after the discovery of a naval shell at Ferryden triggered a multi-agency evacuation of 140 houses

WRVS celebrate at the presentation of cheques for hospital equipment in the revamped café at Perth Royal Infirmary, supported by local actor Martyn James, May 2001

Another community centre is taken over for emergency services in March 2002

Lynn Millar from the Fife Good Neighbours' Project at a display of WRVS
memorabilia at Kirkcaldy's Links Market in April 2004

Linwood pupils Leanne Baxter and Paula Denniston delivering Meals on
Wheels in November 2004

Pictured in July 2005, Margaret Duncan, head of the WRVS rapid response unit for East and Central Scotland, with volunteers Norma Adam, Margaret Scott and Ann Marshall

Chief executive Mark Lever receives a cheque from WRVS facilities manager Heather Bett, left, and volunteers Hazel Lamond and Nan Trevett at Queen Margaret Hospital, Dunfermline, August 2007

WRVS Long Service Medal, ribbon and clasp

and British troops did not depart Korea until July 1957. Throughout this long deployment WVS and other organisations did all in their power to make the men's service more tolerable – 1,000 garments sent out by WVS in Scotland alone before the end of 1951, for instance – with Stella Reading encouraging the membership to "knit, knit, knit . . . in your baths if need be." As well as the usual mobilisation of work parties and parcel collectors, a more novel departure involved just that – the departure of a handful of WVS volunteers to the front line in Korea, where they reported finding "the most glorious muddle of masculine disorder."[3]

The best known of the WVS deputation was Margaret Murie of Alloa, who was the only member to serve two terms in the shadow of the 38th Parallel. Murie arrived with advance forces in northern regions of South Korea in 1952. Before then, no British woman had been allowed in the isolated forward camp located in the peninsula's 'no man's land'. Men produced outdated pictures of children and wanted to send messages home. Others wanted to be photographed with her. Murie and two colleagues from England sat for hours by candlelight and torch taking down hundreds of messages. In addition she wrote personal letters to relatives of over 100 Scots soldiers. Korea tested the women's endurance to the limit. Living conditions were primitive and the weather ranged from intense heat to bitter cold. Riding in open jeeps through snowstorms, they took books and magazines sent by WVS at home to men on the front line. Murie told how she went to bed in a hut nicknamed 'Balmoral' with a balaclava, two sleeping bags, bedsocks, hot water bottle, half a dozen blankets and a quilt. Her five-week stints of leave in Scotland were mostly spent visiting relations of soldiers she had met in the Far East. Described as a 'mother' to hundreds of soldiers and known to thousands as Maggie, by 1955 she was still running the British Commonwealth camp's night-club in a converted hut called The Castle Inn at the furthest point north in South Korea, making cakes for men's birthdays and beating them at darts. As to the commitment of this remarkable volunteer, when The Black Watch arrived in Pusan, she was waiting at the station at four in the morning to greet them, wearing WVS uniform topped by a Red Hackle.[4]

The Countess of Cadogan, district organiser for Perth, was another of the WVS contingent overseas. Lady Cadogan had driven vans and ambulances in the war, but then volunteered for overseas work in Kenya. There she worked in canteens, scrubbed floors, drove cars, and carried out "dangerous jobs in Mau Mau territory." She looked after service families when there were sudden troop movements, re-united families who became separated, cheered up homesick soldiers, saw that they wrote home regularly and "provided them with every-thing from books to table tennis balls." Another part of her role was to organise games and dances. She recalled on her return: "Sometimes the dance is attended by 100 men and 20 girls. That can be very exhausting for the girls – especially if there are rock 'n' roll enthu-siasts among the troops."[5]

Overseas welfare work for the Forces was pioneered by such women, but unexpected calls to emergencies closer to home frequently saw the peacetime machinery of WVS mobilised. In the spring of 1952, a hurricane swept across the Orkneys leaving 25 families homeless and their bedding decorating telegraph poles. Headquarters immediately dispatched gifts of clothing donated by the public for the islanders involved. Difficulties in heavy snow also brought calls for help. In 1954 members at the Stromness centre in Orkney rallied during a blizzard which swept the Northern Isles and delivered food through drifting snow and impassable roads. The organiser noted: "Friday dawned with deep snow, and still no hope of opening the road outwards. This was our day for hot meals for the old people. We set off, clad in Wellingtons and mackintoshes, carrying the pails packed in handgrips. Despite the snow and winds the job was done." Further south, Dundee WVS was called into action when a prefab in the city was destroyed by fire. A widow and her three children were left homeless, but an appeal by the centre brought in pots, pans, bedding and clothing for their replacement house. It was no unusual sight, reported the local organiser, "to see a member carrying household goods around, including a roll of carpet begged from one of the large stores, and surplus pieces of china from their tea-room." With typical efficiency she was able to add that all the family's needs had been seen to, including light bulbs purloined from the garage where the WVS van was kept, and everything "down to a toothbrush".[6]

A typical week's activities by the mid-1950s looked like this for a busy centre:

1. **Meals on Wheels.** Three or four times a week vans would set off with hot lunches – 170,000 of them annually in Scotland at this time. The service provided more than a meal . . . contact with the outside world and a visitor willing to listen and ready to help with problems.
2. **Trolley Shops.** Manned in hospitals across Scotland, stocking everything from cakes and sweets to soap and overalls. Patient visits also carried out.
3. **Welfare Foods.** Work at various depots, helping the Ministry of Health to distribute a range of vitamins and health supplements.
4. **Clothing Stores.** Maintained in case of emergency – also issued to needy families recommended by local authorities.
5. **Salvage.** Milk bottle foil tops collected from schools, organisations and individuals and sold for scrap. Money raised used to buy birthday cards and presents for Meals on Wheels customers, or to pay for holidays for the elderly or children. Typically, this was the only source of WVS branch income at this time.
6. **National Savings.** Weekly collections of savings, including sole-responsibility WVS street schemes.
7. **Hospital Car Service.** Mothers and babies brought home from hospital, children taken to clinics and sick people driven to consultation at clinics and hospitals.
8. **The Forces.** Parcels each week sent to clubs in Germany, Hong Kong, British Guyana, Malaya and Korea . . . magazines, books, jigsaws and games.
9. **Christmas Cards.** Old cards cut up and made into scrapbooks for hospitalised children.
10. **Civil Defence.** Members trained and always ready.
11. **Emergency Feeding.** Procedures maintained by regular lectures and mock exercises.

Commitment varied. Some volunteers might spend two hours a week on WVS duty and others offer a considerable amount of their personal time. On one visit to her troops in the east of Scotland Lady Reading remarked that she "had talked to women who told her they would be a tower of strength to her when the time came, but right now they had to get their golf handicap down." She had told them bluntly that it was necessary for them to take training there and then.[7] Another story, recorded in a note to Headquarters from the Dumfries centre, demonstrates the dedicated service many WVS volunteers continued into the post-war era. There the centre organiser had initially volunteered for a few hours a week. Gradually this became all day and every day. When her husband took up fishing he started going out all night. When they saw each other in the street he saluted her and asked where they had met before!

The next test for members came in 1956 when over 20,000 Hungarian refugees poured into Britain following the Communist crackdown. Food, bedding and clothing was readied for them in hastily-prepared rest centres and WVS was given the task of dispersing arrivals to the decentralised network of support groups. Of the 1,500 WVS offices across Britain, it was estimated that 1,300 were involved in some way. WVS also produced phrase sheets to cover everyday expressions and needs, which were not only used by the Hungarian refugees but by WVS billeters and at clothing depots, by the police, landladies, employers, doctors and dentists. Trains carrying Hungarian refugees arrived in Scotland at the end of 1956 and they disembarked at two camps set aside for them. WVS had established clothing issue stores in both camps 24 hours before the expected arrival and were at the stations and in the camps to help them settle in. A novel arrangement was instituted in Banffshire, where the local council provided WVS with a six-month itinerary of its mobile library and gave permission for clothing and gifts for the refugees to be handed into it anywhere along its travels across the scattered community. Another example of practical co-operation occurred in the Borders, where an appeal was made to set up a home for an incoming family. Roxburgh WVS started the wheels moving with provision of the property, in came Selkirkshire with beds, china and cutlery, next came Kelso and Yetholm with chairs and sheets, Bonchester measured for curtains and Hawick collected beds, pillows and a chest of drawers. WVS at its most effective!

Welfare had replaced wartime work and this was made clear in returns to Headquarters from Scottish centres during the mid-1950s. Sometimes it was essential, longer-term activity, such as that involving the Hungarian refugees, the Meals on Wheels service, petrol rationing information during the Suez crisis, Darby & Joan clubs or holidays for children. And sometimes it was urgent emergency work concerned with civil accidents and disasters. Such an occasion arose in September 1959 when a fire started deep underground at the Auchengeich Colliery in Lanarkshire. Forty-six trapped men died. It was Scotland's worst pit disaster of the century. Rutherglen WVS was first on the scene and the Food Flying Squad at Chapelhall, near Airdrie, was scrambled, picking up milk donated by concerned farmers on the way. As the drama unfolded, teams of WVS from surrounding centres volunteered for duty over three days and nights to feed the 1,200-strong crowd gathered at the pithead – the firefighters, rescuers and officials, and the women with children wrapped in shawls waiting in silent dread for news of the outcome.

On other occasions WVS was turned to because it had the trust of the people to get things done. Grangemouth WVS was asked to repair and iron 200 dresses belonging to the touring Ballet Rambert. Largs WVS found a wireless for a blind elderly woman, and at Shotts the centre organiser managed to obtain oxygen for another vulnerable lady, thereby saving her life. Dumfries helped with the Royal Highland Show, while Yetholm members fed snacks to over 1,000 actors and spectators at an historical pageant. Edinburgh laid on interpreters to help overseas troops performing at the Tattoo. Mallaig members collected books for fishermen. Glasgow centre helped with the training of guide dogs for the blind and Perth helped a local X-ray information unit. Dingwall ran a mothers and babies club, to which the local authority, who knew it was on to a good thing, quickly added a clinic. A minister on holiday called at the Fort William office to ask if he could have a button sewn on. He said he saw 'WVS' on the notice board and knew he would get help. He did!

The late 1950s would also bring the first-ever national confer-ence of WVS to be held in Scotland, presided over, as ever, by the indestructible Stella Reading. At that gathering in Edinburgh a commitment to supply 100 tons of clothing for the United Nations' World Refugee Year (1959–60) was made by Scottish centres as part of the WVS UK target of 1,000 tons. A report noted: "When UNWRA wrote and asked whether WVS could collect and dispatch 1,000 tons, it was first thought to be a typographical error, and that what was really meant was 100 tons." As it turned out, clothing in excess of the total requested was sent, with Scotland punching well above its weight by offering Headquarters 175 tons against its promise of 100 tons – a total of 2,800 bales of clothes measuring 2ft by 2ft by 2ft. Shop windows had recreated scenes of the homeless with replicas of refugee camps. There were local 'refugee weeks', door-to-door collections, leaflets, posters and loudspeaker appeals – with everyone from Scouts and Girl Guides to elderly SWRI members helping the crusade against international poverty and oppression. The Scottish clothing organiser reported: "In Aberdeen the whole house up to the top was stacked with men's suits, and it was the same in Edinburgh."[8] The Olympic runner Christopher Chataway, by then a Conservative MP, praised the remarkable response: "It is reason-ably easy to send two vests and a pullover to the WVS, but for the WVS to send a thousand tons of clothes, which is about 2,500,000 garments, to the Middle East, is a different matter. And this is what it has done."[9] Once again, WVS had vastly exceeded expectations – though Lady Reading was hardly likely to let the achievement go to her members' heads. Touring America when the 1,000-ton total was met, she telegrammed Headquarters: "Grand news. Congratulations to every single person concerned. Suggest five minutes rest before next job. Love to all. Reading."[10]

To round off the decade, Women's Voluntary Services celebrated its coming of age in 1959. Amongst many 21st parties across the country was one hosted by the Queen, the WVS Patron, at Buckingham Palace, to which 500 members were invited by ballot, while its President, the Queen Mother, attended a celebration at the Service's spiritual home in Westminster Abbey. And that year Stella

Reading was deservedly elevated to the House of Lords as Baroness Swanborough. She took as her coat of arms a design featuring two women WVS volunteers, as she felt the honour "belongs to you, for it is you, the members of WVS, who have earned it." Between the two figures the arms were displayed on a lozenge because, "As women do not engage in actual battle it would be illogical to display feminine arms on a shield!" She added that the two bees contained in the design "naturally" stood for the industry of WVS and "their true readiness to go about the business of the community, ignoring self." On the lower part of the lozenge were three sprigs of rosemary, not only for remembrance, but because rosemary had so many feminine qualities, used as a scent, in cooking and in medicine, for example. The design rested upon a motto reading "Not Why We Can't But How We Can". Colour copies and an explanatory letter were sent by Lady Reading to every centre in the country, with the explanation: "To you belongs this Coat of Arms, and all the pleasure and happiness which has come with it. As I can never thank WVS for what you have given to me, I hope in this way I have for all time given back to you one of the things which you have created and for which you are entirely responsible."

However, it was the Cold War, the international superpower stalemate between America and the Soviet Union, and involving Britain to a considerable extent, which doggedly took up the time and energies of the membership after the announcement of the formation of the Warsaw Pact in 1955. The resulting arms race and stockpiling of nuclear weapons threatened wholesale destruction and alarmingly placed Scotland in the front line of what many thought was impending oblivion. By the spring of 1960 the US Navy had established the Holy Loch as a forward operating base for submarines carrying Polaris nuclear missiles. Two years later British submarines carrying the same deadly arsenal were stationed at the adjacent Gare Loch. Between these deployments, the Cuban missile crisis heightened fears of a nuclear exchange.

At its new Scottish headquarters at 14 Frederick Street in Edinburgh emergency policies were reviewed and nuclear fall-out surveys organised as the global gloom deepened. Backed by the Scottish Office,

WVS established courses for community feeding and clothing, and many members undertook and passed home nursing tests. The main input of WVS, however, was an initiative intended to allay the fears many women had of a nuclear explosion on British soil. The WVS One in Five Scheme was launched in 1956 with the agreement of the Home Office to inform one-fifth of the female population what to do in the event of a nuclear attack. In effect, the WVS membership set themselves the task of talking to one in five of the 15 million women in the country aged between 17 and 70 in the hope that they would go on to form groups to disseminate the wisdom further. It was not a practical proposition to talk to every woman in the country, hence the scheme's name and target of three million women. From 1959, speakers toured the country to tell women of nuclear warfare precautions and how to mitigate the effects of an atomic bomb. WVS specifically targeted difficult-to-contact women who were not attached to clubs or guilds and who perhaps did not mix socially, or go out to work. Later, government departments, factories, firms, banks, stores and other workplaces allowed the talks to be given during working hours. One electronics factory in Dundee held the lectures on a Sunday and attracted an audience of over 500. Topics included the effects of radiation, shock and burns – but always concentrated on the basic essentials of survival within people's homes. Flora Kirkland, a One in Five speaker, recalled that it was not always possible to keep the talks focused on their serious subject. She once told members of a Perthshire WRI that radiation spread could be limited if windows were white-washed. All eyes in the room turned to one individual, and there were guffaws of laughter. The poor woman was the wife of the Warden of Glenalmond College – where several hundred windows awaited her![11]

Various leaflets carrying the One in Five logo – of silhouettes of five women in line holding each other's hands – supported the scheme. They told their readers: "For protection against fall-out items in the larder must be canned or covered." They gave advice for flame-proofing everything from thatched roofs to interior doors. They showed how to plan a refuge room and how it could be made safer by thickening outside walls and windows with earth. Optimistically they suggested that rooms should be equipped "with the things your family would need for a stay of up to two weeks." An unconvincing leaflet called *Survival*, issued in November 1962, provided details of a nuclear blast. It pointed out that, apart from broken windows, the maximum extent of damage to property caused by a 10-megaton nuclear bomb – twice as powerful as that dropped on Hiroshima in 1945 – would be between 20 and 25 miles from the point of burst. It did warn of the possibility of exposure to radiation If people were downwind of the explosion, but reassured the public that alerts would be given to those locations which fall-out was approaching. If caught in the open, it suggested lying face down on the ground.[12]

Meanwhile, One in Five speakers, who numbered 3,000 by the end of 1962, were re-trained as more information on nuclear contamination became available. That year marked the Cuban missile crisis, and with the world on the verge of nuclear war it was no surprise to witness a surge of interest in the WVS information scheme. By the end of 1962, over one million of the national target of three million had heard the talks, with Scotland's total by then an impressive 300,000 women. Continuing her role as a speaker in Perthshire, Flora Kirkland recalled a visit to the Convent of the Sacred Heart School at Kilgraston, Bridge of Earn, where the nuns who ran the school were keen to learn what sort of roofing on their new extension could protect them from an atomic attack. "One (of many) pertinent questions was 'Have you brought a Geiger counter with you?' I hadn't, but promised to do something about it." Mrs Kirkland duly returned with a Geiger counter and operator. Its use was explained but the nuns wanted to see it in operation . . . "The operator switched on the machine and slowly walked along the line of nuns. Suddenly, the thing broke into the most ghastly clattering noise. The operator and I and some of the nuns were very startled, some giggled, and the offending nun stood there, eyes cast down, looking as if butter wouldn't melt in her mouth. Slowly she took from her sleeves a paper bag which she tipped out on to the ground – a small heap of chunks of rock – all highly radioactive. Her archaeologist brother had sent them from Egypt. She was the science teacher – how she stored them I didn't ask."[13]

Throughout the years of training and practising for nuclear attack WVS centres engaged in a remarkable range of other activities. Welfare, in the form of helping the elderly, the hospitalised and the homeless, were the priorities inherited from the 1950s. But entry to the 1960s had brought a release from post-war austerity and the membership revelled in the new challenges facing them as the dawn of consumerism finally loosened the belt-tightening that had stifled Britain since the end of the war. When, for instance, an appeal to help Polish soldiers stranded in Germany was announced, centres across the country rushed to assist them. Many of the Poles had tuberculosis and had been placed in and out of sanatoriums with little chance of repatriation. Soon WVS in Scotland had adopted over 60 patients, resulting in dozens of letters and food and clothing parcels being sent overseas. Records show individuals being helped for several years after initial contact. Later, centres adopted overseas orphans and disabled young people, continuing a tradition of helping displaced and abandoned children, once at the heart of its under-fives wartime work.

The beginning of the new decade also proved significant for members in a personal way. Early in 1961 a Long Service Medal was struck to be awarded to volunteers on completion of 15 years' service. The medal showed a portrait of the Queen on one side and on the other a design of rosemary, ivy and roses with the inscription 'Service beyond Self'. Its ribbon was green and maroon. The award gave "a great deal of pleasure throughout Scotland," and within a year 150 volunteers had been nominated for the medal, some of whom had survived the most difficult and dangerous days of war. Yet many women did not aim a thought towards medals or any form of official approbation. The Scottish chairman, Lady MacColl, commented at the time, "All we offer is work. Sometimes I don't understand it myself."[14]

Membership had increased, not to wartime levels, but to far healthier numbers than in the intervening years. Ranks had been swelled during the East Coast floods of 1953 and the Hungarian refugee crisis three years later. A rush of members resulted from the Cuban missile drama in 1962, with WVS in Scotland "greatly assisted in their One in Five campaign by the publicity given to the Russian nuclear tests." On the other hand, Lady MacColl told a television interviewer that in some districts, "The Ban the Bomb movement countered with a few letters to the editors." Recruitment generally became a central priority and various leaflets, posters and other promotional materials were introduced in the early 1960s, along with countrywide appeals for volunteers to come forward. Typical of the 'new' centres to open was Lesmahagow. A branch had been established in the town during the war, operating a canteen in the Masonic Hall to entertain soldiers stationed locally, but it had disbanded when hostilities ended in 1945. In May 1962, at the height of the Cold War, a meeting of concerned women was held in the Old Age Pensioners Hall under the direction of the Lanarkshire organiser and a WVS hospitals expert from Glasgow. Afterwards the branch was reformed with 18 members enrolling. Among its early priorities was to establish a visitors' canteen in Birkwood Hospital in the town – an aim met successfully and carried on for the next 37 years.[15]

Away from the delivery of meals and commitments in hospitals, WVS endorsed and embraced a wide sweep of activities across Scotland, ranging from staffing the Festival and Fringe information desks in Edinburgh, to despatching its Food Flying Squads to various exercises across Britain. The Holiday Scheme to provide holidays for city children proved popular and in 1960, for example, 337 children were sent on holiday by WVS in Scotland, mostly recommended by social work departments, courts, council homes or the RSPCC. By that year Scottish centres had adopted 70 overseas refugees and a constant stream of gifts and money was sent out. Services welfare continued in the form of bundles of knitted goods, books and magazines for troops abroad while American servicemen were helped at several facilities in Scotland, such as at the WVS coffee bar in the US Army air base at Kirknewton in Midlothian. One in Five talks continued into the early 1960s, as did prison welfare, civil defence work, clothing collections and national savings. At the end of each year the membership could look forward to the annual visit north by the founding mother of the service, Lady Reading – who was usually happy to pose for local newspapers with tea towel in hand.

Some work was hidden from public gaze. There was little fuss, for example, when the Milngavie centre was contacted about the arrival of two Polish families in 1961. Council houses next door to each other were allocated to them. WVS arranged to clean the homes, lit fires, provided flowers, laid tables for supper and ensured larders were fully stocked. WVS arranged for an interpreter and later found work for three of the family on arrival. Such attention to detail was typical. Another 'hidden' contribution was the continued collection, assembly and despatch of layettes for newborn babies in troubled locations ranging from Beirut to Burma. By 1961 WVS Scotland had sent over 2,000 complete layettes, comprising towels, nappies, vests, pins and soap, to far-flung communities in need. Indeed, much centre work was routine and repetitive . . . as extracts from the minutes of a Lanarkshire branch demonstrate:

"Payment for hall light to be discussed."
"Two dozen tea towels to be bought."
"Magazines sent to the troops."
"Five new drivers volunteered for Meals on Wheels."
"Funds low at £1.15/-."
"Four members passed home nursing test in Civil Defence.
"Party postponed because of mumps in hospital."
"More pies to be bought for canteen."[16]

Rachel Purvis of Earlshall, near Leuchars, a North Fife councillor, took over as Scottish chairman on 1 March 1963. She had previously administered the East District of WVS and had later acted as vice-chairman. For three months in 1962 she had stood in as chairman when Margaret MacColl was advised to rest after an illness. Another appointment at this time was Veronica Crabbie to the position of children's welfare officer for south-east Scotland, and it would not be long before Mrs Purvis would elevate her to children's welfare officer for Scotland, based at Edinburgh HQ, and thereafter vice-chairman.

Under Rachel Purvis WVS moved its Scottish headquarters once again, taking up a three-storey former Army records office at 19 Grosvenor Crescent in Edinburgh in 1964. Further significant changes followed. Scotland's five Districts, established soon after WVS was formed, were now to be known as Divisions and arranged as follows:

Eastern Division – based at 19 Grosvenor Crescent, and comprising the counties of Angus, Fife, Kinross and Perth, and the large burghs of Arbroath, Dundee, Dunfermline, Kirkcaldy and Perth.

Highland Division – based at Caberfeidh Avenue, Dingwall, and comprising the counties of Caithness, Inverness, Ross and Cromarty and Sutherland, and the large burgh of Inverness.

North East Division – based at 41 Union Street, Aberdeen, and comprising the counties of Aberdeenshire, Banff, Kincardine, Moray, Nairn, Orkney and Shetland, and the large burgh of Aberdeen.

Western Division – based at 13 Newton Terrace, Sauchiehall Street, Glasgow, and comprising the counties of Argyll, Ayr, Bute, Clackmannan, Dumfries, Dunbarton, Kircudbright, Lanark, Renfrew, Stirling and Wigtown, and the large burghs of Airdrie, Ayr, Clydebank, Coatbridge, Dumfries, Dumbarton, East Kilbride, Falkirk, Glasgow, Greenock, Hamilton, Kilmarnock, Motherwell & Wishaw, Paisley, Port Glasgow, Rutherglen and Stirling.

South East Division – based at 19 Grosvenor Crescent, and comprising the counties of Berwick, East Lothian, Midlothian, Peebles, Roxburgh, Selkirk and West Lothian, and the large burgh of Edinburgh.

A momentous year awaited the restructured organisation. On 22 July 1966 the Queen honoured WVS by conferring 'Royal' to its title, after which the Service was known as Women's Royal Voluntary Service, or WRVS. One of her first duties as Queen had been to salute the women who had won the right to wear her father's crown as she followed the king's funeral procession in 1952. Immediately afterwards she had agreed to become WVS Patron. The granting of the 'Royal' accolade 14 years later was an honour richly deserved by the Service and to mark the occasion 2,000 volunteers, including a Scottish contingent led by Rachel Purvis, gathered for a service of dedication at Westminster Abbey. For nearly 30 years WVS had freely provided the nation with willing and capable volunteers, and at last it had received public recognition of the highest kind. As Lady Reading once said, "I don't think you need to go out with a drum to recruit women. You only need to explain to them where the need is and what the job is and women will come forward."[17] In Scotland members waited excitedly for the new badges and cloth shoulder flashes to arrive and sewing groups were soon busily employed applying the 'WRVS' initials on uniforms and berets. Another important development was the departure from the founding headquarters at 41 Tothill Street and a move to an elegant property at 17 Old Park Lane, just off Piccadilly. There must have been many regrets at the desertion of the familiar building close to the Houses of Parliament. It had been barricaded and bombed during the war but had emerged to become the nerve centre of WVS operations for many eventful years. From there, WVS had grown into a million-strong motherhood of women volunteers, a powerful force in the nation's response to emergency and aggression, made up of countless women unsuspecting of their capacities and talents but destined to prove themselves again and again.

If WRVS members were chuffed at stitching the WRVS badge to new felt hats created by a Leicestershire member, above yet another new grey-green uniform designed by Digby Morton, they were also on the verge of removing another of their insignia. Just two years later, in 1968, the decision was taken to disband Britain's Civil Defence Corps. Stood down at the end of 1945, only to be reactivated on the same local-authority-run, volunteer-manned basis in the face of the increasing Soviet threat, it was decided as the 1970s approached that the global threat of the nuclear ballistic missile had left the corps with no meaningful role to play at local level. Nonetheless, WRVS continued to prepare its members to respond to emergencies of all kinds and local authorities were advised by the Home Office to make use of the training provided by WRVS for themselves and for relevant personnel in other organisations.

A booklet running to 96 pages, titled *A Handbook on WRVS*

Emergency Welfare, issued in 1967, explained how the organisation should mobilise in the event of a peacetime disaster. It stressed the difficulties which might have to be surmounted and the improvisation which would be required. It re-emphasised the need for close co-operation with councils and other agencies. Essentially it was a training manual, telling women about the jobs they should do. These included fire prevention, cooking in an emergency, clothing in an emergency, resuscitation, inquiry points and emergency home care. Members were also reminded of the core WVS philosophy – to be prepared to assist where required to do so.

Experience had told WRVS that in almost any disaster the first need of the homeless was shelter. The handbook spoke of how most buildings could be used as a rest centre, though prominent educational buildings were likely to be ideal for refreshment, sanitation, washing, first aid, clothing needs, disseminating information and providing advice. It told how the premises should be clearly marked outside and along the approaches, and how edges of steps should be whitened to avoid accidents. And if centres had to be opened in a hurry, the four elementary necessities were light, heat, water and sanitation. It warned from experience that in grave peacetime emergencies it would be commonplace to find that "the turn of a tap or the flick of a switch do not have the usual result." The booklet went on to give practical advice on feeding by the thousand – 15 loaves per 100 people for bread, and a half hundredweight of potatoes. It showed how to apply the kiss of life, not only in 'normal' circumstances but on someone buried underneath rubble or under water. In the event of nuclear attack it warned members not to look at bright lights but "to throw themselves into shade immediately." And there were many tips on improvisation – a grill pan could be used as a urinal, lipstick instead of chalk for notices, bitter lemon bottles as baby feeders and a megaphone made from stiff cardboard held together by paper-clips.[18]

In 1966 the Ministry of Health began the formal collection of statistics relating to how organisations such as WRVS provided care. The data, published the following year, showed that the number of main meals provided by voluntary workers across the UK was 11.3

million. Of that total WRVS provided 5.5 million meals – in other words it met over half of the country's needs through the contribution of around 25,000 volunteers. There were over 60 schemes across Scotland, with seven centres also preparing meals. And where a place did not have a scheme the WRVS *Blue Guide to Meals on Wheels* advised: "I am sure we ought to start Meals on Wheels in the town. There must be a lot of people who need them and it would be a way of finding new members, but I have no idea how to set about it. What must I do?"[19] A further million meals were provided that year in WRVS-run Lunch Clubs. An internal report also showed that members in 1966 provided clothing for nearly a quarter of a million people, recommended by local authority social services. Six hundred volunteers staffed 20 soon-to-be-disbanded Food Flying Squads and members were serving with the forces in nine locations ranging from North Africa to the Persian Gulf. That year the Hospital Car Service carried 311,487 patients over three million miles and auxiliary non-nursing work was taking place in 1,328 British hospitals. The statistics could go on and on – 2,000 Darby & Joan clubs, 109 mother and baby clubs, 84 play centres, 4,163 children sent on holiday, 673 bales of clothing sent overseas for refugees and victims of disasters, 1,500 groups collecting and sending parcels to troops – adding up to a precious commitment by volunteers in 1,776 centres in the UK, of which 233 were in Scotland.[20]

When the Civil Defence Corps was disbanded, WRVS also became the primary source of volunteers on which local authorities could draw in emergencies. As it was of utmost importance that they were properly trained, three courses for work in emergencies were drawn up and approved by the Home Office and ministries concerned. Stage one of the training laid stress on peacetime emergencies, and covered elements such as blanket packing, mouth to mouth resuscitation, clothing, cooking, fire precaution and emergency home care. Stage two took this training to a higher level, and stage three provided advanced training with war in mind. Training was available to members of the public, not just to WRVS, but before it could begin, intensive training of instructors had to be carried out. By

1967, certificates had been awarded for 711 emergency trainers, 201 'trainers' of trainers, 78 welfare instructors and 151 Headquarters instructors. Over 80,000 WRVS and members of the public had taken the training by the end of its first year in operation.

Wartime membership of WVS had reached 1.2 million women, and Stella Reading had made it known that she could call upon a further 750,000 reservists, if required to do so. Men volunteers, however, were beginning to make their mark by the 1960s, none more so than Robert Dick of Carnoustie. In July 1968 Mr Dick reached a landmark when he became the first man to be awarded the Long Service Medal for 15 years' work with WRVS. Mr Dick had joined as a Meals on Wheels driver in the festival year of 1951. As for his clients, well, if they had a statement from their doctor saying that they were unable to provide their own meals, they could be supplied by Mr Dick and the thousands of volunteers from other WRVS centres with a main course at 5d and pudding for 4d. Times were changing, however. Soup was no longer a staple of the Meals on Wheels service – outlawed since a law was passed saying it was unhygienic to be served from containers.

As the 1970s approached, the transformation of WVS from war to welfare had gained an unstoppable momentum. Yet the public firmly held the organisation in its heart. One year a request came from the RAF for a WRVS member to appear in its display at the Royal Tournament in London. The scene showed a wounded man being evacuated to hospital, and being met by doctors, the Red Cross and a WVS volunteer. A member of WRVS London staff recorded what happened on the opening night of the Earl's Court event. "When WVS appeared in the arena, the Commentator said, 'Ah, here comes WVS,' and before he could say another word deafening applause broke out absolutely spontaneously. As she walked across the arena, entirely by herself, the applause continued and we all felt that it was a real tribute to all the work done by WVS over the years."[21]

8

EXTRAORDINARY ORDINARY WOMEN

The loss of Lady Reading was deeply felt before the 1970s had progressed much beyond their opening year. Stella Reading, who had founded and led her cherished women's organisation for over 30 years, died in May 1971. Her death was unexpected and came as a shock to many thousands of women. She had devoted her life to helping others and her record of public service was magnificent. A solemn House of Lords, where she had sat as Baroness Swanborough since 1959, was told, "The name of Stella Reading will go down in world history." Lady Reading had started her mission with a secretary and built up a volunteer force of 1.2 million able women. Her greatest gift, perhaps, was the manner in which she inspired people with a belief in their dormant capabilities. One of her wartime office staff, Virginia Graham, recalled that she was also a "reformer of great imagination and even greater persistence, a compelling orator, an exuberant gardener, the owner of a powerful and brilliant mind. Best of all, though, she was, to many fortunate people, the perfect friend."[1]

Stella, Dowager Marchioness of Reading had emerged on the eve of war with her Women's Voluntary Services symbolising and embodying the very spirit of women's independence. It had comprised a potent and powerful force, one convinced that if the nation needed help, then WVS gave them a way to act on that belief. WVS work, she said, was a national expansion of what any woman would cope with at home. This was her philosophy and enduring legacy.

Lady Reading was succeeded as chairman by Frances Clode CBE, originally from Cambridge WVS, who had spent 33 years with the Service in a number of leading roles. These included heading the civil defence department at Headquarters and acting as vice-chairman from 1967. Under her sheltering administrative umbrella as the 1970s began were 1,664 offices, 209 of them in Scotland, where Rachel Purvis occupied the chairman's role. And WRVS in Scotland was continuing to help communities in a thousand essential or small but necessary ways where they saw a need.

Some of today's most experienced WRVS and retired members of the WRVS Association joined the organisation in the 1970s and will recall the extraordinary range of activities which centres undertook some 35 years ago. This mid-period – a bridge between the founding of the Service and its 70th anniversary – is a suitable point at which to examine how it had developed in the decades since Lady Reading's inspirational leadership began.

Children and family services

The start of WRVS's work with children was in helping with evacuation during the war, sending the little ones off with sandwiches and milk, and in creating an Under-Fives scheme in London to offer protection to the capital's vulnerable toddlers. In 1970 WRVS recommended foster homes at the request of local authorities, befriended staff in children's homes and helped in emergencies. It supported ante-natal clinics, maternity wards and child welfare centres by weighing babies, carrying out clerical work, minding youngsters and, predictably, making tea. Continuing its post-war Holiday Scheme it sent over 6,000 children from poor or difficult circumstance families on holiday in 1970, over 4,000 to private hostesses, the others to supervised camps, caravans and chalets. WRVS also provided escorts for children going to and from hospitals, homes and special schools and 'sitters-in' to help stressed mothers. By 1970 it was helping to operate over 60 Mother & Baby Clubs, pioneered by Dingwall WVS in 1951, and nearly 200 play centres. As for new initiatives, by the early 1970s over 200 Tufty Clubs, including 30 in Scotland, had been established for local authority road safety committees. Members also provided crèches at major local events, such as conferences, fêtes, festivals and agricultural shows.

Clothing

Thirty years after its creation, WRVS clothing supplies were still regarded as the 'National Wardrobe' – and yet, because of the tiring, repetitive work which went on in its often-dreary depots, clothing work was aptly known as the organisation's 'Cinderella' activity. Garments of all shapes, sizes and colours bombarded volunteers, allowing members in 1970 to distribute clothes to 270,000 people recommended by social work departments. Knitting parties, by then known as "knitting and natter" groups, were wonderfully well supported and hundreds of bundles were dispatched to the needy. Overseas work remained a significant commitment. Over 700 bales of clothing were sent abroad for refugees and victims of disasters through the British Red Cross Society, the United Nations and other relief agencies. Continuing the World Refugee Year initiative, WRVS was by 1970 sending over 1,500 layettes a year for refugee babies in the Middle East.

Health and hospitals

One of the keystones of WRVS activity, Hospital Services confounded forecasters who predicted that the launch of the National Health Service in 1948 would mean hospital volunteers would be surplus to requirements. Instead, WRVS expanded and enhanced its services to health authorities. By 1970 over 500 canteens for outpatients and visitors were run by WRVS across Britain. There were 700 trolley services for patients and 150 static hospital shops and cafes – where mature members nervously awaited conversion to North Sea gas and the abandonment of pounds, shillings and pence! Profits from these enterprises were ploughed back into hospitals. In 150 clinics and outpatient departments, WRVS helped with reception, clerical work and records, or by escorting new patients to their wards. And, after a timid entry into psychiatric hospitals in the post-war era, by 1970 members served in nearly 200 hospitals for the mentally ill, thereby forming an important link for patients with the outside world. A growing commitment was the provision of inpatient library services – which numbered just over 100 in 1970 – and work elsewhere in hospitals. This included writing letters for patients, mending clothes, flower arranging in wards, chapels and waiting rooms, running crèches for visitors' children and providing telephone trolleys. Diversional therapy and handicrafts were arranged in more than 100 hospitals and the Blood Transfusion Service was helped with publicity, clerical duties and the provision of refreshments. Lady Reading on one of her last visits to Scotland had admitted being very "moved" when a hospital matron had told her, "Oh, we do not count WRVS as a voluntary body: we count them as part of our staff."[2]

Old people's welfare

By 1970 WRVS had greatly expanded help given to elderly people who could not be properly cared for in their own homes. Yet the best known and biggest scheme, Meals on Wheels, in which WRVS co-operated with local authorities to provide meals for the elderly and housebound who found difficulty in cooking and shopping, owed its origins to wartime help for evacuated Londoners. Ten million meals were being delivered annually by 1970, around 900,000 of them in Scotland. Drivers and 'mates' had become a familiar lunchtime landmark – though rotas were generally worked from 10.30 a.m. to 2 p.m. Meals were transported in heated containers which fitted snugly into car boots or back seats in the tradition that plates, cups and saucers were once cleverly stowed into mobile canteens. Mileage allowances were paid to members using their own cars. In 1970 what was thought to be Britain's first Prescriptions-on-Wheels service began in Morayshire, linking Elgin to Lhanbryde. Elgin chemists passed on medicines to WRVS members, who then delivered them to patients in the hamlet four miles away. And there was an audible or perhaps edible cheer in March 1972 when Scottish members marked the 25th anniversary of the first meal delivered in Glasgow. This drew a congratulatory letter from the Secretary of State for Scotland in which he described the service as "essential" and said it had been "of tremendous value."[3] Back in 1947, however, the cost of equipping a Morris van was a considerable £35, which covered eight earthenware soup and dessert plates, with two food containers at £6 each. There was also the licence to pay for, plus maintenance, insurance, garaging and petrol (then 1/11d a gallon – about 10p). Members hoping to expand the service had to be reminded that Morris vans "did not grow on hedgerows."

The second major project associated with old people's welfare was clubs for the fit and unfit elderly. Over 2,200 Darby & Joan clubs were operated by members across the country by 1970, providing companionship and recreation for 160,000 fit elderly people who were sufficiently mobile to attend. Luncheon Clubs, where the frail elderly could enjoy a comfy get-together, served a further two million meals by 1970 and over three million by mid-decade. These offered companionship as well as an incentive for folk to get out and about. By 1970 there were also 25 WRVS-run residential clubs for the elderly infirm. Linked to these initiatives were over 300 chiropody services arranged by WRVS. There were also two WRVS-run nursing homes, organised under contractual arrangements with hospital boards. The WRVS Housing Association provided 300 flats for retired people and by 1970 had 130 flats for letting. The association also managed around 1,000 flats for the elderly owned by housing associations and local authorities, including seven in Glasgow. New in 1970 was the pilot of the Good Companion Scheme, in which members carried out tasks like shopping and gardening, which helped older people to go on living in their homes. But Home Helps, a service WVS launched during the war, had largely become a local authority responsibility, and the last Home Help scheme run by members ended in 1974. Once again WRVS had pioneered a welfare initiative subsequently adopted as a routine local government service.

Refugee help

For three decades W(R)VS had helped dispossessed and demoralised refugees who had sought sanctuary in Britain, including from 1972 the organised reception of Ugandan Asians. Tellingly, when a journalist was asked why he did not mention WRVS when writing about Ugandan Asians arriving to settle in Scotland, he replied, "It would be like saying a patient was taken to hospital and there were doctors and nurses there. We just expect you to be there. The green is soothing as a colour and the red shows that you are switched on for action."[4] By then there were also many elderly refugees who were of retiral age and who were finding it difficult to make ends meet. WRVS made a special effort to find, befriend and comfort these troubled people. The 'adoption' scheme, instigated in the 1950s for those refugees who could not return to their pre-war countries, also continued, and in the 1960s WRVS established two full-time workers in West Germany to keep in touch with institutionalised refugees there. By 1970 there were around 600 refugees of this kind who received "pen and parcel" help from centres across Britain.

Services welfare

The brave WVS women who travelled with the wartime Allies into Algiers and Italy in 1944 had been followed by nearly 3,000 overseas volunteers by 1970. In that year, 100 members were serving with British Forces in Germany, Hong Kong, Malaysia, Cyprus and Gibraltar. Eight members also served with the families of Gurkha troops in Brunei, Hong Kong and Nepal. One recalled that Gurkha wives were permitted to see their husbands every two years – "There was always a rash of babies thereafter!" Duties mostly involved organising daily programmes in clubs on sprawling military bases, and in the case of the vast Cold War contingent in Germany, WRVS organisers were appointed to work in cavernous community centres. In Ireland, though, volunteers regularly became surrogate mothers to lonely and unhappy young soldiers. Many were hemmed in by tight security to the extent that the purchase of hard-to-find items for them, such as toothpaste and birthday cards for their girlfriends, made WRVS invaluable contacts.

One daring member accompanied soldiers of the Royal Green Jackets on a Ruhr exercise in which the SAS won the day by raining down smoke bombs and thunder flashes on their position. In the follow-up exercise she helped to turn the tables by being disguised as a rifleman on a bicycle, which lured the SAS into an ambush, after which this unlikely decoy was snatched by her jubilant comrades and whisked away by helicopter. This perilous role was not seen as setting a precedent! Meanwhile over 1,000 WRVS centres at home supplied parcels of magazines and newspapers to units serving overseas. In Britain, too, by 1970, WRVS had assigned 24 members to undertake full-time welfare and club organisation at various Forces facilities. The following year three volunteers were despatched to start a central welfare agency for troops stationed in Northern Ireland, travelling to camps to visit soldiers, taking with them books, games, sweets and messages from home as the 'Troubles' began to loom large in our daily lives.

Transport

In the darkest days of war transport was an unsung but vital component of WVS work. As years passed, the provision of drivers remained a low-profile but important activity across the organisation. In 1971, WRVS vans and members using their own cars covered 1,805,787 miles collecting clothing and carrying equipment or people on essential service. Members also travelled countless miles on Meals on Wheels outings for local authorities. The Hospital Car Service eclipsed all other commitments, however, and accounted for an enormous amount of members' time. It was organised in Scotland by WRVS, the Red Cross and the St Andrew's Ambulance Association in support of ambulance committees and regional hospital boards. Each year thousands of patients were driven to and from appointments and, by 1970, five million miles annually were covered on their behalf.

Information

The clever idea of providing an information desk at the first Edinburgh International Festival in 1947 had extended by the seventies to embrace a wide range of events across Britain, from popular sporting fixtures such as Wimbledon and the Royal Show at Warwick to other gatherings where large crowds were in need of sustenance or support, such as the Royal Highland Show at Ingliston where, in 1972, the favourite request from youngsters concerned the whereabouts of the Daleks on the BBC stand! Moving with the times WRVS also helped at the first of the cold, wet, miserable, outdoor pop festivals, where it provided washed-out youngsters with warm blankets and clothes from its stores. It was often found useful to attend such events as a means of practising for an emergency. For example, members regularly fed over 2,000 participants at the Lord Mayor's Show in London, working out over time that such an exercise took WRVS teams roughly two hours. This was duly worked into response times in planning for major disasters.

Drug advice

Emerging from the Swinging Sixties, requests began to be made by anxious parents for WRVS speakers to explain the dangers of illicit drugs. In 1971, trained members gave over 300 talks and spoke to 37 groups about proscribed drug use. At the end of that year WRVS had 103 authorised speakers, two of them spending a fortnight with the Army in Germany talking to families about the dangers of drug misuse. This was such a new departure for the Service that Headquarters agreed with the Home Office that it should receive quarterly updates to enable it to keep pace with social trends and changing legislation.

Prison welfare

Prison welfare schemes owed their origins to a handful of WVS volunteers who spent Saturday afternoons in 1947 visiting Holloway women's prison in London to look after the interests of its inmates. Then, in 1954, WVS formally began work on an experimental basis for prisoners' families and, in 1963, a home run by WVS for ex-Borstal boys was opened in a converted council house in Glasgow, an initiative watched and eventually copied across the country. By 1970 members worked in the biggest prisons, remand centres and borstals, mostly operating canteens but involved in many less-publicised activities, such as running crèches, helping with handicrafts, visiting families at the request of Probation services, escorting girls and women to and from institutions, collecting and delivering prisoners' luggage and forming prisoners' wives groups. One initiative at HM Women's Prison Gateside (now HMP Greenock) in 1970 saw 20 of its inmates undergoing training from four WRVS instructors to learn how to feed large numbers of people in an emergency situation. And by 1970 tea bars were established in court houses up and down the country. Many a sleepy sheriff since has settled down to the last case of the day with a WRVS mug anchoring the charge sheet![5]

These activities are a snapshot of how the Scottish Women in Green operated as the 1970s began. They illustrate the organisation's evolution from emergency civil defence to welfare support for isolated and vulnerable people, particularly the elderly. Activity was still determined by need, by women working side by side and capable of an immense load, though duties had been revolutionised by the shifting sands of society.

What actually happened inside the larger branches as the modern era dawned? How did they operate?

WRVS centres were often located in civic chambers or town houses, or in rooms set aside or rented in public or private buildings, such as libraries or church halls. Purpose built, stand-alone or outright-purchase centres were less common. Offices were requested by Headquarters to be "well-ordered, tidy and to present a friendly welcome" to callers. They had to be well signposted, and all offices had to be in "a state of readiness to open in an emergency."[6] Most were operated on a volunteer rota system, with their opening hours advertised by notice outside. Organisers were provided with a WRVS Guide describing strategy and policies, a Day Book in which activities or action to be taken was noted, and a Finance Manual in which income and expenditure procedures were explained. They were, of course, awash with the essentials of any busy office – desks, storage cabinets, typewriters, notice boards and mounds of staples and paper-clips.

Centre activities were listed in reports compiled by organisers and copied to divisional representatives, Scottish headquarters and London staff. From the WVS formation in 1938 these were known as 'Narrative Reports' and they were collected and stored in Tothill Street. By the 1970s reports generally covered a three-monthly period and were sent quarterly. Narrative Reports consisted of a standardised front sheet to which additional pages could be attached as required. The form was headed *Women's Voluntary Service for*

Civil Defence Narrative Report and changed very little over the years, with many centres using old WVS forms well into the 'royal' era. Centre organisers also received a separate circular outlining how the Narrative Report should be properly filled in. This suggested headings and contents and what the report should and should not include. It pointed out that report completion was "vital" to the work of WRVS and that its "value should not be underestimated." It told local organisers that reports would be read and analysed "at every level" and that the chairman aimed to read them all. It also encouraged organisers to note items of special interest, and a sprinkling of branch activities and anecdotes eventually found their way on to the pages of WVS/WRVS newsletters and publications. Narrative Reports ranged from the carefully typed to the informally handwritten and much of their content concerned routine activities – just as it had done in the salvage, savings and knitting days of the wartime WVS.

Two examples of Narrative Reports from Bridge of Allan – one from 1956 and another from 1970 – illustrate the changing nature of activities spanning the early-to-middle period of WRVS history in Scotland. During August to October 1956 WVS in Bridge of Allan was much concerned with civil defence. Seven of its members had taken the CD course at Stirling, and another had started training for the Food Flying Squad at Falkirk. A further six members were about to begin the "schooling for 1-in-5 speakers" to instruct other women on the aftermath of nuclear explosion. The distribution of 'welfare foods' was undertaken every second Tuesday by two members at the local clinic for mothers and babies and "eighteen beautifully knitted jackets" had been sent to a maternity hospital. Two people benefited from the post-war Garden Gifts Scheme and the centre organiser noted: "We are making plans for the donation of a number of plants in the spring to those who expect to be making their gardens then." National Savings was also part of the centre's post-war work and after years of rationing and austerity it found people "very willing to start saving again." Two members had sold National Savings stamps from house to house. In three weeks they had collected £18, equivalent to around £200 today. Many letters of thanks had been received from troops for magazines and knitted items sent overseas. Visiting the elderly and housebound was also part of the centre's work. One member called upon an old lady to shampoo her hair one week and to attend to her feet the next. Another member addressed envelopes to the relations of an old man. His wife, who used to do it for him, had recently died.

The 1970 Narrative Report for Bridge of Allan, covering February to March, shows members being asked to help out at an old folks' home because of a staff shortage. The centre's Tufty road safety club was flourishing and monthly get-togethers for local elderly people were taking place. Knitting and mending were carried out by members at home and they worked in association with the clothing depot at Denny. Parcels were sent overseas regularly, but the branch felt they were not appreciated by one unit of the Forces, which was said to be well provided for, and decided to send them elsewhere. Transport for OAPs to and from hospital and the Darby & Joan club was provided. Six members worked on a rota at the baby clinic. A trolley service at Bannockburn hospital was established, but the Food Flying Squads, born from the destruction of the Coventry bombing, had been withdrawn two years earlier. Meals on Wheels numbers had risen to 10, but one old man had recently died. Before passing away he had given £1 to the meals organiser to spend on the other recipients. With this she was able to present each of them with a half-pound of tea in his memory. For Narrative Report categories marked 'furniture', 'press', 'probation' and (long service) 'medal', the organiser responded candidly with 'nil'. Under 'miscellaneous', she added, "We were given a radio and a TV set, both in good order, for which to find homes. The radio went to a disabled pensioner in Kilsyth, and the television to a local OAP."[7]

The internal workings of a WRVS centre can be gleaned from such reports. They show a strong commitment to training, helping the elderly and children, and being ready to respond to local and national events. There is a consistent preparedness – almost eager impatience – to take on new challenges. Ann McGregor, who took over as centre organiser for Bridge of Allan in 1970, was able to recall how 80 members were on the books, which made life more straightforward for her rota secretary. The branch met in a church but was about to hold meetings at a new leisure centre. She recalled a large board which listed activities to be carried out. It was headed 'Monday to Friday' and was used to remind the busy membership of where they should be on any given day, whether visiting Cornton Vale prison or helping with a Tufty club![8]

Comparable duties were being carried out in centres across Scotland by women wearing the crowned badge and distinctive green overalls of WRVS. Not only Jim fixed things in the 1970s. Members became missionaries through their work, going into parts of towns and the country seldom visited by local authority workers or other support organisations. There were parts of Leith that Agnes Mair visited in the 1970s where the WRVS car was a novelty and she recalled once, disorientated, delivering a heated lunch container to a coal cellar by mistake. Sylvia Morrison recalled "being shocked" that one old lady lived in a single room surrounded by plastic bags – "her life's belongings". One man of 88 years tasted soup for the first time in 27 years when Aberdeen Meals on Wheels called at his house to start deliveries. He had "done" for himself and had lived mainly on cups of tea and oatcakes. Further hardship was witnessed when WRVS in Scotland took over the visiting of First World War widows. Mrs Morrison recollected: "What wonderful women they were. Many had brought up families that had never known their own fathers. I also visited widows who were so strong they were outliving their own families. Some of them deserved to benefit from Meals on Wheels, but needed a reference from a doctor. One 95-year-old had never ever consulted a doctor!"[9]

Surviving Narrative Reports are a reminder of the extraordinary range of activities carried out by WRVS, individually and collectively. One member in Cupar single-handedly sent 1,000 parcels of books and magazines to the Royal Corps of Signals over a period of 22 years. This astonishing effort included donations to bases as distant as Benbecula and Borneo. Each parcel contained an average of four books and 11 magazines – some 15,000 items in total by the 1970s from one determined Fifer! Then there were initiatives which started with an individual and eventually involved many members. This occurred in Glasgow where, in the early 1950s, a small boy arrived at the WRVS office holding a large ball of silver paper. He said he thought perhaps the women might have some use for it. Not wanting to disappoint the youngster, the volunteers thanked him and took it. At first it was thought the ball could be donated to a children's home as a ribboned toy. Then someone had the idea that it might be worth something – and as scrap metal it was. After discussions it was agreed to start collecting silver paper formally, and to devote the proceeds to the purchase of a guide dog for the blind. By the early 1970s, Glasgow WRVS had proudly provided funds for 12 dogs.

Where a great number of members might be involved was in the administration of housing projects. Glasgow WRVS, for example, was responsible for the management of a house gifted to the Service. A typical stone-built villa, it was converted into seven flats with living quarters for a resident warden. Members had to form committees to cover areas such as tenant selection, maintenance, repairs, supervision and rent collection. The same centre also administered seven flats for Glasgow Corporation – including one located at 3 Devonshire Gardens, next door nowadays to a famous hotel. These responsibilities took up a great deal of time but a report to Headquarters in 1971 told how many WRVS had learned new skills "such as handling money . . . not to be afraid of lawyers or doctors . . . and it is about the fabric of the houses themselves that they have become most knowledgeable, downpipes, drainpipes, burst pipes, damp rot, electrical fuses – all extremely interesting and no doubt helpful in dealing with their own homes."[10]

In listing the activities of typical WRVS centres, nothing yet has been said of the emergency work of volunteers in the 1970s. It goes without saying that the Ibrox Disaster in 1971 was the blackest day in Scotland's sporting history. Sixty-six football fans lost their lives when Stairway 13 collapsed towards the end of the Rangers-Celtic match on January 2. Among the dead were 31 teenagers. The immediate rescue operation involved blue-light services stationed at the stadium as well as representatives of the clubs and spectators. Glasgow WRVS quickly mobilised and members made their way to the scene to provide refreshments to rescuers toiling among twisted barriers and handrails, and to the crews of the ambulances stretching along the front of the stadium. WRVS were also positioned to comfort and counsel hundreds of distraught people who had heard news of the unfolding tragedy on television and radio and had made their way to the stadium, some in the terrible quandary of not knowing whether loved ones were involved.

Indeed, 1971 began with WRVS helping deliveries to the needy during that year's national postal strike and ended with support for evacuees from the civil war in West Pakistan, now Bangladesh, of whom 15,000 passed through WRVS refreshment stations during an emergency airlift. In between there was hardly a month without an emergency, including a terrible tragedy at Clarkston in October when 20 people died and more than 100 were injured after an explosion at a shopping centre. During the course of that incident WRVS served 30 gallons of tea to 100 police officers, 20 fire brigade units and the crews of "every available ambulance in Glasgow." On a lighter note, a familiar sight was seen on the roads of Angus in 1971. The fuel crisis that year meant the historic WVS mobile canteen at Glamis Castle, gifted by the Queen Mother in 1943, was again taken into action by WRVS, still with its wartime camouflage and hooded lights. The canteen had been purchased from money placed at the Queen Mother's disposal by the Canadian Cattle Breeders' Society. She had presented the van to Angus WRVS, and in naming it 'Queen Elizabeth' in 1943 she had said, "I hope it will be of great service." Indeed it was – still responding to emergencies nearly three decades on.

Fires, floods, pit disasters, mountain rescues, motorway pile-ups, aircraft crashes and train collisions – WRVS was always on call. Major emergencies where members attended included the explosion at the Flixborough chemical plant in June 1974 and the Moorgate Underground disaster in February 1975. They were present to help as power cuts and oil shortages hit the country and during the infamous 'Winter of Discontent' when rubbish piled up on the streets. Glasgow WRVS and social work teams borrowed candles from churches and enlisted the help of small boys to trek up and down thousands of stairs in multi-storey blocks to deliver food to residents cut-off from power in more than 1,000 skyscraper homes. The boys had volunteered from three of the city's schools – unaware that they would soon have to climb 29 floors in some buildings!

Some of the most unusual call-outs occurred during the national fire-fighters' strike in the autumn of 1977. Members in Central Region, for example, maintained fire-watch patrols in local authority children's and old people's homes for several weeks. No fire-fighting training was given, but volunteers familiarised themselves with the layout of buildings and the location of equipment, telephones and essential keys. One entry in a flimsy log, written by one of the WRVS watchers, stated: "Toured premises and two-hourly rounds with member of staff thereafter. Various cups of tea and coffee. Stayed awake all night – talked and played Scrabble until 6am." During the strike, Glasgow WRVS answered 18 call-outs to help with clothing, staffed rest centres and fed soldiers carrying out firemen's duties. North of Scotland members, wearing fiery-red tabards, performed heroically at a massive blaze at Carrbridge which destroyed thousands of trees. WRVS used emergency equipment kept for mountain rescue and deployed helpers in shifts to cater for the 600 personnel involved, but the heavy smoke and unpleasant atmosphere "made it a tiring job." The local centre organiser later paid tribute to her helpers who had been "willing to come out and stay out," and related "how disappointed" were those who were not needed. At East Lothian, members fed fire-fighting troops in barracks too far from Army kitchens to be supplied. The home cooking was much appreciated by the military crews of the stand-in 'Green Goddess' fire tenders. One officer wrote in thanks, but added, "The men are getting fat."[11]

The first official visit by the Queen to the Women's Royal Voluntary Service division headquarters in Edinburgh took place in 1973. She arrived to be welcomed by a guard of honour of women in green drawn from all parts of Scotland. At Grosvenor Crescent the Queen admired a public exhibition of the organisation's work in the company of the new chairman for Scotland, Veronica Crabbie, who had taken over from Rachel Purvis the previous year. Mrs Purvis, appointed chairman in 1963, had made a considerable contribution – among unmentioned achievements accepting the royal title on behalf of Scottish members in 1966 and co-ordinating the organisation's Cold War information strategy in the backyard of Britain's nuclear arsenal. Mrs Crabbie, the daughter of an eminent Scottish judge, had spent many years with leading children's charities and, during the 1960s, had chaired the Scottish Council for the Unmarried Mother and Her Child, later the Scottish Council for Single Parents. She had joined WVS in 1955 and had been vice-chairman for nearly a decade. Mrs Crabbie explained to her royal visitor in 1973 that "there were a number of useful jobs to be done filling in the gaps of the general social services" and that many of these activities were "better done on a voluntary basis." Among them, she reassured the Queen, was the provision of Meals on Wheels at Ballater, near her royal retreat at Balmoral. Typical of the new work referred to by Mrs Crabbie was a scheme by Scottish centres to send books to the vast numbers of troops now stationed in Northern Ireland.

Related to this was the expansion in the 1970s of the Books on Wheels scheme. This took books to housebound readers and involved not only a range of library skills but often the actual choosing of books to be distributed. The Elgin delivery at this time, for example, involved Moray members carrying County Library books to 22 readers. Each fortnight the members restocked at library headquarters before setting off in their own cars armed with their contact list. At that time, any special books or books on a particular subject were arranged. Books in large print made reading easier for those with failing eyesight and were always popular. No charge was made for the service which, for housebound older people, often living alone, was a welcome pleasure and solace.

Another 'novel' initiative supported by Veronica Crabbie was a short broadcast by the BBC for use in primary schools across Scotland. This began with an Edinburgh woman making her way into Saughton Prison – but when she gets inside the children are told she is not a prisoner: she is a volunteer WRVS helper who spends her spare time at the prison. There, she is seen making cups of tea. The young viewers next see a WRVS volunteer from the Borders and they are told she provides free transport for the vulnerable. The volunteer tells them about a pick-up involving an elderly woman in Lauder who is . . . "crippled very seriously and can walk only with the aid of one of these walkers which they push in front. She has to go to the dentist in Galashiels and she obviously cannot manage a bus in any way. We dropped her at the door of the dentist . . . she stopped for a short time first to look at the shop windows . . . looking at the shop windows gave her a lot of pleasure because she never gets to a town to see these things." The scene shifts to Gartnavel Hospital in Glasgow, and the new WRVS shop there . . . "and here is another way they give a hand," says the narrator, as women in familiar green aprons are seen serving at the counter. He introduces emergency work and gently reminds the children of the tragic fire at Clarkston in 1971 . . . "lots of people were injured and the WRVS and other organisations helped by serving tea, sandwiches, coffee and soup many, many hours through the night to the rescuers and to anyone who was helping to get these people out . . . " Appropriately, the 20-minute film was called *A Helping Hand*. It was broadcast to primary schools in the spring term of 1973.[12]

For former members 1973 was a milestone year. In March that year a group of recently retired WRVS members formed an independent organisation which they christened the WRVS Association and which allowed former members to keep in touch and to take part in activities and outings. Very quickly the association boasted hundreds of enthusiastic members and its own newsletter. Eventually it became a legal part of WRVS, who paid administration costs for its offices in York – with a requirement that although anyone could join, they had to have been a member for five years. Today's WRVS Association continues to offer many opportunities for past members to remain in touch and is an important voice in WRVS circles.

Staying in touch was part and parcel of what WRVS clubs for the elderly were all about. By the mid-1970s, Darby & Joan clubs and Lunch clubs were thriving, with scarcely a community across Scotland not provided for. Activities in such clubs were many and varied. Indeed, Professor Ferguson Anderson, a leading authority on work with the elderly in the 1970s, told a WRVS conference in Edinburgh: "The age at which old age now begins is rising all the time. Sixty-five is the beginning of a happy, active time for many; by ninety years of age they feel elderly." This penetrating comment was reflected in the dual objectives of companionship and quality of life of WRVS get-together clubs. They were a terrific place for the elderly to meet and interact with people of their own generation. Activities included quizzes, concert parties, visiting musicians and magicians, speakers and outings. There were card schools and roulette tables, knitting and sewing, tea and cakes. One favourite game involved arranging men in chairs and wheelchairs in two circles around two waste paper baskets. Table tennis balls were given out and the team which filled the basket first was the winner. WRVS retrieved the balls which missed the target . . . "which causes a splendid confusion and a lot of fun; some members are asking if they can wear trouser suits for this game!" Seventies midi and maxi skirts may have been suitable – hot pants were not an option!

A significant change to WRVS hierarchy came in 1974 when Baroness Pike of Melton was appointed national chairman on the retirement of Frances Clode. Dame Frances, as she had become after somewhat uniquely progressing up the Order of the British Empire via an MBE, OBE, CBE and DBE, will be remembered for her unselfish commitment to voluntary service and talent for dealing with major crises. Mervyn Pike, an economics graduate who had been a sergeant in the WAAF during the war, had spent the previous 18 years as MP for Melton, and she had served as Assistant Postmaster General under Harold Macmillan. Regarded as the most socially-conscious Conservative of her time, she had worked with a number of leading charities and had been a close friend of Stella Reading. Famously it was Mrs Pike as Opposition social services spokesman who had made life miserable for Harold Wilson by highlighting the inadequacies of his concessions to the needy. Yet it was also Mervyn Pike, in her early days as WRVS chairman, who was asked by Edward Heath to draw up new contingency plans for the aftermath of a nuclear explosion as the Cold War continued to threaten. Scotland, meanwhile, was on the cusp of further political gerrymandering and Veronica Crabbie was charged in 1974 with restructuring WRVS north of the border to take account of the reformed local authority boundaries planned for the following year, which saw the end of county and burgh councils and the introduction of two-tier region and district councils. This posed many headaches for the organisation and its centre organisers. Responsibility for much welfare work passed to the social services and education departments of the new authorities. Incident work fell under the control of council emergency planning officers. "Thus a huge task lay ahead in training and re-orientating experienced older organisers in their new role, and giving special training to newer members."[13]

Any national event was still likely to draw heavily upon the membership – and the Queen's Silver Jubilee in 1977 was no exception. WRVS helped at countless functions across the country but, in Scotland, particular mention should be made of its increasing participation in the Duke of Edinburgh Award Scheme through a popular syllabus called 'Work with WRVS' in the scheme's Service section. The anniversary was also used to reaffirm the organisation's commitment to the elderly – a role on which it would focus increasingly in years ahead. Across Scotland, for instance, WRVS expanded the number of properties it owned under its Holidays for the Elderly scheme. At one cottage, at Glenconner, near North Berwick, around 100 senior citizens a year enjoyed a break in a beautiful setting with access to the sea. At the WRVS caravan at Blair Atholl, located on a site gifted by the Duke of Atholl, many people donated treats for the visitors and offered them car trips. Around 50 older people a year spent holidays there. WRVS also helped the Aberdeen Association for the Blind to look after a caravan at Buckie where partially sighted people had a summer holiday. A letter to *The Sunday Post* probably spoke for the many elderly to benefit from the scheme: "We'd like to thank the WRVS Wemyss Bay for kindness to four senior citizens on their first holiday in a caravan."[14]

After successfully overseeing the regionalisation of the organisation, Veronica Crabbie stepped down as chairman in Scotland in 1977, reaching the newly-agreed obligatory retiral age of 65 and after 22 years' service with WRVS. Among achievements not previously mentioned, in 1973 she had helped to run the national organisation in London in the lull before Mervyn Pike was able to take up her appointment as chairman. Mrs Crabbie's links to the Service were not severed. In 1977 she founded the WVS & WRVS Association in Scotland and became its first chairman. The woman to take the reins in Scotland was hardly inexperienced. Brigadier Sheila Heaney had served in the ATS during the war and had elected to follow a path in the military, rising to become director of the Women's Royal Army Corps. She joined WRVS on retiring from the WRAC in 1973.

Both national and Scottish chairmen did not have their problems to seek. Towards the end of the 1970s various county councils in England were starting to query whether they could continue to rely on WRVS volunteers to cope with the ever-increasing number of residents requiring meals at home and other services. Some councils decided to experiment by taking Meals on Wheels in-house, citing the need for "a uniform pattern of provision." Partly, however, the testing of frozen meals had also eroded the need for WRVS deliveries, as they allowed people to heat up food as and when they wanted. The councils' thinking was underpinned by problems in urban areas where WRVS sometimes found it difficult to provide a comprehensive service, largely through interruptions by absence to its volunteer coverage.[15]

On a happier note, WRVS celebrated its ruby anniversary in 1978 with a range of commemorative events around the country, among them the creation of a splendid floral arrangement in George Square, Glasgow, around a monogram which spelt out 'WRVS-1938'. As the 40th birthday candles were blown out and countless cakes cut across the country, the calls on the Service were as great as they had been when WVS was formed. WRVS had 25,000 helpers in 1,100 hospitals, 22 residential clubs and over 2,000 other clubs for the elderly, three homes for ex-borstal boys, over 2,500 workers in prison canteens, and some 650 escorts for prisoners' families. Its clothing depots issued near two million garments, all cleaned and mended by working parties, and 51,000 members carried nearly 17 million meals to people in their own homes.

And yet, as ever, some of the most valuable work was done quietly, week in week out, by individual volunteers among vulnerable people. They were the backbone of the organisation – the members who never forgot what the 'V' in WRVS stood for.

9

THE CHALLENGES CONTINUE

Many look on the 1980s as the beginning of 'modern times' – a watershed marking the end of a 'Dark Ages' decade of oil shortages, the three-day week and platform shoes. Britain was on the cusp of rapid technological advance – a decade which began with the birth of the home computer and ended with the launch of the internet age. Where stood WRVS at this exciting time?

By 1980 national headquarters was located at 17 Old Park Lane, a converted nursing home overlooking Hyde Park in London, where an incoming chairman, Barbara Shenfield, was finding her feet in a role which habitually thrust public prominence on its incumbent. Mrs Shenfield was a remarkable catch for WRVS. Her first husband had been killed in action only three months after their wedding in 1941. The grieving Shenfield threw herself into work for the Women's Land Army in Staffordshire. A gifted scholar, from 1946 she lectured in social studies at Birmingham University and, in 1951, married distinguished barrister and economist Arthur Shenfield. Between overseas lecturing appointments she contributed to government studies on social service and wrote extensively on services for the elderly and on social security issues. She had become vice-chairman of WRVS in 1976 after stepping down as chairman of the National Old People's Welfare Council, now Age Concern. Conversely, it was with considerable regret that the Service said farewell to Baroness Pike of Melton, who had led WRVS diligently and with huge enthusiasm, warmth and humanity since 1974. Her retirement, to take up an appointment as the first chairman of the Broadcasting Complaints Commission, was marked with countrywide presentations and messages of goodwill.

Scotland was also to get a new chairman in 1980 when the Honourable Mary Corsar took over from Sheila Heaney who had held the role since 1977. In her years as chairman Miss Heaney had offered unstinting service and had introduced several far-sighted projects, including the Good Companion Scheme, in which members gave a few hours, undertaking to assist with small chores to help keep a person living at home, which evolved into today's Good Neighbours home support project. She was also particularly proud of introducing a toy library in Edinburgh in 1975, an initiative eventually adopted by many larger centres.

Mary Corsar, the daughter of Lord Balerno, brought up on a dairy farm and married to a farmer, had a practical and methodical streak to her, an honours degree from Edinburgh University, and was ideally suited to the modern era of WRVS activities. A former Deputy Chief Commissioner for Scotland of the Girl Guides, she had become involved with WRVS after the youngest of her four children went to nursery. She began as a volunteer on Meals on Wheels and graduated to a hospital trolley shop, then Books on Wheels, before learning the administrative side of the organisation at Midlothian district office. Thus a second good catch could be claimed.

Scottish headquarters remained at 19 Grosvenor Crescent in Edinburgh's West End. There, in her office overlooking Edinburgh Castle and with views to the Pentland Hills beyond, Mrs Corsar and two vice-chairmen co-ordinated the organisation north of the border. Located within Scottish head office were experts for the widening WRVS specialties – clothing, emergency services, hospitals, housing, membership, premises, publicity, Services welfare, statistics, transport, welfare for the disabled, welfare for the elderly and welfare for offenders and their families. WRVS in Scotland had by now abandoned its district structure and was organised into 10 regional offices shadowing local government boundaries. These were Borders, Central, Dumfries & Galloway, Fife, Grampian, Highland North, Highland South, Lothian, Strathclyde and Tayside. Each had an organiser, reporting to Grosvenor Crescent. Within these regions were county and burgh centres, from which members organised and provided services to local communities. Scottish affairs were also supported enthusiastically at this time by Dame Susan Walker, a Scot, who had been appointed vice-chairman of WRVS in London.

Membership was open to "reliable and caring people" of school-leaving age and upwards, and it was publicly promised that a telephone call or letter to a local organiser would "receive immediate response." References were normally requested, unless an applicant was known to members. Two to three months of regular voluntary work was a prerequisite before a membership card was issued. As before, uniforms could be purchased, but they were not essential and the WRVS badge could be worn out of uniform. There was no joining fee or annual subscription but, by the 1980s, members could join the WRVS personal accident insurance scheme and take out a special policy which covered owner drivers. Record cards, which were begun for each recruit, were important tools in the day-to-day running of the organisation. These were used to note personal details of members and training they had undertaken. They were passed to another centre if a volunteer moved and continued membership. In a throwback to the founding structure, the national chairman remained the only person with the authority to terminate the service of a member.[1]

WRVS remained unique in the voluntary sector as it continued to receive a Home Office grant towards emergency commitments. This enabled it to formally assist government departments, local authorities and statutory agencies in organising 'national coverage' welfare and emergency work on behalf of the community. Proudly – and controversially – it continued to make no appeals for money on its own behalf at this time and many members bore minor expenses personally with great willingness. Continuing its founding mantra, WRVS remained non-sectarian and non-political, happy through the years, and under governments of different hues, to make available to the community the part-time service of its women and men volunteers.

The core concern of WRVS was also unchanged. Where there was a need, members strove to fill it. What was different by the 1980s was that WRVS activity was meaningfully linked to local authority social work departments and NHS projects. While during the war and the post-war period WVS was much its own mistress and its Women in Green recognised as an independent force for good, by

1980 volunteers were encouraged to accept invitations to serve as co-opted members on local authority committees, to co-operate with organisations working in the same field, or to attend workshops related to WRVS ventures – though it was always advised that members could only express views in line with policy.

Networking was demonstrated in the early months of the new decade during a major international project which drew in the government, statutory authorities, voluntary groups and charities and occupied the energies of thousands of WRVS volunteers. This was the International Year of Disabled People in 1981. Members across Scotland opened their hearts and gave generously of their time during the special year. One highlight was a holiday at the Trefoil Centre near Edinburgh for 40 able-bodied and physically handicapped teenagers, four from each WRVS region in Scotland. Members, who hugely enjoyed the experience, supported the teenagers by organising various activities. Extra excitement was caused by a couple of visitors who dropped in – the Queen and the Duke of Edinburgh. Elsewhere, WRVS Borders provided a meal for eight mentally handicapped boys from Airdrie, and staffed a camp for disabled children at Kelso racecourse. Stirling organised a visit to Scotland for a handicapped teenager from its twin town in Germany. She was warmly welcomed by a member and her family and a new friendship was formed. Dumfries & Galloway opened a garden for the blind in Stranraer in the presence of the newly retired Baroness Pike and Sheila Heaney. Aberdeen staged a fashion show titled Clothes Adapted for the Disabled, after which members were asked to lecture to the city's occupational therapists. Aberdeen also helped at a jamboree for 2,000 disabled children and adults. Highland South increased efforts to visit handicapped children and some of its village volunteers started 'birthdays-on-wheels', taking cards, presents and even parties to the disabled housebound. The year might be best summed up by the word "remarkable" – used to describe the experience of 14 mentally handicapped boys from inner Glasgow taken by WRVS on a never-to-be-forgotten sailing holiday.

Little has been mentioned so far about WRVS Christmas activities. Every year since its foundation members have contributed with freshness and energy to festive period projects, from little gifts to hospitalised children to major initiatives embracing the wider voluntary sector. Typical enterprises from the early 1980s included, for example, support for an appeal by local radio stations to 'Buy an Extra Tin'. This popular project encouraged the public to contribute to parcels for recipients of Meals on Wheels – and who better to pack the parcels than WRVS? Many a lonely person in Scotland answered a knock at the door to a WRVS badge-holder bearing a Christmas gift, generosity which inspired this return 'offering' from an anonymous Meals on Wheels client in the Borders Region in 1981:

> To hear your rat-tat on my door,
> I know it's you who's there,
> How well I know your footsteps,
> upon my little stair.
>
> Then in you come with smiling face
> which brightens up my room,
> Just like a little summer rose
> when it is in full bloom.
>
> Then out you bring my lovely lunch
> as welcome as before,
> What more comfort could one ask
> into one's very door.
>
> A word, a laugh, is then passed
> "not much time to spare",
> Then off you go, with cans in hand,
> back down my little stair.
>
> May the good Lord bless the WRVS
> for all the work that's given,
> And folks like me be grateful for
> this little bit of heaven.[2]

WRVS acted as a conduit for festive goodwill and many Christmas and New Year gifts were handed into centres for dispersal to the needy. Typical in 1981 was the 20 bags of coal donated by a kindly coal merchant to WRVS Fife for distribution to the elderly. A donation of end bales of Harris Tweed was described as a "windfall" and "a joy for the work parties." And when a bullock was presented to the Aberdeen centre by the city's Lord Provost, the district organiser apparently hardly turned a hair! Similarly, members have seldom been slow to support other voluntary and charitable organisations with Christmas activities, such as late-night shopping, lunch outings, gift schemes and festive parties. Residents of old people's homes and Meals on Wheels clients across Scotland continue to receive presents from Santa, alongside others bearing the label, "from the ladies of WRVS". And on launching a volunteer-manned festive-period internet advice line – titled Christmas Wiseline – towards the end of 2007, chief executive Lynne Berry said: "Christmas is a time when people clearly need help and advice and who better to offer this than older people who have lived through most scenarios?" She was able to point out that WRVS volunteers had three million years of experience between them and an average of 65 Christmases each![3]

Such activities have reinforced the good name of the organisation, bolstered morale and inspired public confidence in the Service. While the original activities of the wartime Women's Voluntary Services depended on patriotic Pathe cinema clips, heavily censored press releases or the occasional propaganda film, publicity-conscious centre organisers in the 1980s were happy to tell their stories to newspapers, local radio stations and regional television broadcasters. Indeed, the 1981 WRVS Guide urged centre leaders "to get to know the editors of local newspapers" and advised that there "was no need for members to be frightened" of local radio. Long gone were the days when in response to a Headquarters' directive to get as close as she could to the local authority, a centre organiser responded, "I've got as close as I can. I'm marrying the Town Clerk!"[4]

Media coverage in the 1980s greatly helped to expand membership – a concern of the chairman Barbara Shenfield as early as 1981 when she boldly suggested targeting "people made redundant" to replace those retiring.[5] Recruitment interviews were given to the media by centre organisers, and listeners and viewers encouraged to come forward as volunteers to fill shoes emptied by the retirements and resignations of valued members. Membership opportunities were also highlighted when Jill Archer (Patricia Green) played the role of a WRVS organiser in that everyday Radio 4 story of country folk. The presence of orange tabards at emergencies also attracted new volunteers. This happened, for example, after members dealt with evacuees from the 1982 Falklands War, for which WRVS was given full responsibility by the Home Office. Perth was asked to look after the welfare of a woman from the Falklands who had been in hospital in Argentina and who was evacuated to Scone. Following a desperate 'help' call from London Headquarters, Glasgow WRVS offered to look after a Falklands evacuee who was going to relatives on Ulva, a tiny island off Mull. She had travelled 8,000 miles clutching her brand-new food mixer which she was determined would not fall into the hands of the Argentinian military. In an impressive mobilisation the woman was safely 'delivered' to Glasgow, was driven to the west coast and clothed by Oban WRVS before being passed on again to another driver to catch a ferry to her island family. The publicity gained from such activities acted as a recruitment sergeant for the organisation but much leafleting still had to take place in supermarket car parks, libraries, shopping malls and hospitals to get the message across about what WRVS stood for and the breadth of community work it carried out.

To this end, exhibitions were organised all over the country to inform people about WRVS services. One exhibition in Dundee took over a floor of the city library and was manned from 8 a.m. to 6 p.m. On a table beside promotional material two blank sheets were left for people to submit their names and addresses as prospective members, or when they could visit the office, or how they would like to help. The Dundee organiser commented: "To our delight both these sheets were filled every day. We were inundated with offers of wool and clothes. All of our projects have gained new 'bodies' and many of the volunteers have already asked if there are other things for them to do."[6] At a particularly successful exhibition in the House of Commons in 1983 Members of Parliament were reminded of the usefulness of the 45-year-old organisation, and over 500 MPs were each given a short summary of WRVS work in their constituencies.

Recruitment was seldom straightforward. More women than ever before were entering the workplace, notably into rapidly-expanding local authority social work departments, the NHS and voluntary and charitable sectors. Even when there were sufficient members, centre reports noted how difficult it was to persuade volunteers to accept positions of responsibility. In 1983, for example, the Highland North regional organiser visited Skye to tell people there about WRVS work, but noted: "It has been uphill work over the years to expand membership on the island." On the other hand, Highland South gleefully reported that an Afternoon Club had been started on the Outer Hebridean island of Benbecula. To rub salt into its northern neighbour's wounds, Highland South was also able to confirm "over one hundred new members, including some very able organisers."[7] This was a phenomenon uncommon at urban centres, however, where labour-intensive activities such as Meals on Wheels and hospital welcome work frequently struggled to maintain volunteer coverage.

The 1980s raised the percentage of men in the organisation to nearly 10% and also saw a marked increase in the work of school-children with WRVS. The latter occurred primarily in connection with the Duke of Edinburgh Award Scheme, where pupils as young as 14 helped WRVS, and during national Meals on Wheels Weeks when many schoolchildren dipped their toes into the world of volunteering on delivery runs. In 1982 pupils at Linwood High School began helping volunteers with local MoW distribution, becoming the first in the UK to participate in the service as part of their social and vocational skills course. Thus began a school tradition which has seen over the years 500 Linwood pupils helping to deliver 30,000 meals to the housebound in Renfrewshire, bridging the gap between young and old. Balancing teenage humour with the "grey-haired grannies" image of WRVS, the youngsters have delivered meals on roller skates and in shopping trolleys. More seriously, pupils involved have always been aware that if there was no answer at a house they had to report it immediately in case something was wrong. One pupil, Natalie McCann, summed up the feelings of many classroom peers by saying, "This was my favourite placement. Seeing the faces of elderly people light up when we walked in the door was a great experience that I'll carry with me all my life."[8]

It was young people in Edinburgh – some 45,000 of them – who formed the huge welcome party which greeted the arrival of Pope John Paul to Scotland in 1982. Afterwards, WRVS was asked to provide sustenance to the physically but not spiritually exhausted 300,000 waiting to welcome the pontiff to the open-air National Mass for Scotland in Glasgow, which required tremendous planning and organisation. A similar mobilisation was required as the 1980s jogging boom began – WRVS Glasgow turning out to provide hot soup to 8,000 finishers at the first Scottish People's Marathon in 1982. There were no reports of kettle-carrying women overtaking athletes!

On the subject of schoolchildren it is appropriate to re-visit the WRVS Children's Holiday Scheme, which began in 1951 as a continuation of the work to find foster homes for post-war children. The Holiday Scheme, as its name suggests, existed to provide holidays for children with special needs brought about by difficult circumstances. Early placements demonstrated that staying a week or 10 days with a caring hostess and her family, or in a camp or other type of group holiday, greatly benefited a child. In 1951, 20 children were helped in this way. The landmark 5,000th placement was achieved in 1969. The role of WRVS was to 'match' a child to a hostess, transporting the child to and from the holiday, seeing that he or she had sufficient clothing, arranging insurance cover, and generally being responsible for the child's welfare throughout the stay. Children aged five to 15 were eligible for the scheme and, bearing in mind the troubles with wartime evacuation, it was policy to keep siblings together. Hostesses were volunteers and were always interviewed by WRVS. A small 'hospitality' allowance was provided to them and referring bodies and sometimes parents were asked to contribute towards this. Children were recommended to WRVS for holidays from a number of sources – including social workers, health visitors, doctors, teachers, education welfare officers, probation officers and other organisations concerned with caring for young people. Parents were normally asked to sign a medical consent form in the event of emergency treatment being necessary. After the holiday, WRVS usually provided a report to the referring body containing information which might be helpful in the continuing welfare of the child. In 1981, Scottish centres sent 363 children to hostesses and a further 236 children to camps, caravans and other gatherings. This was in addition to the help with holidays provided that year in connection with the International Year of the Disabled. The commitment to the Holiday Scheme was considerable. Yet among members it was frequently stated to be among the most popular and satisfying of duties.

With four of her own, Scotland's chairman Mary Corsar knew all about children. The deserved reward for her drive to establish WRVS as an indispensable volunteer force in Scotland came in 1984 when she was made vice-chairman of the national organisation. This meant, inevitably, that Mrs Corsar, while remaining in charge north of the border, was obliged to attend meetings and functions in England as well as, in October that year, a rally involving 600 members at Bloomsbury addressed by the Lord Mayor of London and the Home Secretary, Leon Brittan. Mrs Corsar also contributed to the Civil Protection in Peacetime Act 1986, which provided specifically for local authorities to use their civil defence resources in responding to peacetime emergencies. The whole idea behind civil defence was that it provided a basic framework of emergency planning which could be developed rapidly into a fuller structure should the risk of warfare materialise. Since the 1940s WRVS had not only been part of the government's rapid-deployment force, but had facilitated training and preparation for those who worked at emergencies. The 1986 Act confirmed the WRVS position of its readiness to serve the community – in what was termed an 'all hazards' approach. And where practicable, WRVS was included in every local authority emergency plan, as it is today, some volunteers to be called out at short notice, others to help in the aftermath of incidents. Brora volunteer Isabella McKay was among many Scottish volunteers to participate in civil defence training in the 1980s and recalled an exercise at Invergordon where she offered orange juice to a small boy – only to be told, "Can't you see I'm dead?"[9]

In the autumn of 1985 members found the first issue of a tabloid-sized *WRVS News* awaiting them at centres, replacing the pocket-sized *WRVS Magazine* which had itself superseded the *Bulletin* and typewritten newsletters from Tothill Street. More new ground was broken in October that year with the launch of National Members' Week. Chairman Barbara Shenfield explained that the initiative would allow the organisation to "think about our membership as a whole, how we can make the best use of the skills and abilities our members have, how we can make sure they feel appreciated, that the jobs they are doing are worthwhile and that they find real enjoyment and satisfaction working for WRVS." The special week also provided an opportunity for members to be publicly thanked for their hard work – and a moment for the organisation to blow its own trumpet. Or, as Mrs Shenfield put it, "Let us flood the country with green uniforms during 'our' week."[10]

In 1986 WRVS Scottish headquarters was chosen as the 'guinea pig' for the introduction of computerisation north of the border. Elaine Smith, secretary to Mary Corsar at that time, recalled that it was not without teething troubles. "During the next few years many hours were spent on the phone to the IT department at Headquarters whenever anything went wrong." She added, however, "The members of that department seemed unfailingly patient, both during visits to Edinburgh and when manning the helpline."[11] By the late 1980s, Scottish division had recruited staff experienced in programming and operating systems, which relieved the pressure and allowed the computerised infrastructure to be enhanced and advanced. Twenty years on, the WRVS website is the centralising element of the national organisation, somewhat in the manner that Lady Reading used to be.

A significant physical change took place in November 1987 when Headquarters moved from Old Park Lane to new offices at 234-244

Stockwell Road in south-west London. The changing character of WRVS could also be seen with the creation of what modern members know as CAMBRIC. This acronym stood for Counties and Metropolitans, Boroughs (London), Regions (Scotland), including Cities. CAMBRIC was essentially an umbrella service within WRVS to allow better administration of its tiers. Among functions it dealt with was the award of the WRVS Long Service Medal after 15 years of regular service. After 27 years' service members could apply for a clasp for the medal, and a second clasp could be awarded for a further 12 years' service, a total commitment of 39 years. Certificates were also awarded to those who had completed 10 years, and over time various approaches have been examined to reward the contribution of volunteers. Few recipients could have experienced the excitement of a Motherwell clothing organiser in 1983 – presented with her medal by the chairman in Scotland, Mary Corsar, at 2.30 p.m., she answered an SOS from the local social work department at 4.30 p.m. Having only time to peel off the top layer of her finery, namely her fur coat, and replace it with her apron, she was to be found in the clothing store, medal swinging from her jacket, pulling and piling clothes and blankets before she had time to come down from 'cloud nine' from the earlier events of the day. And when Sylvia Morrison received her Long Service Medal at a ceremony at Edinburgh HQ she stayed behind at the end to wash all the teacups and plates. "My family couldn't believe that," she recalled.[12]

Clothing may have been the unsung 'Cinderella' work of WRVS but it was always necessary, and never more so than when the organisation had to respond rapidly to emergencies. Alas, the 1980s will be remembered for the tragedies in which WRVS stood out as beacons of help and hope. Members in England were mobilised to assist at the Kegworth air crash in Leicestershire, the Hillsborough football stadium tragedy and severe hurricane damage in London. But nowhere was more dramatically affected than Scotland, firstly by the world's worst oil rig fire and then by Britain's worst peacetime disaster. The explosion and fire which engulfed the Piper Alpha oil platform in the North Sea in the summer of 1988 killed 167 men. It was the world's biggest offshore oil disaster. News of the tragedy was transmitted as a distress call on the evening of 6 July and a huge rescue operation responded. Despite the intense heat and appalling conditions many small ships and standby vessels made heroic attempts to take off survivors. Over 50 of those involved reached Aberdeen by helicopter in the early hours of 7 July and were rushed to hospital. As dawn broke, and the full extent of the tragedy became clear, the whole of Scotland was shocked into silence. By then the WRVS who normally staffed Aberdeen Royal Infirmary had mobilised under the "inspirational leadership" of Grampian regional organiser Muriel Scanlan to look after survivors and relatives anxious for news. This must have involved heartbreaking and at times harrowing duties, but Kristeen (Kirsty) Smith, Emergency Services Organiser for Scotland, recalled modestly, "As only 62 of the 229 crew survived, the main task of the WRVS team was to make 10p pieces available to the distraught relatives to enable them to make phone calls."[13]

Just five months later, nearly 300 WRVS volunteers from three regions served over 50,000 meals to relief workers in the 18 days after a Pan Am Boeing 747 jet carrying 258 people had crashed on Lockerbie. As cameras panned over the sombre town in the aftermath of the disaster, fleeting glimpses could be seen of WRVS teams at work. One police rescue team leader later wrote to say they were "the Angels of Lockerbie". Kirsty Smith, still Emergency Services Organiser, faced the task of reacting with speed to the unfolding disaster. On first news of the explosion of Flight 103, just after 7 p.m. on Wednesday, 21 December, she immediately attempted to call the regional emergency team leader for Dumfries and Galloway, only to discover that contact with local groups in the area was impossible as the telephone exchange in Lockerbie had been damaged. Fortuitously, WRVS personnel in Dumfries and Galloway, Borders region and Cumbria had exchanged emergency contact lists to enable them to assist each other in the event of a serious incident. Mrs Smith contacted the emergency leader in Carlisle and arranged for Cumbria to send the initial response team. Food had been requested for around 250 people evacuated from their homes near the crash site and blankets were hurriedly organised by members from

Nithsdale. There they were joined by the first emergency team, from Longtown in Cumbria, who had gathered their equipment, collected meat from the local butcher and then sped along the A74 behind a police escort. Remarkably, this team was serving refreshments in the corridor of Lockerbie Town Hall by 11.30 p.m., before moving to an emergency control room established in the local academy later in the night.

That was the initial response – the first stage. Over the next days WRVS helped prepare and provide a steady flow of hot meals, with teams standing elbow to elbow serving an endless procession of police, Army, RAF accident investigators, mountain rescue teams, regional and district council staff, and many others. About 100 relatives of the crash victims, along with Pan Am personnel and social workers, were looked after in a separate room and food was taken to them there. As the recovery operations continued, 12 WRVS members with the help of local people worked on each shift for a total of three shifts per day, starting at four o'clock in the morning. Volunteers on the point of exhaustion were replaced by others drafted in from neighbouring centres. WRVS Strathclyde – East Kilbride, Hamilton, Lanark and Eastwood – took over between 29 December and 1 January, for example. The intense WRVS involvement finished at lunchtime on Saturday, 7 January, the team from Cumbria poignantly taking the last shift as they had done every night since the evening of the crash. Members had toiled for 18 days in the aftermath of Britain's worst peacetime tragedy. The response had involved 200 volunteers from Dumfries and Galloway, 31 from Cumbria and 40 from Strathclyde. Between them they had worked approximately 4,000 hours and served 52,000 meals to over 600 people. They had also provided dry socks for young soldiers, food and water for rescue dogs and countless words of comfort and counsel. No wonder tributes to WRVS poured in. Among them, the Strathclyde Police search and rescue leader wrote: "I'm afraid I formed a hazy impression of the ladies' work. The true meaning of the 'Emergency Team' was brought home to me when I attended the Lockerbie disaster ... after spending hours searching and meeting the horror face on, the pleasantness and cheerfulness of these ladies were truly heart warming." As for Kirsty Smith, she says she will never forget the quiet she found on arrival in Lockerbie . . . "not a holy quiet, but no dogs barking, no birds singing and the smell of aircraft fuel hanging over everything . . ."[14]

In the midst of this painful work came the rightful celebration of the Golden Jubilee of WRVS in May 1988, at a time when the organisation still had over 160,000 members regularly volunteering their services in various capacities. It was a double celebration in Scotland, where Mary Corsar took over as national chairman from Dame Barbara Shenfield, moving to WRVS headquarters at Stockwell Road in Brixton. Mrs Corsar left behind in Scotland, "a very close knit, competent staff who operated very well as a team. The organisation had been built up over the years to work in line with a devolved Scottish Parliament, if such a thing should ever come into existence." That this was WRVS thinking in 1988, nearly a decade before the public vote in favour of a devolved parliament, shows how prescient and almost clairvoyant the WRVS leadership was in many respects.[15]

The Golden Jubilee was celebrated in every WRVS centre in Britain as well as more formally at a service at Westminster Abbey in the presence of the organisation's President, the Queen Mother, and at a garden party at Headquarters attended by the Queen, the WRVS Patron, to which members from all over Scotland travelled. To mark the occasion, a decorated WRVS 'Jubilee' float had a place of honour in the Lord Mayor's Show in London. When it reached the Embankment, one of the members on board reported that an "Arab gentleman held up a placard reading 'Five camels for the fat one.' He took one look at me and gave me the thumbs up, and the crowd roared!"[16] It was not all fun. Further along the route, in Maltravers Street, men and women Emergency Services members, who had been on duty from the early hours preparing, were busily handing out refreshments and luncheon packs to the hundreds of people in the parade. In Scotland, a service of thanksgiving was held at Cannongate Church in Edinburgh, at which Princess Alexandra was guest of honour and founder members invited. The 50th birthday was also marked by Scotland's 20,000 members with many floral displays, some of them planted with a new rose, Royal Volunteer, bred by James Cocker & Sons, and several exhibitions of WRVS work. Civic receptions were offered by local councils, but just as enjoyable were spontaneous parties where, perhaps for the first time, the tea urn was left unplugged as bottles of bubbly were uncorked and their contents drunk from commemorative WRVS Jubilee mugs.

As far as the WRVS membership at large was concerned, welfare work continued untouched by the celebration of the Golden Jubilee. In Scottish centre statements dealing with activities in the harsh winter bridging 1987–88, Borders Region reported tramping through deep snow to deliver meals by tractor and sledge, and a similar spirit was required when WRVS was called upon by government to disburse EEC surpluses to the needy. These were organised from Scottish headquarters by Joan Scott, "who seemed to move the European Butter Mountain around the country almost single handedly."[17] Heavy snow also affected Dundee where pioneering owners of four-wheel-drive vehicles phoned in to offer help. Even Glasgow reported impassable snow, and members there had to deliver hundreds of meals on foot. Central agreed in Jubilee year to take over the running of a tea bar and shops at the Royal Scottish National Hospital at Larbert, which meant finding additional volunteers for the new duties. WRVS Fife was represented for the first time at the RAF Leuchars air show and also established a laundry service in Glenrothes. Highland North opened a new shop and trolley service at Wick General Hospital, and increased demand brought the re-opening of the Alness clothing store. Highland South members were interviewed on Moray Firth Radio and BBC Highland about a new 'helpcall' service for the elderly. In Benbecula the highlight of the year for members was a trip to Skye. Some participants had never left the island before and the centre reported that "a whole new world had opened for them." And it was just like old times for Grampian when members borrowed a mobile kitchen from Scottish Gas to cook EEC surplus food, providing 250 meals in a week. Dwelling on bygone days, a member of the Dundee sewing team won a competition run by Radio Forth and Lothian WRVS by making a very neat pair of underpants from one leg of a pair of long johns.

WVS veterans would have nodded approval!

10

THE CARING, SHARING NINETIES

The 1990s was an amazing decade for Women's Royal Voluntary Service. It became a limited company. It was registered as a charity. It had a new chairman as the 90s began and another at their end. It organised Meals on Wheels by computer and invited celebrities to deliver them. It was re-branded, got a new slogan and designed another uniform. It saw men enlist in huge numbers and women resign in droves. At one emergency it served burgers from McDonald's and pies from Waitrose. It absorbed new rules and learned to toe the legal line. And for the first time in half a century, the organisation born from pre-war panic over civilian bombing had to generate its own income, had to compete with other suppliers to tender for hospital contracts – even had to rethink its sandwich strategy to consider ethnic dietary requirements.

The 1990s began like others; with service beyond self for Scotland's 20,000 members. This is how WRVS north of the border looked in 1990.

Hospitals

Canteens/tea trolleys	102
Trolley shops	120
Static shops	46
Ward parcel services	19
Reception services	85
Libraries	20

Clothing

Persons helped	29,800
Garments issued	292,300
In stock	93,700

Emergency Services

Members trained	3,531
Instructors	45

Administration

Premises	72
Vehicles	32

Food

MoW deliveries	1,345,737
Lunch Club meals	122,967

Welfare of Offenders/Families

Prison canteens	8
Court canteens	10

Work with Disabled

Clubs, day centres, etc	46
Trolley services	2
Riding clubs	2
Talking book schemes	28
Holidays	182

Work with Elderly

Clubs all/part day	147
Visiting schemes	48
Trolleys/shops	145
Holidays	266

Home Support

Persons escorted	52,717
Mileage for above	501,426
Books on Wheels clients	2,371
Home from hospital schemes	6

Work with Children

Tufty Clubs	26
Toy libraries	30
Clinics and crèches	34
Camp/caravan holidays	353 [1]

If the organisation's new corporate identity was important, its founding *raison d'etre* still prevailed to help in time of war. In 1991 members throughout the country were put on standby to support the families of personnel involved in the Gulf War. Thankfully, the short duration of the conflict and the low numbers of casualties resulted in the membership being stood down soon after. At home the focus was on Meals on Wheels which celebrated its Golden Jubilee in 1992. It had come a long way from its start of five meals for evacuated London bomb victims in Welwyn Garden City: food prepared at British Restaurants, then school kitchens, then commercial concerns; kept warm by charcoal, then aluminium dishes, then foil, then insulated boxes, then frozen; delivered by foot and pram, then bicycle, then private cars, vans and by dedicated vehicles. During 1991 some 15 million meals were delivered to 120,000 grateful UK recipients.

The delivery of dinners followed an established 'menu' of instructions across the UK. Staff involved were reminded that they had a legal obligation to show due diligence in observing food safety legislation. They were asked to ensure that delivery vehicles were clean inside. They were not allowed to carry pets. There were procedures to follow if the scheme organiser was unwell. Other instructions reminded volunteers not to open insulated carriers until the first delivery was under way, and advised on the time limit for their run. They were also given a band of temperatures, both hot and cold, between which meals must had to be served, and the heating 'danger' zones to avoid. To experienced groups the process became second nature.

During celebrations for Meals on Wheels, Headquarters was diverted by a report for the Home Office which recommended a new system of management for the organisation. Its conclusion was that WRVS should become a registered company with charitable status, comprising seven (later to become six) divisions in England, Scotland and Wales. Thus in 1993 WRVS left behind its 55-year-old status as a member-led voluntary organisation to become a company limited by guarantee and registered as a charity. Under its new structure, a WRVS Council was established to formulate policy for the new company. The council comprised seven members, including the chairman and vice-chairman plus WRVS staff or volunteers, or external people who were invited to join because of their expertise. The new council was accountable to the WRVS company, whose board comprised six divisional directors from across the UK and 24 other members, who could be volunteers or paid staff and who were nominated by the divisional directors. Scotland was designated one of the divisions and a Scottish divisional office was later established at 44 Albany Street, Edinburgh. Elaine Ross, who had joined WRVS in 1982 and who had been Mary Corsar's deputy since 1986, was appointed Scottish divisional director. National chairman Mary Corsar wrote to members, explaining, "This means better support for the wonderful work you do in your communities." Sensing the unease among members, many of whom had recently completed rolling four-hour shifts supporting Windsor Castle fire teams, she added, "The spirit of service remains unchanged."[2]

Mrs Corsar survived in post barely another year before stepping down "when I reached my sell-by-date of 65." She was the only Scottish chairman to lead the national organisation and did so at a time of tremendous change and development. She showed great awareness and – "always sitting with my door open" – she was able to encourage and enthuse volunteers in the unlikeliest of tasks. She also coped with unprecedented national emergencies across the UK, at which her membership responded magnificently. She was aptly rewarded for her services by being created DBE, and, as Dame Mary, she became chairman of the TSB Foundation Scotland. On 1 July 1993, the London barrister Elizabeth Toulson became WRVS chairman. She had been vice-chairman since 1989. Yet if anything characterised and emphasised the speed of the changes engulfing

172

the organisation it was the appointment of a man, the Cheshire accountant Gerald Burton, as the first chief executive of WRVS. Dame Mary recalled: "It was ridiculous. We had a multi-million-pound turnover and I had no financial training. For example, our Home Office grant, about £6 million at that time, was basically for emergency services work, not for projects like toy libraries. So during my time I had to investigate schemes whereby profitable projects like Hospital Services could perhaps subsidise other areas, such as children's holidays. So we went to the Home Office to discuss how we were organised and one of the suggestions we came up with was a paid chief executive. We felt it would allow the chairman to get out and about. Meeting volunteers and finding out what they were thinking and doing really was an important and pleasurable part of my role."[3] Under Mr Burton, WRVS was split into three major areas of activity – local hospital services, local community services and local emergency services – to allow external audiences better understanding of its work.

The re-launch of the in-house *WRVS News* with a new title, *WRVS Today*, in April 1994 coincided with the introduction of the organisation's new identity. One of the historic elements to be lost was the crowned badge worn by members from WVS days. This was replaced by a new oval logo in burgundy which Headquarters said was necessary "in order to make sure that the outward face of the Service is communicating the right message to the people we are dealing with." While the oval design was intended to convey a modern image to potential sponsors, it also subtly altered the identity of the organisation by playing down the 'W' in the acronym and increasing the size of the 'V.' That 16,000 of its members were men justified the change, of course. Also unveiled to the 140,000-strong membership was a new public relations manager, a new external public relations manager, a systems development manager and a director of operations. Contributing to the quickening pace of change was a "vision" in the form of a mission statement: "The members of the Women's Royal Voluntary Service, in partnership with public and private sectors, are committed to being the premier providers of voluntary assistance to those in need of care within their local communities."[4] As it happened, this was not far removed from Lady Reading's hard-won post-war objectives.

Among projects which defined the modernised Service were Contact Centres, where separated parents and their children could meet in neutral surroundings. The first in Scotland was established in Dumfries in the 1980s. By the mid-1990s, there were 50 such centres across Britain providing both tea and toys and much-needed non-statutory help to minimise the trauma caused to the children of separating parents. Local projects also had a bearing on the organisation's changing make-up. Dundee, for example, was the first centre in the UK to introduce a tea-time meals service, for which it had to recruit a new tranche of volunteers. The service operated from its William Street depot, and was aimed at the particularly frail in the community who could not look after themselves. The meals were supplied by eight residential homes in the city and were delivered hot and ready to eat. The service operated seven days a week, with the WRVS shift beginning work at 4.30 p.m.

The unique geography and topography of Scotland, not to mention its unpredictable weather systems, continued to focus the attentions of the near 20,000 WRVS members north of the border on practical work. In January 1993 the River Tay burst its banks after a rapid snow melt and caused what was described as a "week of disaster". As water levels rose, low-lying areas of central Perth and the heavily-populated North Muirton housing estate adjacent to the river on the town's outskirts were put on major alert. The local emergency plan swung into action and the WRVS centre in Perth placed on standby. As waters rose to 12 feet above their normal level and flowed into ground floor windows, the local authority and its emergency plan partners decided to evacuate nearly 2,000 people, including residents from two sheltered housing developments. It was one of the largest evacuations of civilian population in post-war Scotland. Over 1,500 people were welcomed into Perth Grammar School's community wing about half a mile from the worst-hit area, while many others stayed with families or friends. At the school they were looked after by social workers and housing officers, the Red Cross, and a small battalion of WRVS helpers who provided warm drinks and snacks through the anxious waits for high tides.

When the mighty Tay receded, 1,600 homes were left damaged, over 300 of them requiring major repairs. Falling trees and flood-water blocked numerous roads. Several riverside communities were cut off altogether. Two ScotRail bridges were also brought down and farmland badly affected. Priceless paintings stored in the basement at Perth Art Galleries were damaged – even a murder trial at the High Court in Perth had to be postponed because water had soaked exhibits. WRVS eventually served meals twice a day for several days for the homeless, emergency personnel and construction workers, while the WRVS clothing depot at Rosslyn House in Perth turned out thousands of garments to help keep people warm and dry.[5]

Publicity gained through such emergencies helped recruitment, and as 1993 moved over for 1994 WRVS could still call upon 140,000 members, ensuring that it remained the country's largest voluntary service organisation. There were 1,400 members in flood-hit Perth alone, for example, more than 200 of them men. It was not the case that the so-called 'caring, sharing man of the 1990s' was suddenly considered suitable for WRVS. Men had always supported the organisation, from driving Food Flying Squad lorries to acting as 'labourers' on countless Meals on Wheels delivery runs. The organisation across the UK now had 16,000 of them – including the boss. Having said that, Headquarters was well aware the Service relied heavily on the contribution of middle-aged-to-elderly women, often retirees or at-home housewives who could devote time to Meals on Wheels and other activities. Yet even these women were dropping out as they retired or became alienated from the modernised WRVS with its corporate marketing vision, and perhaps more especially because of what they perceived as the loss of Lady Reading's homely public spirit. A reducing, ageing membership was clearly not sustainable and the incoming WRVS chairman Elizabeth Toulson made the point that many younger people were not getting involved "because they are afraid of becoming over-committed." Instead she believed there was a clear need "to make people realise that, because we have so many members, volunteers need only give as little as a couple of hours a week to make a practical difference."[6]

In April 1994, the new recruitment slogan "Make Someone's Day" was introduced to replace its sincere but rather punchless "We Help in Any Way We Can" predecessor. The new catchline was, as *The Guardian* put it, "a nod towards Clint Eastwood's Dirty Harry," but it also reflected the confidence of an organisation moving into the future with unrivalled knowledge of voluntary caring. WRVS also began to re-train its organisers to commercialise the service and to generate more of its own income. Chief executive Gerry Burton admitted that the organisation had to cast off its 'twinset and pearls' image to attract corporate sponsors and commercial partnerships. That December he unveiled the new WRVS corporate plan, whose primary function was to support the WRVS application for a government grant each year, but which could also be used by centres in their contract negotiations with local authorities and other partners. Leading the implementation of the plan north of the border was the new divisional director for Scotland, Anne Boyd of Logierait, near Pitlochry, who took over from Elaine Ross in April 1995. A lawyer by profession, Mrs Boyd had amassed 30 years of voluntary work in hospitals, prisons and courts, and her immediate plans involved streamlining WRVS management in Scotland. Sleeves rolled up, she explained how, "If there is a job to be done, then I just get on with it."

By the mid-1990s, Scotland still had 19,000 members, some 3,000 of them trained for emergency work. Yet the need for younger people to join the Service drove much of its thinking, as did awareness that older volunteers formed its backbone. To them belonged the proud past and busy present. But there was a determination that the organisation should have a national contemporary face for the 21st century. Throughout its operations, though, the new management structure never did things for the sake of it. True to tradition, it was determined to do what was needed, to help where required and to be Britain's public face of voluntary emergency and community aid. The national chairman pointed out: "With every member's support WRVS will offer an even greater service tomorrow than it does today – we will not be just an interesting chapter in a GCSE 20th century history paper."[7]

Changes to WRVS Scotland in 1995 involved the restructuring of centres to mirror the ending of regional and district councils and to reflect the arrival of single-tier local government authorities. WRVS moved away from the old region and district offices run by volunteers and, as the new unitary authorities began to purchase WRVS-run services such as Meals on Wheels, paid 'area managers' were employed to liaise directly with councils. By providing professional organisers able to negotiate locally over contracts of service, WRVS in Scotland was leading the rest of the UK in breaking from the central purchasing power of Headquarters. Director Anne Boyd quickly reassured Scotland's members: "Volunteers will always be needed. It's a question of making ourselves much more professionally accountable, and more professionally run, not because it gives us credibility with local authorities, but because it means we don't let down our members . . . they are the people who matter."[8]

Changes were afoot at central office, too. In 1997 WRVS opened a national training centre at Milton Hill estate near Abingdon in Oxfordshire, and relocated its Headquarters out of London for the first time in 60 years to a low, modern office suite in Milton Hill's wooded grounds. At the same time, the Compass Report, a Home Office review of WRVS ordered by the Conservative government before it left power, recommended a move towards the end of Treasury grant and the gradual introduction of self-funding for the organisation.

This was far from the minds of members north of the border when the terrible events at Dunblane Primary School shook the country in 1996. Many will never forget the traumatised, distraught families who lost children, the heartbreaking work of the police and local authority staff and the sincere sorrow expressed by pale politicians in the aftermath of the tragedy. Kirsty Smith, Emergency Services co-ordinator during the Piper Alpha and Lockerbie disasters, had by 1996 ended that role, but was on the rota of the Stirling centre. She recalled how the police quickly called out WRVS to assist them at "an incident" at Dunblane Primary School. Mrs Smith joined three other members to make up a response team and proceeded to Dunblane. On arrival she was directed, with other volunteer helpers, to a local hotel, where they were to await further instructions. There they helped the hotel provide sandwiches and warm drinks to those coming and going. The emergency response team was then stood down from the immediate aftermath of the awful incident, with Mrs Smith paying tribute to the police for "always trying to protect WRVS from exposure to the worst of the incidents." Over subsequent days, however, WRVS assisted social services at Dunblane community centre by serving refreshments, and spoke to many distressed families. Mrs Smith recalled: "A drop-in centre was opened in the town and manned by WRVS volunteers for many months after the event, providing a meeting place for everyone wishing to talk and share their thoughts and grief with others."[9] Through compassionate actions WRVS and other volunteer agencies offered a burning light of hope in this fateful episode in Scotland's modern history.

August 1997 also brought the death of Diana, Princess of Wales. Some 500 members of WRVS emergency teams were requested to provide refreshments for the queues of people waiting for up to 12 hours to sign books of condolence in London. Following the funeral WRVS members helped clear away 25,000 tons of flowers and thousands of toys left in remembrance at St Jame's and Kensington Palaces. It was one of the biggest mobilisations of the organisation since the end of the war. Again, WRVS had been called upon by government. At moments of crisis, when disaster struck or when a major incident occurred, WRVS worked alongside local authorities, emergency services, public utilities and other aid organisations to provide as efficient, humane and co-ordinated a response as possible. During 1997–98 alone, employees and volunteers across Britain attended and assisted at 128 emergencies.

Arguably, the best WRVS work related not to national disasters and outpourings of grief but to what went on in Britain's hospitals. By 1997–98 WRVS members were running projects in 444 hospitals across the UK. Within this astonishing commitment members staffed 129 reception and guiding services, provided 38 flower arranging services, 29 library and book trolleys, over 500 shops and cafes and 280 trolley services to wards. WRVS Hospital Services

provided a better experience for patients, staff and visitors. At entrances to hospitals volunteers offered a warm and human welcome to people who may have found a visit or stay a daunting prospect. Its information desks told people which door to go through, which corridor to walk along – and where toilets were. It gave sweets to apprehensive children and provided tea to stressed parents. It soothed nerves and offered an environment of cheerful calm. WRVS care also stretched beyond hospital foyers. On wards it provided hairdressing services and manicures, helped patients to unpack or to write letters, arranged flowers, completed menu cards and read books. Through its trolley service it provided snacks, soft drinks, library books, magazines, toiletries and sundry other essentials. These services were not only useful to those immobilised in hospital wards, but provided WRVS with important opportunities to talk to patients whose circle of family and friends was perhaps limited. Outpatients were also looked after, as members gave their time to help reduce the tension of visiting hospital with a comforting word provided here and there where isolation or an element of worry was sensed.

Countless visitors, patients and staff also popped into WRVS-run shops and cafes for anything required during a hospital visit or stay, or anything forgotten – but cafes also became places where people could meet and chat, providing also an oasis of calm for hard-pressed staff. In this 'win-win' work, profits from WRVS retail were churned back into hospitals, and not only to help to pay for vital equipment: "Television sets, hair dryers, electric shavers, seats, wheelchairs and special beds for long-term bedridden patients are in use throughout our hospitals – thanks to the WRVS."[10] In 1998 WRVS donations to hospital trusts amounted to a healthy £4.3 million, mostly used to provide additional diagnostic and treatment equipment and services in the community. Report after report, year upon year, is sprinkled with details of significant WRVS cheque presentations to very appreciative hospital authorities.

Older people often stay in hospital much longer than required because they do not have anyone at home to help them with hitherto manageable tasks such as shopping, cooking and household chores. On countless occasions WRVS was able to provide patients

with information before they left hospital so they could benefit from other services in the community, such as Meals on Wheels or community transport. By the late 1990s WRVS 'after-care' schemes had been added to its list of hospital services, helping those returning home to ensure they had support for a speedy post-hospital recovery.

Yet the defining WRVS service for many people is the provision of Meals on Wheels. By the late 1990s WRVS provided around half of the 26 million served in the UK – and it remained the organisation's most effective generator of publicity. Scottish and national head offices used the flagship service to emphasise WRVS work and as a means of recruitment, principally through national Meals on Wheels Weeks or Volunteers' Weeks, when many celebrities and national figures were wheeled out to accompany deliveries up and down the country. Every year, clever publicity stunts were arranged to draw attention to a service considered a lifeline to thousands of vulnerable older people. In 1997, for instance, Meals on Wheels Week involved as many different types of transport as possible. Throughout Scotland a variety of unfamiliar vehicles was pressed into service. Lord Provosts used official limousines, fire engines joined in, prams, motorbikes, even a milk float. Stirling Council's catering staff prepared a treat of haggis, neeps and tatties, stovies, clootie dumpling and shortbread for more than 200 housebound people, and volunteers delivered the meals in a borrowed vintage car.

WRVS Founders Day – which was designated May 16 – took on special significance in 1998 as it marked the Diamond Jubilee of the Service. To commemorate Lady Reading's launch of WVS, the Speaker of the House of Commons hosted a reception for 100 members at Westminster. In the summer the Queen hosted a garden party at the Service's new home in Oxfordshire where 3,000 members attended despite poor weather to welcome their Patron. Television celebrity Cilla Black agreed to become special ambassador for the year and launched WRVS's Give us a Hand campaign to promote volunteering. In Scotland members attended a service of rededication and thanksgiving in St Cuthbert's Church in Edinburgh. Smaller celebrations took place among the tartan army of volunteers – perhaps the most enjoyable in Stonehaven where Aberdeenshire

Council turned the tables on WRVS by waiting on members at a sumptuous 60th anniversary tea party in the town's St Leonard's Hotel.

Anne Boyd, director of WRVS in Scotland, wrote to volunteers to congratulate them on the year's efforts: "Not only have you kept projects going, started new ones, attended training courses and meetings, but many of you have put in long hours to helping celebrate our Diamond Year." Among new projects referred to by Mrs Boyd was Meals with Care, whereby food was provided with 'Safe and Well' checks to those temporarily or permanently housebound, or those who found shopping difficult. Another was Travel Companions, launched in 1998, in which volunteers accompanied people to get out and about. All participating members were trained in emergency first aid, disability awareness and leading blind people.

On its 60th anniversary, the modern-day WRVS maintained many of the services it had carried out after its inauguration in 1938. Others, like Darby & Joan clubs and Meals on Wheels, had celebrated their own milestones – 50 years of helping the elderly able and disabled. WRVS ran over 1,000 clubs, operated nearly 100 prison tea bars and 150 tea bars in courts by its diamond jubilee year. It provided over 300 trolley services in residential homes, and carried out over 1,600 Books on Wheels rounds, benefiting 18,000 people. It ran 65 clothing stores, nearly 100 contact services for separated parents and 50 toy libraries. It had teams in nearly 500 hospitals. It arranged holidays for 805 families, 384 children and 28 elderly people. In partnership with the Army it had 72 trained welfare officers, nearly half of them based overseas. It was involved in transport schemes to help people get to shops or visit relatives, good neighbours schemes in which it collected prescriptions or walked dogs, home from hospital schemes where it helped recovery, and organised library services for the housebound.

As the millennium neared, WRVS priorities remained the five great areas of work developed by its founding chairman Lady Reading – community services helping the old and the young, hospital services serving the ill and infirm, food services to help the needy, Services welfare to support men and women in the Forces, and, of course, emergency services assisting at incidents and major events. All activities offered the possibility for members to stop for a chat, as they served snacks, scrubbed urns, cleaned blinds, did their stock-taking or entered figures in their ledgers – while experiencing the special rewards of teamwork and shared responsibility. Agnes Mair, who joined WRVS in 1970, recalled working on the rota of "mainly retired ladies" at Astley Ainsley Hospital in Edinburgh, where: "The Lyons man came in with wee sponges and four-in-a-box apple tarts" and regular customers included local funeral directors. One day an undertaker complained to her that the apple tarts were getting smaller. "So I said, 'I'll get a measuring tape.' 'Don't worry,' he replied mischievously, looking me up and down, 'we've already got a meas-uring tape.'"[11]

The decade was still to produce one of the most tumultuous years in the organisation's history. In November 1999, while its members dealt with thousands of Kosovan refugees entering Britain after the conflict in the Balkans, a vote to change the WRVS structure was carried out at its annual general meeting at Milton Hill. Drastic changes were made to the way WRVS operated. A new structure, the Vice-Chairman's Committee, was launched and this comprised a group of 30 regionally-based WRVS volunteers who became the vice-chairman's representatives in their areas. This committee, under vice-chairman Alice Cleland, effectively formed one third of the organisation's hierarchy, and was fronted by new volunteering and communications officers, who were paid staff. Another part of the structure was formed by the company's board members, known as the Board of Trustees, which comprised the chairman, vice-chairman and up to 12 other trustees, including some members from the Vice-Chairman's Committee. To complete the new structure, external individuals, picked for their expertise in areas relevant to the work of WRVS, were also invited on to the board, as were volunteers or external candidates, depending on the skills required by the trustees.

Allied to the changes was the publication of a WRVS 'manifesto' late in 1999. This document, titled *Partnership in Action*, set out to present the organisation to its partners – whether that was government, local authorities, the NHS, business and commercial organisations or the people and groups it served in the community. In short it was aimed at streamlining WRVS integration into the welfare state, working with local authority departments for the benefit of vulnerable groups, primarily the elderly, and developing packages of care to support them. The manifesto was launched in Scotland in an Edinburgh cyber cafe which allowed the charity to show it was at the forefront of technological change by inviting the public to "log on to volunteering" using the WRVS website. As Lady Reading had done so effectively in 1946, the manifesto also provided a reminder to the country of WRVS skills and expertise, and one of its objectives was to explain how relationships between WRVS and its partner organisations – "whether you represent a multinational company, a local authority, a hospital trust, a group of constituents, or simply yourself" – should always be beneficial to both parties. In other words, WRVS was selling itself.[12]

To many seasoned WRVS volunteers, the rapid pace of change was deeply unsettling and some said so. Adding to their sense of insecurity, a debate began over the very name of the organisation, with some arguing that a change should come about to reflect the significant number of male volunteers. The obvious option was to drop the 'W' from the acronym but this did not find favour with many volunteers, including men. The matter was set aside. The last year of the decade also brought the retiral of Elizabeth Toulson after six years as chairman. She was replaced by Tina Tietjen, formerly chief executive of an arts organisation and adviser to the government's Business in the Community think-tank. Ms Tietjen explained the remodelling of the organisation to members in this way: "Our clients and customers are changing, as are their needs, so we need to change also if we are to continue to help."[13]

Income was the pre-eminent concern. Some £6.5 million a year of funding met by the government was to be lost through a decision to reduce WRVS's funding year by year. The erosion of Treasury grant began in 1998–99, with an intention that it would continue to be reduced until 2007, at which point it would be around £1 million. It meant the charity had to generate a substantial income to replace lost money. Fund-raising became a core priority and a procession of WRVS cards, paperweights, teddy bears, tea towels, folding umbrellas, key-rings – and, of course, mugs for tea and coffee – were produced as the merchandising drive got into full swing. The public was asked to take part in abseiling, parachuting, wild-water rafting and go-karting on behalf of WRVS to generate income. It piloted its first direct mail campaign as another initiative to raise funds – the envelopes marked 'Red Alert' and not surprisingly focusing on emergency services. The mail-out took place in Wiltshire and raised £15,000. It was estimated, however, that Wiltshire's share of the reduction of funding that year was £65,000. The sums did not add up.

Changes, which included fund-raising, but also the closure of WRVS offices and clothing stores, paid managers and public relations staff and the introduction of microwaved freezer meals, did not always sit well with those whose remedies for ills used to be tea with lots of sugar. One Scottish member of 34 years' service, who handed in her resignation in November 1999, recalled, "At that time a lot of paid organisers arrived on the scene, and we weren't told what was happening. The office closed – no more monthly meetings. Meals on Wheels organisers reported directly to Edinburgh. The Government had cut our grant, we were all into fund-raising. We had become business-like. It was all very sad . . ." Another long-serving member said: "Restructuring at the end of the 1990s had eventually caught up with me, all my jobs having been taking over by other, highly-paid staff, all of whom have since moved on to other things."[14]

As the charity appeared to distance itself from the public-spirited past – the "disciplined corps of volunteers ready to undertake tasks at the bidding of central and local government" – another senior member of divisional office staff in Edinburgh said, "It was quite a shock to go into work one morning (in 1999) and discover that I did not have any jobs to do . . . all my jobs having been taken over by other, highly-paid staff. That's when I decided to call it a day."[15] As many of the remaining centres across the UK were earmarked for closure, clothing depots mothballed and members followed their post-war predecessors by melting back into the Women's Institutes, another disgruntled volunteer wrote: "Up there, somebody is rubbing his/her hands with glee – no rent, no overheads and more months to spend on rubbish like 'how to sell draw tickets'."[16]

Yet Britain would always need volunteers to make society tick – as companions, as helpers, as partners, as surrogate mums. WRVS still had a role to play. It had a future. Besides, this extraordinary organisation still had 160,000 members – a total more than that of the Armed Services it had originally enlisted to support.

11

THE GLUE OF SOCIETY

It is 3 a.m. The telephone rings. Emergency – can the WRVS attend?

WRVS has responded to such calls for 70 years, and today it stands prepared and organised on a local and national basis 24 hours a day throughout the year. Across television screens and newspapers as recently as November 2007, lines of distraught fire-fighters watched as a van took the bodies of three colleagues away from the scene of a warehouse fire near Stratford-upon-Avon. Standing shoulder to shoulder with them were saluting police officers and the solemn volunteers of WRVS, who had already assisted at the cordoned-off site for three days. Just hours later WRVS were mobilised again to help with evacuation as a North Sea surge threatened vast swathes of the east coast.

What is it like to be part of an Emergency Services team, or to be responsible for deploying members, or to establish a rest centre, or to be early on the scene of a tragedy and to face the distressing sight of casualties or weeping relatives? How is it possible to train to become a focal point for a community's grief, as happened at Dunblane in 1996, where volunteers comforted the bereaved for many weeks after schoolchildren and a teacher were killed by a gunman?

No one can say when the call will come. Often it is not at a convenient time. It is never comfortable work and nobody knows how long you will be on your feet. It can be emotionally draining. But WRVS has been at the scene of every major catastrophe in the UK since Women's Voluntary Services was established in 1938, and today its rapid response services are built into 98% of Britain's local authority, blue-light services, Network Rail and utility company emergency plans.

Towards the end of December 1989, Kristeen Smith looked into Headquarters in Edinburgh to wish everyone a happy Christmas.

She then spent the whole of the festive holiday organising the WRVS response to the Lockerbie tragedy. Mrs Smith faced the task of reacting with speed to the unfolding events, as she had done at the terrible Piper Alpha disaster a year earlier. And at 2 a.m. on a Saturday morning in December 2002, Margaret Duncan was asleep at home when her phone rang – her second emergency in a month. A huge blaze had struck at the heart of historic Edinburgh. Quickly she alerted local members and gave them the details – firing information to them over the location of a suitable rest centre, her estimated arrival time and the need for an early assessment by the first team on the ground. Dressing swiftly she checked a map, jumped into her car and raced to the capital from her home in Clackmannanshire, mentally working out a rota of volunteers as she drove. As manager of WRVS Emergency Services for East and Central Scotland, she was always on call – always ready to react to incidents and disasters. For the next 20 hours, WRVS teams served hot drinks and soup to 80 firefighters and dozens of police, and set up a rest centre for 100 residents evacuated from Edinburgh's Old Town.

The WRVS contribution in these situations allows fire-fighters, police, public utilities, local officials and other specialists to concentrate on their tasks in the knowledge that the victims of such awful incidents are being looked after by trained volunteers. It ensures emergency teams will have food and drinks – and often temporary welfare support – as required. It offers rest centres as a haven for people to retreat to. It means that local authorities have the confidence to telephone at ungodly hours aware that an unflappable response will be triggered, and a range of skills – from emergency feeding to rest centre management to general welfare support for those affected – will be expertly deployed and managed by WRVS.

As their attendance at Dunblane showed, the value of WRVS work also lies in providing emotional comfort, offering a human touch while helping a community's recovery. This is partly achieved by restoring people's dignity after a crisis. Held in high esteem, WRVS can achieve this by its attention to detail after a tragedy – looking after medication, feeding pets, keeping a note of people evacuated from their homes so that family and friends can be told they are safe, working closely with housing departments and social services for the best outcomes for victims. It is about making a happier difference through Emergency Services roles planned and exercised with local authorities as part of a rest centre response.

Kirsty Smith's and Margaret Duncan's responses would have been formulated long before emergencies happened. From prior planning they knew what to do and how their volunteers would integrate into emergency management procedures. With 3,000 WRVS colleagues across Scotland they had undertaken exercises alongside police, fire, ambulance, local authorities and transport organisations, continuing a tradition started by their stoic, heroic sister-members during the Blitz. Regular meetings and advance planning would have taken place to agree local authority and pan-authority responses to major incidents, as happens today. Always the worst possible scenarios are considered – a bomb blast, bus or rail crash, floods, landslides, incidents at football matches or a major terrorist strike. Every catastrophe is simulated and contingency plans made to tackle it. Exercises using actors and recreating disaster situations and conditions hone the skills of emergency management teams and allow them to establish blueprints for procedures to follow in all eventualities. This harks back to the origins of the organisation and the warm summer of 1938 when Women's Voluntary Services marshalled the first schoolchildren to take part in an evacuation dress rehearsal in Fife.

Margaret Duncan and other emergency leaders would face another 34 incidents nationwide in the first three months of 2002 alone, living up to the WRVS promise to be available 24/7. Thus, along with charities including the British Red Cross and the Salvation Army, WRVS petitioned the government over the new Civil Contingencies Bill, which was intended to set the pattern for emergency planning for a decade, and to form the core response to events such as the Twin Towers terror attack on New York in 2001. WRVS argued that in response to a national emergency its trained volunteers could play a more formal role in relief operations. In making its case, WRVS could state that for 60 years it had helped to prevent emergency and statutory services from becoming overwhelmed during crises. Preparing for and dealing with large-scale incidents was the purpose for which the Service was created, and large numbers of its membership were trained to provide food, shelter and emotional support for victims and survivors, while working alongside other services. Local authorities, fire services and the police were consequently obliged to consult with voluntary organisations in the preparation and activation of emergency plans for civil emergencies or national disasters, yet the government was reluctant to set into legislative stone a formal role for volunteers, rather leaving it to councils to determine as and when emergency teams were mobilised.

Nonetheless – and with apologies to the Automobile Association – WRVS has consistently shown itself to be Britain's trained and easily mobilised fourth emergency service, and one which copes smoothly with multi-agency collaboration in support of blue-light services. To this end WRVS is a member of the Voluntary Sector Civil Protection Forum, an umbrella group of support agencies that reinforces the importance and commitment to work together in emergencies. WRVS has also exhibited in recent years at the annual Emergency Services Show, an event dedicated to organisations that offer specialist work in response to emergencies. This has allowed WRVS to parade a raft of its members' talents, including managing and staffing support centres, emergency feeding, crisis support and the delivery of rest centre management training to external organisations. These skills do not happen by chance. Every Emergency Services volunteer completes a foundation course which ensures that they are trained in responses such as call-out procedures, integrated emergency management and rest centre operations. Each Emergency Services volunteer periodically attends a refresher course or takes part in an appropriate exercise to ensure skills and knowledge are up to date. In that way, some 7,000 WRVS volunteers around Britain, formed into 500 Emergency Services teams, are always ready to help local or national government. A further 400 members are trained as team leaders to take on extra responsibilities, many of them attending courses delivered by WRVS which take them through the process of setting up emergency support centres, the new generic term for rest centres.

Elsewhere, the millennium began with WRVS in a state of flux over restructuring, and with the loss of many seasoned members through resignation and retirement. Some 100,000 volunteers remained, of which 18,000, or nearly 20%, were men. Double this number had been enrolled a decade earlier. After a major review of the organisation's 275 remaining premises, dozens of centres and clothing depots were earmarked for closure. Of its £4.75 million Treasury grant in 1999, some £2.8 million was spent on premises and administrative staff. In the new economic climate this could not be sustained. Letters to the new WRVS magazine *Action* reflected members' disappointment and frustration at the changes. One member warned in the summer of 2000 that closing clothing stores would "abandon the vulnerable".[1] WRVS responded by telling members that it had to focus its resources on areas where it excelled, which principally concerned services for the elderly. Clothing, for example, was something which other agencies, such as the Salvation Army and Oxfam, handled very well.

Drastic action was deemed necessary to achieve savings. A financial review of the organisation looked something like this. Income came from a Home Office grant, Meals on Wheels contracts, sales in court tea bars and prison visitors' centres, receipts from attending emergency events, MoD grants to run Services Welfare, income from property and investments, fund-raising income, legacies and hospital services, including shops, cafes and trolleys. Expenditure included the costs of Meals on Wheels, hospital services, emergency services, services welfare and community projects and the costs of publicity, administration and staff. WRVS accounts to March 2000 showed an income of £57 million and a total expenditure of £55 million.[2]

Intent on replacing £5 million of declining government grant with £5 million of income, raising money became a WRVS priority. An annual raffle was created, generating sums of around £150,000 annually in the early years of the decade, with Scotland producing the highest receipts. The Mad Hatter's Tea Party was launched on

1 March 2000. This involved hundreds of volunteers staging fund-raising tea parties across the country. A WRVS community lottery was promoted and direct mailings extended, taking in prosperous areas of Scotland such as Edinburgh and Perth. The public was encouraged by sympathetic celebrities to leave money to WRVS in wills. A corporate event held at Edinburgh Castle in the presence of the Princess Royal, with tables costing £1000, and another at Gleneagles Hotel, added to the coffers. In what incoming chairman Tina Tietjen called "our new world of self-sufficiency" many individual members ran marathons, took part in sponsored cycles or engaged in more hair-raising events, which not only generated income but kept WRVS in the public eye at this belt-tightening time.

Perhaps the most poignant funding event was the first WRVS choral event in the historic surroundings of Guards Chapel, close to Buckingham Palace, in December 2000. The service was hosted by WRVS member David Jacobs and readers included Terry Waite, Alan Titchmarsh, Dame Diana Rigg and Una Stubbs. Music was provided by the Guards Chapel Choir and the Band of the Scots Guards. The chapel had an incredibly moving link with WRVS. On a warm June Sunday in 1944 it had suffered a direct hit by a flying bomb. Over 120 soldiers and civilians lost their lives. Only the chapel's altar was left undamaged, with its six candlesticks still burning after the building had crashed into ruins. It was WVS volunteers who washed the hands and faces of the dead and catalogued their clothing so they could be identified.

The casualties of war have never been forgotten by WRVS. Over many years volunteers have travelled to London to take part in the annual Cenotaph Parade on Remembrance Sunday, marching out from the Foreign Office as part of the civilian contingent at the start of the commemoration and as part of the civilian services guard of honour at the Centotaph. In 2000 and 2001 WRVS had the honour to feature both at the front and back of the veterans' march-past, to prolonged applause from thousands of spectators. Members also lay poppies each year at the WRVS plot at the Field of Remembrance ceremony at Westminster Abbey led by its Patron, the Queen, and, since 1971, have been invited in rotation with other wartime organisations to the televised Royal British Legion Festival of Remembrance at the Royal Albert Hall. Across the country, too, WRVS are represented at many local remembrance services, including a presence at the annual wreath-laying in Edinburgh.

Yet, half a century distant from the war, Lady Reading might have barely recognised the Service she created. WRVS was now a business and in 2000 'business objectives' were circulated to members. Targets, as they were called, covered seven areas: community services, emergency services, food services, hospital services, volunteering, fund-raising and communications. Community service targets included negotiating more packages for community projects with local authorities, and developing training. The first studies for a network of community centres around Britain were planned at this time. Emergency service targets included generating income from community assistance events from each of the WRVS regions and from new clients in emergency work – made more achievable by widespread flooding in 2000. In terms of food services, an investigation was proposed into centralising supplies and to establishing 18 new Meals with Care projects. It was planned to expand hospital services with a minimum of four new hospitals, to refurbish some tea bars and cafes and to generate nearly half a million pounds from such projects. Proposals involving volunteering included a desire to promote equal opportunities, to support the European Year of Volunteering in 2001 and to produce a handbook for project managers on best practice for volunteer management. Fund-raising targets included establishing corporate sponsorships of WRVS parent-child contact centres and emergency teams, to promote WRVS scratchcards, to increase the number of fund-raising activities and to introduce a members' benefits club. Communications objectives involved internal and external targets – communicating the direction and changes to members, and raising the profile externally of WRVS as a relevant, reliable and modern provider of quality services.

In management terms, WRVS had resorted to being a centralised organisation. Outside the Milton Hill head office in Oxfordshire

five key centres across Britain were established, each with a professional administration team to run projects in its region. The Scottish
office at another Edinburgh address, 96 Clermiston Road, was one
of the regional centres and from there core and support service
managers were co-ordinated. Yet, under the watchful cost-cutting
regime, even this structure did not last beyond a decision in October
2002 to amalgamate the administrative functions of the five regions
into a new National Customer Service Centre at Cardiff, a one-stop
contact point for project managers with a dedicated phone number.
The Edinburgh administrative centre was a casualty and the Scottish
presence reduced to an admittedly plush office in the city's Albany
Street. Former Scottish and national chairman Dame Mary Corsar
recalled of this time: "Although a representative for Scotland was
appointed, it was felt that the nation had been downgraded."[3] As if
it were a sign of the times, a major WRVS conference in Manchester
comprised not volunteers, but 200 paid employees of the organisation
from across the country. The millennium had impacted on WRVS
in a dramatic and transforming manner. In an age of political,
economic and technological change, it had evolved with all the
internal debates and dilemmas faced by Stella Reading and Ruth
Balfour on the eve of peacetime.

Morale was boosted in 2000 when the organisation took to the
cat-walk to launch its first major uniform change for 62 years. As
with the push to revamp WRVS management, the new image did
not chime well with traditionalists. Purple and orange 'work wear'
replaced the famous green uniform. Gone were the military-style
A-line skirts, tweed jackets and felt hats. In, with the help of
Edinburgh designer Betty Davies, were body-warmers, polo shirts
and discreet logos. The admission that WRVS was to phase out
formal uniforms on the way to being "a non uniformed organisation"
unsettled many members. In a letter to the in-house magazine *Action*
one volunteer wrote: "Are we all ashamed of WRVS clothes and
don't want the public to know who we are?" There was certainly a
feeling in Scotland that uniforms helped, rather than hindered WRVS
work. One experienced member said: "We used to walk into rooms
and everyone knew who we were. When we stopped wearing the

green uniform we weren't recognised. This made recruitment difficult. We weren't able to get the volunteers through word of mouth that we used to."[4] WRVS responded by reminding members of the continuing requirement to wear the organisation's badge when 'on duty' or acting on behalf of the Service. It also advised volunteers that clothing bearing the WRVS logo should not be donated to charity shops or to any place where it might be used to misrepresent the organisation. This followed concern after an article in a *Scotland on Sunday* supplement used a WRVS uniform as a fashion accessory. In fact, as far back as the start of the war WVS had advised against any slovenly or incorrect use of its uniform. "Wearing jewellery, wearing the uniform hat with civilian clothes or vice versa, using the scarf as a turban round the head or wearing a different colour blouse with the suit – were all contrary to the conditions under which permission to wear it was given."[5]

Image became increasingly important. WRVS came under scrutiny for epitomising what *The Guardian* called the "lack of diversity in the voluntary sector," and the newspaper highlighted its 100,000-strong "army of typically white female volunteers."[6] It was not a characterisation with which the membership would have necessarily agreed. Former chairman Dame Barbara Shenfield, for one, was dismissive of complaints that WRVS was only for middle-aged, middle-class do-gooders. She regularly pointed out that the Service drew women and men from all walks of life. WRVS actually tried hard to reflect society generally within its membership and to become more representative. Among millennium initiatives, it embarked upon a two-year Home Office-funded twinning partnership with two black and minority ethnic (BME) organisations aimed at training volunteer managers to engage BME communities and so gain a better understanding of these groups. A further aim was for individuals from these groups to join the organisation. The WRVS director of community services said at the time: "Where the people who use our services are from different ethnic backgrounds, we need to make concentrated efforts to recruit from these communities to ensure that the needs of vulnerable people are properly met." To support this aim, WRVS printed recruitment posters with Arabic, Punjabi and Urdu translations.[7]

Morale was further boosted in 2000 with the 100th birthday of Queen Elizabeth the Queen Mother, who had linked her person and passion to WVS and WRVS for over 60 years. Naturally WRVS was integral to the birthday celebrations and, as a personal gift, presented its President with a leather-bound album featuring many archive photographs of her visits to WRVS projects. More formally, WRVS took part with the 200 organisations associated with the Queen Mother in a parade through London on 19 July. Thirty brightly-clad WRVS employees and volunteers from around the country and representing all sections of the organisation were involved in the parade, marching in fine style behind a chaperone of Coldstream Guards. Yet only one organisation was called upon to make sure the hot, sultry day did not take a physical toll. WRVS emergency services were exclusively responsible for ensuring that the 7,000 paraders were served lunch, a drink and a souvenir programme. Who else . . .? And who else could possibly have rushed from that celebration to dealing with the most serious floods in Britain in 400 years, among other arduous duties standing in support of railway workers for 24 hours as subsidence threatened to swamp the main line between Glasgow and Edinburgh. Across Britain 30 rest centres were activated and nine WRVS emergency teams placed on standby. Soon after, 127 volunteers were called out to support fire-fighters and emergency personnel at the scene of the Selby rail crash, which caused the deaths of 10 people. A temporary refreshment centre was staffed for eight days from 6 a.m. to midnight, the women involved putting their own comfort and needs aside to support the rescue and recovery operation in freezing conditions. The volunteers were praised by Prince Charles and received flowers and notes of appreciation from emergency personnel involved. Afterwards 40 WRVS attended the memorial service in York Minster for victims of the tragedy, invited in recognition of the organisation's selfless contribution.

Important work continued in Scotland across a broad range of activities. Early in 2000 WRVS was awarded a grant of £15,420 to establish a social transport scheme in Berwickshire. The scheme meant that those who could not use public transport, such as the elderly or infirm, could call upon WRVS to take them shopping or to hospital appointments. The grant covered running costs and the salary of a project manager, and was typical of the new era of project-centred WRVS activity. Another tender secured that year against competition from three other organisations was to run the first prison visitors' centre in Scotland. Prior to its inauguration, Edinburgh Prison's 1,200 weekly visitors, most of whom were women, faced having to stand in long queues in all weathers before its gates were opened. WRVS had, of course, already run a tea bar inside the prison – as shown in the BBC documentary for primary schools in 1973. Needless to say, the new facility was 'warmly' welcomed. Further west, WRVS itself funded a new shuttle bus between Paisley and the Royal Alexandra Hospital, which members had been running privately for 10 years. The bus complemented the tea bar, shop, ward trolley service and book service it operated on the site – and in 2000 WRVS gifted £106,000 back to the hospital to be used to provide new equipment. Not too far away, the biggest WRVS shop in Britain opened at the new Hairmyres Hospital in East Kilbride, with two full-time managers and a rota of 65 volunteers – boasting new lines such as costume jewellery and designer sunglasses. Yet even this was eclipsed by the magnificent efforts of WRVS employees and volunteers at Crosshouse Hospital in Kilmarnock. These remark-able public servants began ploughing back money into their hospital in 1982. Sixteen years later, in 1998, they reached the extraordinary total of £1 million in donations from profits from their shop, tea bar and ward sales – the first WRVS hospital service in Britain to achieve the landmark sum.

Uplifting millennium news also came from Shetland where, nearly 40 years after its presence on the islands ended, WRVS established a development worker and two social clubs for the elderly at the request of the local authority. During the war Shetland centres had boasted over 200 members. Perhaps to honour the return of the Service to the islands, the men of Lerwick Fire Station dressed up in blonde wigs and aprons and posed as WRVS look-alikes during the Up-Helly-Aa festival in 2001. WRVS also stole the show at another festival that year – taking part for the first time in the Edinburgh Cavalcade, the traditional launch-pad for the world famous Fringe. The WRVS float was brightly painted and "managed to gyrate the full length of the journey" in front of 200,000 spectators. Members also walked behind the vehicle to hand out over 1,000 WRVS goodie bags to the crowds. How life for volunteers had changed from the days when WVS predecessors made heroic attempts to enter blitzed and ruined cities with their life-giving canteens.

In 2001 the contribution of WRVS in Scotland was marked in a motion to the Scottish Parliament by Dorothy-Grace Elder MSP, who congratulated members on their "outstanding commitment and contribution to public service." She also told MSPs that WRVS contributed the equivalent of £12 million in free working hours annually.[8] Ironically, as it was being signed by MSPs, the first frozen meals to be delivered by WRVS in Scotland were being eaten by elderly 'guinea pigs' in Dumfries and Galloway. The six-month pilot scheme involved 46 clients, each of whom received frozen food in batches of 14 meals, which could be microwaved or heated in a conventional oven. This was regarded by many volunteers and clients as an alien form of delivery and, amid irked scepticism in the press, local authorities were forced to defend accusations that stockpiling frozen meals would leave the vulnerable isolated and without social contact. Little wonder many experienced members looked with considerable nostalgia at the ITV drama Back Home, televised at this time, which showed Sarah Lancashire as a wartime WVS driver and mechanic struggling to cope with her normal life at the end of the war. Later, kindred memories would have been awakened by Victoria Wood's brilliant portrayal of Nella Last in the ITV drama of the housewife and WVS volunteer whose wartime diaries recorded life for the Mass Observation study. Such memories, precious to WRVS, would eventually form the core of a successful WRVS lottery application to the Home Front Recall scheme, through which the exceptional and unprecedented experiences of pioneer volunteers would be recorded for posterity at memory-gathering events across the UK.

Food was in the news for different reasons as the 21st century began when Britain's farming community was struck by a devastating outbreak of foot and mouth disease. Meals on Wheels organisers on rural routes were badly affected and had to take drastic measures to prevent the possible spread of the infection. At the start of the emergency WRVS took advice from the Ministry of Agriculture and either avoided infected areas, made alternative arrangements or delivered meals following strict disinfecting routines. In Dumfries and Galloway, one of the worst affected areas, WRVS volunteers staffed helplines at the local authority command centre. Others served refreshments to ministry, council and emergency personnel. Forty members were involved in support activity in the Borders region, but many rural colleagues were not allowed to leave their properties, being themselves affected by the distressing disease. Jan Christie, Emergency Services manager for the West of Scotland, which covered Dumfries and Galloway, was a witness to fields full of cattle one day, and empty the next. She said: "The situation is appalling, but the volunteers are coping magnificently despite having to deal with some very harrowing calls."[9]

There were further demands on the organisation following the terrorist attacks on New York and Washington on 11 September 2001. As the terrible scenes unfolded on television WRVS began to take calls from distressed members of the public whose relatives may have been involved but also from people motivated and anxious to help in some way. In the hours following the attacks, WRVS assisted by coping with passengers from planes diverted from hurriedly closed American airports. Later they supported many fund-raising events, notably those organised by sympathetic UK fire-fighters. WRVS also wrote to counterparts in New York to offer advice based on its experience. Thereafter WRVS was involved as national and local government here reviewed plans for potential and previously unprecedented levels of crisis and disruption. The following spring, however, in a rather restrained announcement, WRVS revealed that employees and volunteers would "no longer take part in community assistance events, for example county shows."[10]

In February 2002, WRVS disclosed that it was to narrow its role considerably to focus services on Britain's elderly. It revealed a new mission "to help people maintain independence and dignity in their homes and communities, particularly in later life."[11] It made known that it was to pull out of around 400 family-oriented schemes, such as contact centres, toy libraries and prison visitor facilities, and that it would establish a 'New Futures' team to oversee the transfer of projects to what it termed 'independence' or to new 'parent' operators. Projects earmarked for closure – at least under a WRVS banner – were to include over 200 coffee shops and tea bars in courts, 90 child contact centres for estranged families and 42 toy libraries. In prisons, the charity planned to withdraw from running five visitors' centres, six play areas and crèches and 67 tea bars. As the news of the shift in focus sank in, chairman Tina Tietjen offered reassurance that hospital shops and tea trolleys and Meals on Wheels would continue and would be expanded where possible. Emergency planning functions would also remain. As might be expected, there was considerable surprise at the moves among members who had previously expressed concern about the modernised management style of the organisation. One volunteer communicated how the changes were "creating a huge division between the paid staff and volunteers." He added: "No doubt WRVS is run more efficiently, but at what expense? What this reorganisation has boiled down to is that it has been totally cost driven." WRVS responded by saying that pressures were created by "both our internal response to the government grant being phased out, and the need to comply with an ever-increasing range of regulations and legislation."[12]

The new focus on helping older people, the housebound and the disabled to maintain independence and dignity in their own homes was to revolve around community points of contact which would encompass services such as home visiting, Meals on Wheels, community transport, shopping and prescriptions collection. But it also meant that many volunteers were required to give up the duties they had carried out, in some cases, for many years. Indeed, some of the 900 WRVS paid staff among the 95,000 volunteers at the time lost their jobs. There was considerable unease, and incoming chief executive Mark Lever admitted in an interview that internal problems included a lack of communication between Milton Hill and WRVS project managers, poor payment of volunteers' expenses, lack of financial information for project managers, lack of communication to volunteers about the direction of WRVS and low recruitment levels.[13] Early in 2003, the Board of Trustees attempted to reassure the membership by issuing four short-term priorities: to recruit, retain and motivate volunteers and staff; to continue to develop and deliver attractive services; to communicate what WRVS did; and to make operations cost effective and thereby achieve financial viability. The most public priority was recruitment and, in November 2003, WRVS launched its first national recruitment campaign for volunteers since the Second World War. Among promotional ideas recommended to centres were general mail-outs, sending leaflets and posters to schools, generic talks on WRVS, display stands in supermarkets, adverts on buses, open days and press releases.

The wider image and public perception of the new-look charity had unsettled WRVS management. *The Times*, in February 2004, outlined the organisation's 'difficulty' in this way: "Mention of most charities will conjure up a picture of their beneficiaries. Oxfam, for example, is linked in the public consciousness with the developing world, Shelter with homeless people and the RSPCA with animals. But mention the WRVS and the image that pops into most people's heads is not of the 250,000 people whom they support every week, but of the volunteers themselves."[14] In other words WRVS continued to evoke images of the mostly retired, mostly female, mostly middle-class membership serving up tea and sympathy. To address this perception WRVS launched an overlapping purple and orange logo in the spring of 2004 and, for the first time in its history, abandoned its female credentials by stating that it wanted to be known by the initials WRVS only. The sleeker acronym was intended to reflect the contribution of male volunteers but it was also felt necessary to dispel the genteel image which had shadowed the organisation since its creation. Mark Lever, previously director of strategic development, also said the organisation wanted to "attract more ethnic minority and young people."[15]

The transformed identity and a powerful new slogan, 'Make it Count', which replaced the decade-old 'Make Someone's Day' and 'Simply Caring', could not dispel the membership's perception of a haemorrhaging of traditional WRVS values and roles. Even its core Meals on Wheels service striving for independence for older people was under pressure, dropping from a high of around 17 million meals to just nine million by 2002. That year it delivered only around a quarter of meals on wheels across the UK, reflecting competition from commercial operators for council contracts. By 2007 this had fallen to six million of the UK total of 40 million meals – amounting to deliveries to "just" 31,000 vulnerable people from the 200,000 recipients nationwide. Indeed, in trying to win local authority business, WRVS found itself not only competing against the commercial sector, it was also competing with the two main suppliers of the meals it delivered!

In the same vein that it celebrated the Queen's 50th year on the throne, and her 56th as WRVS Patron in 2002, it was with great sadness that the membership marked the passing of Queen Elizabeth the Queen Mother earlier the same year. In respect of the former, Golden Jubilee events took place across the country, and in London volunteers were invited to take part in the biggest national parade since VE Day. WRVS featured in the 22,000-strong march-past in a section representing those who gave service to the country and the community. The WRVS entry was headed by a standard-bearer flanked by members wearing 1950s uniform. They were followed by two Home Choice Meals vehicles, a larger float with displays of emergency work, a hospital trolley and a coffee shop – all accompanied by cheerleaders and roller-skating youngsters carrying Meals on Wheels trays! As usual, WRVS had a more serious undertaking; a team of 250 administered to those in the million-strong crowd who had camped out overnight and served refreshments to the multitude of paraders. Among other achievements they bravely manoeuvred 20,000 chocolate bars through the tight security cordon!

It was with deep pride, however, that members were also asked to staff the official lying-in-state for the Queen Mother, who had been involved with WRVS from its formation. Over 300 volunteers served refreshments to the thousands who queued outside Westminster Hall waiting to pay last respects in what was described as "a huge honour" for the organisation in providing this final service for its President. Many of the world's media took a special interest and WRVS featured on News at Ten, Sky News, the BBC World Service and on the bulletins of many overseas broadcasters. On the day of the funeral WRVS volunteers were just as busy, providing refreshments to the crowds gathered in London and manning a welfare station at Windsor. One member on duty recalled how the public had responded to WRVS: "People recognise us in our orange tabards. They know we treat people with respect . . . we are always welcomed wherever we go."[16]

The Queen Mother was always interested in WRVS and warmly encouraging over its myriad activities. The organisation's one-time deputy-chairman Dame Susan Walker once recalled: "During the war she would often ring Lady Reading and suggest ways in which we might help people."[17] One story illustrates the fondness the Queen Mother had for W(R)VS during her 60-year association with the Service. When WRVS celebrated Meals on Wheels Week in 1997 the Queen Mother was reportedly upset that she could not receive a delivery of lunch from volunteers at Clarence House, as she had a prior lunch engagement with the Canadian High Commissioner. Nonetheless the Meals on Wheels van appeared on time outside her London home. It was met at the side of the road by the nation's most popular and famous pensioner, who lifted the lids of its food containers and nodded her liking for the beef and vegetables and apple pie on offer, allowing the nation's press to record this very public seal of approval. Her spokesman explained, "She would have happily eaten the meal but she had this long-standing engagement. Even so, she was insistent that the van should be seen at Clarence House as she supports the scheme." As a footnote, it was revealed that the royal verdict was that the modern WRVS menu was more appetising than the suet dumplings she ladled out when delivering emergency meals during the Blitz.[18] Further links with the past were severed in January and July 2004, with the deaths of Baroness Pike of Melton and Dame Barbara Shenfield, both aged 85. The two former chairmen had combined the social conscience of enlightened intelligence with a personal involvement in many voluntary organisations, but most impressively as formidable figureheads of WRVS.

WRVS managers fought hard for new projects, attempting to recoup reducing government income by entering into contracts with local authorities, or by winning external funding, often through National Lottery opportunities. In 2004, for example, the organisation was awarded £600,000 by the Charities Minister to promote the involvement of older volunteers, particularly the over 65s, to help them to realise their potential in the community. Mark Lever sensed that there was a place for elderly people in the building of a more inclusive society: "Older volunteers bring vital social contact, skills and experience to their communities. If this contribution is not effectively encouraged, supported and recognised, the voluntary sector is failing both older people and their communities."[19] Such a statement might have been met with wry amusement in centres across the country. Internal statistics showed that fewer than 2% of volunteers were under 25. In Scotland, 11,000 of 12,000 members were over 50. As one volunteer pointed out: "All our helpers are over retiral age, the eldest was 89 last year."[20] But the bottom line was that WRVS still had 95,000 members in 2004 and in its new drive to help people maintain independence and dignity in their homes and communities, particularly in later life, it was running that year 3,500 projects. This core work, tackling social isolation and deprivation in Britain's communities, formed part of what Mr Lever said demonstrated "the magic our volunteers bring".

Despite relying to a considerable extent on external funding and on statutory authority contracts for staple projects, WRVS bravely retained its independence in the charity sector. Evidence of this came in 2004 when it issued a challenge to society to bring an end to social isolation and to ensure that all older people in the UK had daily human contact by 2010. The challenge followed its shocking revelations that 12,000 pensioners died alone and unnoticed in their homes every year. WRVS also revealed that three million people over the age of 65 could go a month without speaking to a single friend or neighbour. Such a lonely and isolated life often led to depression and despair. For others it meant moving out of the home they had lived in all their life if they were unable to get help to maintain their independence. In a passionate appeal which generated widespread media coverage, WRVS called for an end to this isolation and for support for its latest crusade, by urging members of the public to either establish regular contact with an older person they knew or to join a WRVS project in their community. This was valuable work WRVS had proudly carried on for nearly 70 years, making a difference to people's lives while initiating change – introducing new blood and fresh ways of doing necessary things; plugging welfare gaps as they appeared.

Meanwhile, members continued to respond to emergencies wherever they occurred. After the dreadful Boxing Day tsunami which struck Asia at the end of 2004, Emergency Services volunteers assisted disaster relief by staffing a helpline funded by the Foreign Office. Members took calls over several days, providing information and support to people affected by the disaster. They also offered advice to victims on how to return to Britain or where to find other expert assistance. Across the country volunteers also helped in the massive operations of collecting, packing and sending parcels, boxes and crates for the relief effort. On the Home Front, WRVS in 2005 mimicked the pioneering recycling efforts of its 40,000 wartime salvage stewards by asking its volunteers, employees and supporters to recycle printer cartridges and mobile phones. Ready to help, often first to help – though some mature members had seldom seen a mobile phone!

The historic role of Women's Voluntary Services was also rekindled in the summer of 2005 at a special ceremony at Holyroodhouse. As part of UK-wide commemorations to mark the 60th anniversary of the end of the war, the Princess Royal joined 750 veterans and guests at the palace for a 'World War II Tea' that was prepared by WRVS. Using items available during the war the 40 Emergency Services volunteers from Lanark, West Lothian and Edinburgh got through more than 100 gallons of water, 600 tea bags, 730 sand-wich packs and more than 600 fairy cakes and scones! In September that year, Edinburgh's 2,000 WRVS employees and volunteers were honoured by the Lord Provost and the City of Edinburgh Council at a civic reception.

By 2005, WRVS was again petitioning the government over its role and relevance. At a large gathering of voluntary organisations in London in February, WRVS argued that it lay at the heart of British society and the welfare state, and that it had demonstrated successfully how it could change and progress. Yet it was only part of an enormous voluntary contribution. By then there were over 200,000 charities and half a million community groups across the country. The sector had a paid workforce of 600,000, the total income of registered charities exceeded £27 billion and the leading service providers boasted an army of six million regular volunteers. In other words, WRVS had no divine right to deliver public-funded services or to hold the welfare safety net. It was only one of many social care charities and its services were constantly under threat from a range of business-minded competitors or siphoned off to single-issue voluntary organisations.

On the other hand, social services in Scotland relied on the contribution of WRVS to help people maintain health, dignity and independence. As membership fell across many parts of England and a small number of redundancies among paid staff was announced, Scotland could still boast 17,000 volunteers who, between them, worked on 750 projects across the country. One prominent addition to its armoury was the provision in 2005 of an emergency response vehicle, the gift of Central Scotland Fire and Rescue Service. This impressive truck, adorned with a large 'WRVS' logo, was equipped with two microwaves, a fridge and a variety of kitchen mod cons. As befits a charity often regarded as an official emergency service, the truck was readied for a 24/7 response to incidents. It also became a celebrity in its own right at the annual Truckfest event at the Royal Highland Showground in Edinburgh as the only non-blue-light emergency vehicle on display.

As it happened, emergency work dominated WRVS activities in 2005. In the first half of the year WRVS employees and volunteers helped 7,000 people at incidents across England, Scotland and Wales – providing professional support in situations such as floods, fires, power failures and evacuations. This support included the assistance given to 1,000 stranded passengers following the cancellation of ferries between Stranraer and Belfast. Then, in July 2005, WRVS was called out in numbers rarely seen since the Second World War. In the space of a month, emergency teams were summoned to a total of 51 situations. These ranged from world-leading news stories such as the 7 July terrorist attacks in London to help given during a dramatic domestic siege. The London bombings in particular saw WRVS working flat out. Help was required with refreshments for victims, police, NHS, social services and other agencies. WRVS also provided makeshift accommodation for stranded commuters and set up a family assistance centre in Enfield for children whose parents could not get home to collect them because of transport difficulties.

The world also looked in on Scotland that month as Gleneagles Hotel hosted the G8 summit of political leaders. WRVS teams across Central Scotland had been placed on standby weeks before the event. Police and other emergency services were also on heightened alert – as roads were closed, train services re-organised and campsites established for the expected influx of demonstrators. As part of the integrated plans, over 200 WRVS volunteers were placed in readiness to operate rest centres in towns in the venue's hinterland. These members were all properly trained, insured and equipped – drawing upon items from their emergency kits such as torches, flasks and fluorescent tabards. During the summit itself, WRVS was called out to feed 200 police based in and around Stirling. A further 80 volunteers helped social services in Perth, where many of the protesters detained during G8 demonstrations made court appearances and found themselves in need of help. Within a few days the same volunteers were back on duty for the T in the Park music festival at nearby Balado!

Meanwhile, the winds of change were blowing across the north, forcing WRVS in 2005 to put its three-floor headquarters in

Edinburgh's Albany Street on the market and to move its city hub, in February 2006, to a ground-floor office in Hill Street. In response to criticism within the voluntary sector that Scotland was being downgraded by WRVS, management at Milton Hill explained that it had used only two basement rooms in the three-storey property and that it did not require such a large building for its operations. It added: "There should be no alarm about our ability to support existing or develop new projects and our work is continuing as scheduled."[21] To this end a new Scottish advisory group was established in 2006 to influence work and opportunities in Scotland. This team comprised WRVS directors, Scottish employees and volunteers and was co-ordinated in Edinburgh by the incoming media and public affairs manager for Scotland, Rachel Cackett. As 2006 reached its hot summer, the focus of WRVS work – indeed its official mission – was 'to help people maintain independence and dignity in their homes and communities, particularly in later life.' It was undoubtedly a farsighted and courageous decision by WRVS to concentrate much of its volunteer effort on helping the elderly. Every demographic indicator suggested that Britain's population was ageing. Over six decades WRVS had witnessed the issues and problems faced by growing numbers of vulnerable and isolated people. As people aged it discovered that "keeping up interests and social networks can get harder; work activities and connections are lost; mobility is reduced; friends and family get ill and die; disposable income can reduce significantly."[22] When WRVS surveyed 500 of its service users in the summer of 2006 it was told that the biggest worry as people grew older was declining health and mobility and losing their friends, family and social network. Mark Lever responded to the survey by saying: "Our services are geared exactly to helping people deal with these issues."[23] Thus modern-day objectives have been promoted towards providing essential community projects with the aim of ensuring that older people remain well, healthy and in comfort through their later years, with WRVS arguing the case that structured support to the elderly should be appreciated as a long-term national investment. To that end older people have been encouraged by

WRVS to engage in new learning, to take part in health initiatives and to participate in social events.

While some services have had to be sacrificed, harming WRVS's long-won reputation and its relationship with some veteran foot-soldiers, WRVS frequently had to fight its corner to prevent hospital services being absorbed by private operators and high street chains who could maximise profits and thereby offer to pay higher rentals to NHS trusts. Although it generally paid modest rents for the hospital space it occupied, WRVS had a history of ploughing tea bar and trolley profits back into local healthcare projects. For example, by 2006, the combined efforts of volunteers over 19 years at the Royal Alexandra Hospital in Paisley had matched Kilmarnock's Crosshouse in benefiting local health services by another £1 million. There, some 200 volunteers helped to run four projects. But WRVS had to take the threat to its historic role seriously. Mark Lever pointed out that it had 28,000 volunteers working in more than 400 hospitals and that: "I would hope the NHS can see that although we can't place a monetary value on what we do, it is very precious."[24]

The wonderful goodwill created in hospitals over many years certainly helped to prevent some popular WRVS projects becoming casualties. When, for example, WRVS was told it was to lose its shop at Bedford Hospital a doctor there commented publicly: "For as long as anyone who works in our hospital can remember the WRVS have run a small shop selling drinks, chocolate, sweets, and over the years they have given us tens of thousands of pounds. They perform a vital social function and are always happy to chat with distressed relatives and patients. Now they are being asked to move to make way for some high street store. But the service will be worse and everything will cost more."[25] One newspaper added to the weight of support for those volunteers by forcefully stating in a Leader comment: "Entering some British hospitals today, you could be mistaken for thinking that you had walked on to the concourse of a railway station or into a shopping mall. High Street names furnish the shopping needs of patients and their relatives. Consumer choice is prolific. But at what cost?" The article answered its own question: "The NHS may be facing a period of financial austerity, but the value added by an army of loyal and dependable volunteers is self-evident, even if it does not show up on a balance sheet."[26]

WRVS also had a fight on its hands with councils who wanted to replace volunteers with alternative suppliers for Meals on Wheels. During the present decade local authorities across the UK have frequently absorbed WRVS delivery runs or contracted them out to third-party providers. Justification for this has taken many forms – Scottish councils have argued, not always convincingly, that it was for better efficiency, because the workload was too great for WRVS, because of government red tape, for health and safety reasons, to meet moving and handling procedures, even because of concern over civil court claims against them if an accident occurred while a volunteer was making a delivery. When the 60 volunteers who regularly visited 100 householders in Dundee were told they were no longer required, the city council explained its action by saying: "We are looking at respecifying the service to take into account the pattern of demand and the needs of all the people concerned." At the very least the council had invented a new word. When it was also hinted, however, that WRVS were not up to modern hygiene requirements, there was a frosty public rebuttal from Mrs D. M. Norris, honorary chairman of the Dundee branch of the WVS & WRVS Association: "Through all the years WRVS has adhered to all regulations, especially hygiene. We have worked and cared voluntarily, and to be thrown out with no apology or thanks is a disgrace."[27]

Alas, as the decade progressed, more battles were lost than won. Towards the end of 2006, for example, Aberdeenshire Council became the latest local authority to opt for a cost-cutting private fortnightly drop-off of frozen dinners to Meals on Wheels clients. The contract for the new service was awarded to a private supplier in Ellon, and the 600 WRVS volunteers, who gave 24,000 hours a year to Meals on Wheels delivery across Aberdeenshire, were told to stand down. On the day of the emotional hand-over to the microwave service, one WRVS volunteer at Insch commented, "To exchange this service for an impersonal fortnightly frozen meals delivery at higher cost seems short change for our old folk."[28] WRVS teams did not give up without a fight. A protest letter was fired off to the local MP, and one Aberdeenshire volunteer publicly criticised the manner in which the service had been terminated, pointing out that only one of her clients had been informed of the change-over to the new arrangement. She said: "Our old folk were left in the dark by our 'caring' council and were left wondering where their next meal was coming from." Aberdeenshire Council's 'thank you' to the women and men who had provided the service for 65 years was a civic reception where certificates were presented to those involved. And when Angus Council transferred its Meals on Wheels scheme from WRVS to paid staff, the *Dundee Courier*'s Leader columnist commented: "At the very time one might expect the council to welcome volunteers to keep down costs, it is politely showing them the door."[29]

Indeed, across the country WRVS was caught up in the debate over how meals were to be supplied to the vulnerable and elderly. Many sympathetic editorials praised the service which WRVS had diligently provided over four decades and said the councils' agenda was based on the premise that frozen batches of food were a cheaper option than sending them house-to-house every day. In a thumping attack on local authorities headed, "Sorry, but you'll have to cook them yourself," *The Daily Telegraph* claimed that the increasing practice of supplying pensioners with frozen meals and microwaves had been "condemned by pensioners' groups and thousands of elderly people, including those who are wheelchair-bound and suffering from arthritis and dementia." It told how "outraged pensioners" groups feared that councils would eventually foist stockpiles of frozen food on residents, "leaving elderly people isolated from the outside world." This was a fear shared and expressed by Mark Lever, among others. "Our concern is that older people will lose the social contact and that levels of loneliness will increase." He was able to point to a survey carried out on behalf of WRVS in which an astonishing three-quarters of older people said that the daily visit from the WRVS volunteer was the only social contact they had. He added: "Clearly the frozen option is cheaper and is being taken up by more and more councils, but we see this daily contact as vital for many vulnerable people."[30]

Impressively, WRVS stood by its volunteers and announced in late 2005 that it would not tender for contracts from local authorities prepared only to use frozen meals. Janet Lawrenson, WRVS head of food services, explained the decision: "It's not just about food, it's about providing regular human contact to someone who may otherwise not see anyone that day. It is also about providing a helping hand. Moving to a situation where people can only receive infrequent deliveries of frozen meals robs the most isolated people in the community of vital contact and much needed support."[31] In this principled stance WRVS was heartily backed by employees and volunteers up and down the country who had first-hand experience of the benefits to users of routine deliveries of hot meals, and how regular visits helped to break the monotony of isolation. It was a position again put forward by WRVS in February 2008 when Perth and Kinross Council embarked upon a tendering process which would see firms bid for a contract to deliver frozen meals on a less frequent basis than WRVS volunteers already provided.

In 2006, WRVS treated itself to another range of work wear – which included fully-lined fleeces, gilets, long and short sleeved blouses, and sweatshirts in purple and lilac. Much to members' relief, the popular pinny and tabard were retained. An important facet of community work also received a make-over with the introduction of sophisticated plastic-topped trolleys bearing the purple and orange WRVS crest to hospitals across the country. Despite fears of privatisation, a core service and a major source of income remained the WRVS network of 350 retail and catering outlets and 250 trolley rounds within NHS hospitals. Another important service was the delivery of seven million Meals on Wheels for 130 local authorities, which made life better for thousands of older people. By mid-decade, WRVS also ran 837 lunch and social clubs where over 8,000 older people could catch up with old friends and meet new ones. It continued to launch community-based services for older people, including new multi-activity community centres. Thanks in part to the launch of its internet website, it had stemmed a long-trend fall in recruitment and had added 5,000 new volunteers. Its emergency teams had helped thousands of people caught up in emergencies and disasters, including those at the London bombings and the Buncefield oil depot fire in 2005, where 50 volunteers worked in shifts for six days following Europe's biggest fire since the Second World War. It still supported the welfare of the Armed Forces through its subsidiary WRVS Services Welfare Ltd. It provided home library services and Books on Wheels which offered DVDs, CDs, audio tapes and books, and which were as welcome as a meal to many isolated people. And in a modern mirror of the wartime Housewives' Section it had nearly 100 Good Neighbours projects, helping older people with tasks like shopping, gardening, collecting prescriptions or pensions.

In February 2006 WRVS appointed London solicitor Ruth Markland as chairman of the Board of Trustees. This was followed in October 2007 with the appointment of Lynne Berry as chief executive. Mrs Markland was no stranger to WRVS – her mother had delivered Meals on Wheels in Cardiff. Lynne Berry was previously chief executive at the General Social Care Council. But the membership's attention quickly turned from staff changes to a major flood crisis in England, where once again WRVS personnel worked alongside the emergency services, assisting with evacuation, setting up rest centres and providing food and drink to everyone affected. Angela Currie, head of Emergency Services for WRVS, paid tribute to the members of the Gloucester, Tewkesbury and Cheltenham teams who had been at the forefront of the drama: "Our volunteers have been phenomenal. They fought through flood and traffic gridlock to get to rest centres to make sure that people had the support they needed."[32]

September 2007 brought another new home for WRVS in Scotland when Hill Street was abandoned in favour of a property in Rose Street. There, a single WRVS representative shared open-plan offices with other Scottish charities. Media and public affairs manager Rachel Cackett explained the apparent downsizing: "We found that we weren't using all the facilities in Hill Street as often as we'd thought, so it made real sense for us to share facilities with others and only pay for what we use."[33] The organisation as a whole still faced significant challenges. Its trustees at Milton Hill, led by Ruth

Markland and responsible for the policy, governance and direction of WRVS, and its management team of executive directors, were aware that the charity had to expand its range of community services. It was also conscious of the age profile of its volunteer base and believed it urgently needed to recruit the next generation of voluntary help. Only 1,400 out of 60,000-plus volunteers in 2006 were under 25.[34] Funding remained an issue, and a major challenge was securing the means to allow development. Its stated aim that year was to realise an "unrestricted" surplus of £250,000 yearly, growing to £2 million per annum by 2010.

As WRVS celebrates its 70th anniversary, a throwaway judgement on the organisation might amount to describing it as a social care organisation. It is much more. It is irritating for a reader to be confronted with statistics time over time – but numbers can be an important tool in revealing the facts behind commitments and contributions. The facts supporting WRVS are that it regularly helps 75,000 people to live independently at home and to stay active locally. Its Good Neighbours projects help around 10,000 people every week. Over six million people still receive Meals on Wheels deliveries from paid or volunteer WRVS staff. Some 20,000 people benefit from home library services, 40 community transport schemes help thousands of people to get to shops, doctors or to meet friends or to take part in social activities. WRVS has 11 community centres and helps to run over 600 social or lunch clubs. It now operates over 500 shops and cafes in more than 300 hospitals, gifting back over £5 million annually to the NHS to buy equipment and improve facilities and patient care. Trolleys still supply patients with essentials and luxuries, making their hospital stay more comfortable. And some 6,000 volunteers – almost one in 10 of enrolments – are trained to provide support in an emergency.

In Scotland in 2006–7, WRVS helped 14,000 older people remain active and independent, raised £900,000 for hospitals, helped over 2,000 people during emergencies and delivered 800,000 Meals on Wheels – yes, nutritionally balanced, with reduced salt, lower fat, but tasty and easy to chew. Of note in recent times has been its campaigning role in influencing and modifying proposed Scottish

Parliament legislation. It submitted, for example, a thoughtful argument for amendments to the Protection of Vulnerable Groups (Scotland) Bill in 2006. That year, with the help of volunteers across Scotland, Edinburgh staff also responded to the Scottish Executive's proposed *A Scotland with an Ageing Population* strategy by putting forward a range of ideas to address negative perceptions of older people. WRVS has also lobbied the Scottish Government to ensure that Scottish laws and policies in areas such as transport and population provide the best possible outcomes for its service users and volunteers.

MSPs, in turn, have given vocal support to WRVS campaigns to raise the profile of Britain's elderly and support the work it does to alleviate loneliness in older age. Current politicians have joined predecessors by eulogising the organisation's achievements – a Scottish Parliament motion in 2001 praised its "outstanding commitment and contribution to public service," while another that year highlighted Meals on Wheels deliveries across Scotland. A motion in 2004 congratulated its efforts "to demonstrate that volunteering counts in order to serve the needs of vulnerable members of society," yet another in 2007 noted its proud history and that even after "60 years of hard work" WRVS was "still helping people to enable choice, independence and dignity."[35]

Remarkable change has been witnessed and absorbed by the powerful WRVS presence in Scotland across these 70 years. The wartime member enrolled at a time of crisis and ticked a box to determine where she would serve. Today's volunteer, as likely male as female, is managed with induction, initial and intensive training, satisfaction surveys, volunteering audits, reward and recognition, even an exit strategy for those who want to leave. And today's society has increasingly become cash rich and time poor – the amount of time Britons spend on voluntary work has fallen dramatically over the past 20 years. Record levels of employment have emptied the reservoir of potential volunteers. People have been forced to work longer through societal influences such as debt, family break-ups and rising house prices. The result has been that voluntary agencies across the country have struggled to provide comprehensive services to vulnerable groups as people have found themselves unable to sign up for large chunks of time. Mark Lever told an interviewer how, once, the traditional volunteer was a woman in her fifties whose husband worked and whose children had grown up and left home. "That is changing," he said. "More and more homes have got both people working long hours."[36]

Another significant factor is that traditional agencies such as WRVS, the Salvation Army and the Red Cross have lost the modern volunteer to more 'sexy' campaigning and social-issue organisations, such as Oxfam and Greenpeace. This has been the case with many young people, who not only have demands on their time from sport, hobbies, entertainment and holidays but who often appear to prefer protest volunteering to the older-fashioned kind. It is perhaps also the case that increasing professionalism among volunteers, driven by local authority and legislative directives – the debate over criminal disclosure, for instance – has acted to deflect the traditional volunteer from coming forward. Similarly, employee volunteering has become a 21st century phenomenon, whereby larger companies first encourage their own staff to take part in schemes to which the company promises funds, at the same time benefiting from the range of skills developed outside of the firms' time. This, too, has affected the numbers offering their time and energies to WRVS, and yet it can lead to significant benefit to the organisation. In January 2008, for instance, WRVS received the remarkable sum of £800,000 from the HBOS Foundation at a ceremony in Edinburgh. This huge sum was gathered during fund-raising activities by over 30,000 HBOS employees, customers and supporters across the UK and represented one third of an even larger total divided between three receiving charities. Every pound raised by employees and supporters was matched by the bank. While this may diminish recruitment potential, it was reported that a brand-new Emergency Services team was formed comprising HBOS employees. Chairman Ruth Markland commented that the £800,000 donation would "make such a difference to WRVS and the thousands of older people we help get more out of life."[37]

Seventy years on, WRVS remains unique in meeting the government's desire to build resilience and to ensure that communities have the wherewithal to respond to disasters. It continues to offer the country a nationwide network of trained emergency workers that can support both victims and rescue workers. No one can galvanise local communities like WRVS and few organisations are committed to raising the bar of voluntary service in the manner of WRVS.

Thus WRVS must break down the barriers currently deterring people from volunteering, widen the range of opportunities available, make volunteering more relevant and exciting, broaden the range of work done, make it more challenging, and underline the value of voluntary contributions and achievements through publicity and qualifications. To this end the WRVS website will become more important in the years ahead. Through its portal new faces come to the organisation and information is disseminated. It is also hoped that a new WRVS presence on Britain's high streets – the first in Scotland at an information centre and cafe in Paisley – will provide a very public face for the organisation and stimulate interest in it.

Where stands Scotland in this story? Just as Lady Ruth Balfour did not see the future of Women's Voluntary Services stretching beyond the end of war on the basis that it had its own role and identity in Scotland, so succeeding chairmen – perhaps north and south – must often have wondered whether WRVS in Scotland was an independent entity with its own autonomy, and not a branch of the London-driven organisation. Scottish centres followed national policy and procedures, yet by and large 'did their own thing' under the scrutiny of Edinburgh headquarters – though they smartly fell into line on Lady Reading's peregrinations north!

The only Scottish chairman to assume the national role, The Hon Dame Mary Corsar, recalled: "There was no written constitution for WRVS – it was very loose and the way things were interpreted in England and Wales may not always have been the way we interpreted them. So I had a free hand in Scotland. For instance, if I felt strongly that someone deserved an honour, I didn't go to London. I spoke to our point of contact in the Scottish Office, who in my day was Sir William Kerr Fraser. Similarly, our hospitals organiser would go to the Scottish Health Department. We are different. The whole culture in Scotland is different."

Dame Mary believes now that had Scotland voted for devolution in the first referendum in 1979, an independent Women's Royal Voluntary Service might have evolved north of the border. "There was nothing in writing, but we knew that the Scottish Office would support us. The same might have happened during the reconstruction of WRVS in the 1990s, which was deeply unpopular among many staff and volunteers across Scotland. I am not saying that WRVS did not have to change. After the war we were the umbrella organisation that took everything under our wing. Now other agencies specialise in work that we once carried out. So WRVS was bound to get smaller. It was the way that it got smaller that hurt feelings."[38]

Scotland's 12,000 membership punches far above its weight in forming nearly a quarter of today's WRVS roll-call. Its work takes place within Scotland's geographical boundaries and within social, cultural, political and legislative frontiers established within Scotland. In its mission for social welfare reform it has also empowered and changed the people who embodied it.

Ever since WVS emerged north of the border in response to the Second World War, membership has shown to wider society the benefits of volunteering; how opportunities to contribute through WRVS have helped to develop confidence and realised untapped potential. Volunteering has reduced isolation among members and provided a conduit for skills to be used in a productive way for those less fortunate. This is a hidden aspect of WRVS work. There is no record of how members grow in stature and confidence through the duties they undertake, just as there is no doubt that personal development occurs. All sorts of members of all ages from all types of backgrounds have become rich in the multitude of things learned. WRVS is both supportive and empowering, offering potential for a significant sense of self worth. That potent symbol of growing independence, Nella Last, noted 70 years ago: "After all these years I've discovered I've got a suffragette streak in me." And as the war progressed she became "more soldier than a fifty-one-year-old housewife." In the modern era Elaine Smith started work as the chairman's secretary at Edinburgh HQ in October 1984, the start of more than 15 years with the Service. She recalled how the trust placed in her by Mary Corsar, "gave me confidence to develop skills and grow in assurance of my abilities." Miss Smith saw this growth of confidence in others around her, too. She recalled, "I think of one colleague in particular, a married woman who had been away from the workplace whilst bringing up her children. After a few years she had acquired sufficient self-assurance to be able to return to teaching."[39]

In the way that war work created opportunities for WVS women, WRVS has allowed volunteers to engage with others through projects in schools, with families and vulnerable groups to play a prominent and conspicuous part in the life of this country. It has allowed them to attend training and learning opportunities, to grow in capacity, to be receptive, to think clearly and to act practically. It has offered them opportunities to stay active and healthy citizens through the fruits of their voluntary contributions. In a spirit of co-operation it has allowed them to take part in multi-agency projects, to form networks and links and to play many valuable roles, thereby contributing to the economic, cultural and social well-being of Scotland. Even after retirement the WRVS Association, the 'Old Girls' Club,' allows former volunteers to remain in touch and to relive and relate some of the happiest and most fulfilling times of their lives.

The tantalising notion of Scotland's own WRVS-styled support organisation has to be left for future historians to discuss. In the meantime, the last words of this book are dedicated to past and present volunteers, the men and women – but mostly women – from all walks of life who have worn one of Britain's most enduring and recognisable symbols of help – the badge of WRVS.

For 70 years they have faced and overcome challenges with characteristic determination and resourcefulness – from those wartime staff who had to butter bread for hours on end during the Clydebank Blitz – and who never knew what went between the slices – to today's volunteers with their distinctive and precious mission to perform safe and well checks and to offer dignity and happiness to the nation's growing numbers of elderly and vulnerable.

This history salutes them and their story.

REFERENCES

CHAPTER 1

1. Jeffrey, Andrew, *This Time of Crisis; Glasgow, The West of Scotland and the North Western Approaches in the Second World War*, Mainstream, Edinburgh, 1993, p28.
2. Sir Samuel Hoare to Lady Reading, 20 May 1938.
3. Memorandum, Lady Reading to Sir Samuel Hoare, 29 April 1938.
4. *Idem.* See also, Graves, Charles, *Women in Green; The Story of the W.V.S. in Wartime*, Heinemann, London, 1948, p3.
5. Graves, p5. See also: Mills, J., *Within the Island Fortress: The Uniforms, Insignia & Ephemera of the Home Front in Britain 1939–1945. No 1, The Women's Voluntary Services (WVS)*, Wardens Publishing, Orpington, 2005.
6. *WVS Bulletin*, No 44, June 1943, pp2–3.
7. Sweet, Leslie, 'Women's "Voluntary" Services, Some Comments on a New Organisation', in *Red Tape*, the magazine of the Civil Service Clerical Association, July 1938, p781. This rather negative article railed against the apparent lack of democracy in the new organisation.
8. Mills, p1.
9. *WVS Bulletin*, No 44, June 1943, pp2–3.
10. Lady Reading to John Colville, Secretary of State for Scotland, 20 May 1938. See also: Lady Reading's letters to Ruth Balfour, 21 May 1938 and 4 June 1938.
11. *Report on Scotland*, by LKH (Mrs Lindsay Huxley) for Headquarters, Tothill Street, 24 November 1939.
12. Sir Charles Cunningham, in (Anon) *Stella Reading, Some Recollections by Her Friends*, London, 1971, p28.
13. Griselda Tomory to Lady Steel-Maitland, 19 July 1939.
14. *WVS recruitment leaflet*, undated, National Archives of Scotland, GD1/171/1. *Dundee Courier*, 7 March 1939. Ruth Balfour letter to *The Scotsman*, 5 October 1938.

15.   Home Office, *ARP Circular 243/1939.*

16.   Graves, p17.

17.   Beauman, Katharine, *Green Sleeves; The Story of WVS/WRVS*, Seeley, Service & Co, London, 1977, p13.

18.   *Dundee Courier* 22 February 1939. I am indebted to Eileen Moran of Dundee Central Libraries for her help in tracing WVS archives.

19.   Broad, Richard and Fleming, Suzie, *Nella Last's War, The Second World War Diaries of Housewife, 49*, Profile Books, London, 2006, p30. 'Lady Reading's broadcast to the United States', October 1939, in Anon, (Pauline Fenno), *It's The Job That Counts, A Selection From The Writings and Speeches of the Dowager Marchioness of Reading*, Private Circulation, 1954, p5. (Pauline Fenno was Lady Reading's wartime friend and driver.)

20.   Beauman, p19. *The Scotsman*, 1 October 1938.

21.   Stella Reading, *Some Recollections*, pp13–14.

22.   Graves, p30. Mills, p5.

23.   *WVS Bulletin* No 44, June 1943.

24.   *WVS HQ Memorandum to Centres on issue of Uniform*, London, 1939.

25.   *Department of Health for Scotland Circular*, 15 June 1939. William Boyd (Ed), *Evacuation in Scotland: A Record of Events and Experiments*, University of London Press, Kent, 1944, p4.

26.   Graves, p20.

27.   *Perthshire Advertiser*, 16 August 1939. *Minutes of Dundee Education Committee*, August 1939, Dundee City Archives.

CHAPTER 2

1.   Lady Reading to George V, and his return telegram, 3 September 1939.

2.   *The Scotsman*, 6 September 1939.

3.   McPhail, I.M.M., *The Clydebank Blitz*, West Dunbartonshire Libraries, 1974, p2. Jeffrey, *This Time of Crisis*, (1993), p27.

4.   *WVS Report on 25 Years Work*, HMSO, 1963, p21.

5.   *Perthshire Advertiser*, 20 September 1939.

6.   Dundee Education Cuttings Book, p52, Dundee City Archives. *Inverness Courier*, 24 January 1940.

7.   'Life on The Home Front', *Readers Digest Journeys into the Past* Series, London 1993, p15. Memories of Helen Jackson in Robertson, Seona, and Wilson, Les, *Scotland's War*, Mainstream, Edinburgh, 1995, p11.

8.   'WVS Report on Scotland', by LKH (Lindsay Huxley), 24 November 1939, in *Scottish Headquarters Report No 2*, 1938–39.

9.   Ruth Balfour to Agnes Henderson, 2 October 1939.

10. *WVS Scottish News Review No 2*, Jan–Feb 1940. *WVS Bulletin No 2*, December 1939. *Women's Voluntary Services, Report on Ten Years Work for the Nation, 1938–1948*, London, 1948, p21.

11. Graves (1948), p39. *The Scotsman* 15 September 1939.

12. *WVS Scottish News Review No 8*, August 1941. *The Scotsman*, 20 December 1939.

13. Jeffrey, Andrew, *The Time of Crisis*, p21.

14. *Ministry of Home Security Intelligence Report*, 20 March 1941.

15. Robertson and Wilson, 'Scotland's War', p7–9. *Press & Journal* 17 October 1939. Also Jeffrey, Andrew, *This Present Emergency, Edinburgh, The River Forth and South East Scotland and the Second World War*, Mainstream, Edinburgh, 1992, p119.

16. *Daily Sketch*, 16.1.1940.

17. *Nella Last's War* (2006), p49.

18. Interview with Stella Jackson, 2007.

19. Ellis, Jennifer (Ed), *Thatched with Gold, The Memoirs of Mabell Countess of Airlie*, Hutchison, London, 1962, p213.

20. *The Orcadian*, 21.3.1940. *WVS Bulletin No 5*, p15. 'Mary Work to her sister Ida, 24.3. 1940', *Orkney Archive* D32/1/1. *WVS Scottish News Review No 3*, March–April 1940. I am grateful to *Orkney Archive* for allowing access to the Work family papers.

21. *The Sunday Post*, quoted in *World War II, The Scottish Home Front*, National Archives of Scotland, Edinburgh 2004, p13.

22. *WVS Bulletin No 7*, May 1940.

23. Memories of Clemency Greatorex, in Goodall, Felicity, *Voices from the Home Front*, David & Charles, London, 2004, p178.

24. Lady Reading message to County Organisers, May 1940.

25. *Scottish News Review No 4*, May–July 1940, pp2 and 7.

26. *WVS Allied Information Bureau memorandum*, undated (1941).

27. *Idem.*

28. *WVS Bulletin No 59*, September 1944, p4. Also Graves, p162.

29. *People's Journal*, 3 October 1942.

30. Graves, p83.

31. Graves, p58. *Scottish News Review No 4*, May–July 1940, p4.

32. Mia Allan, 'What Happened to My Frying Pan', in Nicholson, Mavis, *What did you do in the war, mummy?: Women in World War II*, Chatto & Windus, London, 1975, pp189–190.

33. *WVS Bulletin No 23*, September 1940, p4.

34. Graham, Virginia, *The Story of WVS*, HMSO, London, 1959, p15. Graves, pp120–121.

35. *Nella Last's War*, pp42 and 130.

36. Mary Work file, *Orkney Archive* D32/1/1. Also Clemency Greatorex in *Voices from the Home Front*, p176. See also Beauman, Green Sleeves (1977), p38.

37. Press statement by Herbert Morrison, praising the work of WVS, Home Office, 16 June 1943.

CHAPTER 3

1. MacPhail, *The Clydebank Blitz*, (1974), p25.

2. Jeffrey, *This Time of Crisis*, (1993), p74.

3. Ministry of Information, *Report on the Clydeside Raids*, March 13 & 14, 1941, p1.

4. Jeffrey, *This Time of Crisis*, pp72–73. MacPhail, p36, Ministry of Information. *Report on the Clydeside Raids*, p1.

5. Kathleen Hanton Coffey to author, 2007.

6. *WVS Bulletin No 19*, May 1941, p5. MacPhail, p57. Interview with Agnes Mair, 2007.

7. McPhail, p58.

8. Jeffrey, *This Time of Crisis*, p65. See also Finlay, Richard, *Modern Scotland*, Profile Books, London, 2004, p187.

9. Lindsay Huxley to Lady Reading, 28 March 1941. MacPhail, p34.

10. *Ministry of Information Report on Clydeside*, p2. MacPhail, p66.

11. *Ministry of Information Report on Clydeside*, p3. MacPhail, p66.

12. *WVS Bulletin No 19*, May 1941, p5.

13. Lindsay Huxley to Lady Reading, 28 March 1941. *Nella Last's War* (2006), p142. See also Titmuss, Richard, *History of the Second World War, Problems of Social Policy*, Chapter XV, 'The Attack on Ports and Provincial Cities', London, 1963.

14. Lindsay Huxley to Lady Reading, 28 March 1941.

15. Boyd (Ed), *Evacuation in Scotland (1944)*, p120.

16. Mary Denholm to author, 2007.

17. *WVS Bulletin No 20*, June 1941, p4. *WVS Renfrewshire Quarterly Report*, July 1941. *WVS Scottish News Review No 8*, August 1941.

18. *WVS Scottish News Review*, August 1941.

19. 'Memories of Nan McLaren' in *People's Journal*, 24 October 1942.

20. MacPhail, pp50 and 53. *WVS Bulletin No 19*, May 1941, p4.

21. *Preparation for Heavy Attacks Next Winter*, HMSO, London, 1944.

22. *WVS Scottish News Review No 8*, August 1941.

23. *WVS Bulletin No 23*, September 1941, p5.

CHAPTER 4

1. *WVS Bulletin No 26*, December 1941, p1.
2. Graves (1948), p169.
3. *WVS Bulletin No 22*, August 1941, p5. *WVS Scottish News Review No 11*, September 1942, p4.
4. *War Cabinet Memorandum on the rationing of clothing*, W.P. (41) 105, June 1941.
5. Board of Trade, *Official List of Coupons*: needed for clothing and footwear, 1 July 1941.
6. *Dundee Education Cuttings Book 6*, 28 September 1943, Dundee City Archives.
7. Graham, (1959), p15.
8. 'Memories of Nan MacLaren', *People's Journal*, 24 October, 1942, p13. See also: Graham, p17. *WVS Scottish News Review No 6*, February 1941.
9. Lady Balfour and Lady Reading messages to volunteers in, *WVS Scottish News Review No 9*, 1941. See also: *It's The Job That Counts* (1954), pp19–20.
10. *WVS Glasgow Quarterly Report*, March 1941. *Interview with Flora Kirkland* 2007.
11. Memories of Mrs R.A. Young in *People's Journal*, 3 October 1942.
12. *WVS Scottish News Review, No 11*, September 1942.
13. *Scottish Headquarters Report*, September 1942, p1. *Nella Last's War* (2006), p89.
14. Reading speech to Centre Organisers, *WVS Bulletin No 45*, p3. See also Hinton, James. *Women, Social Leadership, and the Second World War*, Oxford University Press, 2002, p29, and *WVS Scottish Newsletter No 11*, September 1942, p1.
15. Press statement issued by Herbert Morrison, Home Secretary and Minister of Home Security, 16 June 1943.
16. Hetherington, S.J., Katharine Atholl 1874- 1960, *Against The Tide*, Aberdeen University Press, p221.
17. *Aberdeen Monthly Narrative*, April 1943.
18. *Idem*.
19. Report on the Evacuation of Tarbat Training Area, November-December 1943, by Janet Douglas, Ross-shire County Organiser, Conon-Bridge Centre, December 1943. See also *WVS Bulletin No 59*, September 1944.
20. *WVS Bulletin No 59*, September 1944, p5.

CHAPTER 5

1. *WVS Bulletins No 36*, October 1942, p6, and *No 50*, p3.
2. Cupar WVS, *minute of monthly meeting*, 12 September 1944, p1.

3. *WVS Bulletin No 11*, September 1940. 'Memories of Stella Jackson'. See also: *WVS Scottish News Review No 10*, April 1942.
4. Graves (1948), p203.
5. *WVS Bulletin No 33*, July 1942, p5.
6. *Interview with Isabella McKay*, 2007.
7. *WVS Report on 25 Years Work*, London (1963), p35.
8. *Glasgow Evening Citizen*, 20 December 1944. Graham (1959), p25. *Daily Record*, 23 March 1945. *WVS Scottish News Review No 10*, April 1942. Fraser, Eugenie, *A Home by the Hooghly; A Jute Wallah's Wife*, Mainstream, Edinburgh, 1989, p92.
9. *Scottish Headquarters Report*, September-November 1943. Dunfermline Landward Area, Report for August 1944, p1.
10. *It's The Job That Counts* (1954), p61.

CHAPTER 6

1. *WVS Bulletin No 74*, December 1945, p3.
2. Department of Health for Scotland to Ruth Balfour, 14 May 1945.
3. Lady Reading to Centre Organisers, 4 May 1945.
4. Lady Balfour to Joseph Westwood, 21 August 1945.
5. Lady Balfour to Joseph Westwood, 21 August 1945. *WVS Scotland Headquarters Report,* January-June *1945*, p1.
6. *Home Office Memorandum on future of WVS*, 23 August 1945.
7. Lady Balfour to Joseph Westwood, 27 August 1945.
8. *WVS Bulletin No 65*, March 1945, p3.
9. *The Future of the WVS, Home Office*, 28 August 1945.
10. Hinton (2002), p163.
11. *Department of Health internal memorandum*, 30 August 1945.
12. *The Future of Voluntary Services, Report to Cabinet*, 9 September 1945.
13. *Cabinet decision paper B (45)*, 7 September 1945. See also: Chambers, Rosalind, 'A Study of Three Voluntary Organisations' in D.V. Glass (Ed), *Social Mobility in Britain*, Routledge & Keegan Paul, London 1954, p387.
14. Secretary of State for Scotland's record of meeting 7 September 1945. Lady Balfour's confidential reports for January-June 1945 and July-September list resignations and sickness of senior staff and that Scottish headquarters was "very short staffed".
15. Lady Balfour to Joseph Westwood, 12 September 1945.
16. *It's The Job That Counts* (1954), p63.
17. Lady Balfour to Joseph Westwood, 12 September 1945. See also: *WVS Scottish Headquarters Reports*, July-September 1945 and October-December 1945.

'Mary Smieton's memories' in *Stella Reading, Some Recollections by Her Friends*, (1971), pp15–16.

18. *Red Tape*, the Magazine of the Civil Service Clerical Association, July 1938 p782. Hinton, p162. *Department of Health Memorandum*, 23 January 1946.

20. Balfour, Lady Ruth, *Note on the Future of WVS in Relationship to the Community*, Edinburgh, 21 February 1946.

21. *Lady Reading circular to Scottish WVS centres*, Edinburgh, 15 May 1946. See also: *Future of Women's Voluntary Services in Scotland, report for the Secretary of State for Scotland*, 5 July 1946.

22. *Future of Women's Voluntary Services in Scotland*, 5 July 1946.

23. *Under-Secretary's memorandum to Secretary of State for Scotland*, 12 October 1946.

24. *Welwyn Garden City narrative report*, December 1943. See also: McMurray, Matthew, *The Origins of WVS Meals on Wheels*, WRVS Oxfordshire, 13 October 2007. This information sheet, by WRVS archivist Matthew Mc Murray pins down the start of Meals on Wheels in Welwyn Garden City to October 1943.

25. Home Office to Secretary of State for Scotland, 4 December 1946.

26. *The Scotsman*, 5 December 1939. Secretary of State for Scotland to Home Office, 5 December 1946.

27. James Chuter Ede to House of Commons, *Hansard*, 24 April 1947, Vol 436, No 90.

28. *Report on 25 Years' Work* (1963), p4. Lady Reading to Centre Organisers, April 1947.

29. *Secretary of State for Scotland's memorandum of meeting with Lady Reading and May Campbell*, Edinburgh, 13 June 1947.

30. *WVS Bulletin No 97*, November 1947, p2.

31. *The Scotsman*, 6 March 1945.

32. Beveridge, Lord and Wells, A. F. (Eds), *The Evidence for Voluntary Action*, George Allen & Unwin, London, 1949, p140.

33. *WVS Bulletin No 113*, May 1949, p2.

CHAPTER 7

1. *WVS Bulletin No 152*, August 1952, p13.

2. *WVS Bulletin No 152*, August 1952, p1. Beauman (1977), p69.

3. *Report on 25 Years' Work*, p71. *It's The Job That Counts* (1954), p112.

4. *Dundee Courier*, 7 August 1954. *Scottish Daily Mail*, 4 July 1955.

5. *Dundee Evening Telegraph*, 22 October 1956.

6. Beauman (1977), p126–7. *WVS Bulletin No 137*, May 1951, p9.

7. *Dundee Courier*, 4 October 1956.
8. Beauman, p145.
9. Anon. *WVS Contribute One Thousand Tons of Processed Clothing to World Refuge Year 1959–60*, British Library 8298.e.90, p1.
10. Beauman, p146.
11. Interview with Flora Kirkland, 2007
12. *Survival!*, HMSO, November 1962. I am indebted to Falkirk Council Cultural Services for alerting me to WVS leaflets in the Robb family papers.
13. Flora Kirkland to author, 2008.
14. *Daily Mail*, 24 October 1958.
15. *WVS Scotland Advisory Committee Report 1 February – 31 July 1962*. Affleck, Tom, *A Short History of Lesmahagow WRVS*, 1999. I am grateful to Agnes Affleck for allowing me to quote from this unpublished paper.
16. Extracts of minutes of Lesmahagow WRVS, 1962–66, in *A Short History of Lesmahagow WRVS*.
17. *It's The Job That Counts* (1954), p126.
18. *A Handbook on WRVS Emergency Welfare*, WRVS, London, 1967.
19. *WVS Blue Guide to Meals on Wheels*, London, 1965.
20. Annual Report of the Ministry of Health for 1967, in Morris, Mary, *Voluntary Workers and The Welfare State*, Routledge, London, 1969, p48–50. *WRVS Factsheet, 2004*, WRVS Archives, Milton Hill. *WRVS An Outline of the Work of Women's Royal Voluntary Service in 1967*, London, 1967.
21. Beauman, pp154–5.

CHAPTER 8

1. Beauman (1977), pp162.
2. Beauman, p100.
3. Secretary of State for Scotland to the Chairman for Scotland, 4 March 1972, in *WRVS Magazine*, May 1972, p21.
4. *WRVS Magazine*, January 1973, p23.
5. *WRVS, An Outline of the Work of Women's Royal Voluntary Services in 1971*, London, June 1972.
6. *WRVS, A Guide to the Organisation and Administration of Women's Royal Voluntary Service*, London, 1981.
7. *Bridge of Allan Narrative Reports*, 1956 and 1970.
8. Interview with Ann McGregor, 2007.
9. Letters to author by Agnes Mair and Sylvia Morrison, 2007. See also: *WVS Bulletin No 205*, January 1957, p8.
10. *WRVS Magazine*, June 1971, p9.

11. *WRVS Magazine*, January 1970, p13. Bridge of Allan WRVS centre notes on fire-watching at Allan Lodge, November 1977. I am grateful to Ann McGregor for drawing my attention to this document.

12. *A Helping Hand*, by Stanley Maxton, Twenty Minute Broadcast for Primary Schools in Scotland. Transcript in *Women's Royal Voluntary Services at Work in Scotland*, undated, (1973). See also: WRVS Magazine, April 1973.

13. Beauman, p165.

14. *WRVS Magazine*, January 1970, p8.

15. Mears, Robin, Morby Hazel and Smith, Randall, *From Community Care to Market Care; The Development of Welfare Services for Older People*, Policy Press, London, 2002, p104.

CHAPTER 9

1. WRVS, *A Guide to the Organisation and Administration of Women's Royal Voluntary Service*, London, 1981.

2. *WRVS Guide* (1981).

3. 'Welcome to WRVS Christmas wiseline', *WRVS Press Release*, 3 December 2007.

4. *WRVS Guide* (1981).

5. Chairman's message, *WRVS Annual Report*, 1982.

6. *WRVS News No 1*, Autumn 1985, p5.

7. *WRVS Scotland Information Sheet No 71*, May/June 1983.

8. *WRVS Action No 16*, August 2000, p23.

9. Interview with Isabella McKay, 2007.

10. *WRVS News*, Winter Issue, 1985.

11. Elaine Smith to author, 2007.

12. Sylvia Morrison to author, 2007.

13. Kristeen Smith to author, 2007.

14. 'The Angels of Lockerbie' *WRVS News No 11*, Spring 1989, p1. Interview with Kristeen Smith, 2008.

15. Interview with Dame Mary Corsar, 2008. Elaine Smith to author, 2007.

16. 'Such style for the big parade', *WRVS News No 11*, Spring 1989, p1.

17. Elaine Smith to author, 2007.

CHAPTER 10

1. *WRVS Scottish Report*, Edinburgh, 1990.

2. *WRVS News No 24*, Winter 1992, p1.

3. Interview with Dame Mary Corsar, 2008.
4. *WRVS Today*, April 1994, pp4–5.
5. *Perth Emergency Flood News*, issues one and two, February, 1993.
6. Elizabeth Toulson in, 'Widening horizons', *Dundee Courier*, 5 April 1995.
7. *WRVS Today*, August 1994, p7.
8. Anne Boyd in, 'There's a job to be done', *Evening Telegraph*, 20 July 1995.
9. Kristeen Smith interview with author, 2008. Kristeen Smith to author, 2007.
10. *WRVS Bulletin*, November 1971, p22.
11. Agnes Mair to author, 2007.
12. Partnership in Action, *WRVS Manifesto*, London, 1999.
13. *Action 1999*, p3.
14. Former members letters to author, 2007.
15. *Idem*. See also: Hinton (2002), p90.
16. *WRVS Action No 13*, Winter 1999, p28.

CHAPTER 11

1. *WRVS Action No 15*, Summer 2000, p26.
2. *Action No 17*, Winter 2000, pp13–14.
3. Interview with Dame Mary Corsar, 2008.
4. *Action No 14*, Spring 2000, p26. Interview with Kristeen Smith, 2008.
5. Mills, *Within the Island Fortress (2005)*, p19.
6. *The Guardian*, 10 October 2001.
7. *Action No 16*, Autumn 2000, p8.
8. Scottish Parliament Motion S1M-2053, July 2001.
9. *Action No 19*, Summer 2001, p30.
10. *Action No 22*, May 2002, p11.
11. *Idem*, pp10–11.
12. *Action No 20*, Autumn/Winter 2001, p38.
13. *Action No 24*, Spring 2003, p9.
14. 'WRVS campaigns to change its image of volunteers to services', *The Times*, 23 February 2004.
15. Mark Lever interview in 'Funding cut forces charity to revamp its dowdy image', *The Guardian*, 3 March 2004.
16. *Action No 23*, September 2002, p19.
17. 'Success to Women Volunteers', *Women's Weekly*, 8 July 1978, p9.
18. 'Wheeling in a tasty dish to set before a queen', *The Times*, 13 November 1997.
19. Mark Lever interviewed for Home Office press statement: 'Volunteering Grants will Boost Individuals' Impact in Communities', 25 August 2004.

20. *Action No 17*, Winter 2000, p26.
21. WRVS Press Statement, 13 April 2005.
22. Rachel Cackett, WRVS Response to 'Age and experience: developing a strategy for a Scotland with an ageing population', 2006, p7.
23. *Action No 29*, Autumn 2006, p66.
24. Mark Lever in, 'Burger bars replace NHS coffee shops', *The Guardian*, 28 May 2006.
25. *Idem.*
26. 'Hospital cafes offer more than tea and sympathy', *The Observer*, 28 May 2006.
27. *Dundee Courier*, 27 June 2000 and 3 July 2000.
28. *The Press & Journal*, 21 April 2007.
29. 'Eased out', *Dundee Courier*, 20 May 2002.
30. 'Meals on Wheels? Sorry, but you'll have to cook them yourselves,' *The Daily Telegraph*, 22 May 2005.
31. *WRVS Press Release*, 7 November 2005.
32. *WRVS Press Release*, 'WRVS help people caught up in floods', 23 July 2007.
33. *WRVS Press Release*, 22 August 2007.
34. *Action No 27*, Spring 2006, p39.
35. Scottish Parliament Motions, S1M-1391 January 2001, S1M-2053 July 2001, S2M-1024 May 2004 and S2M-5497 January 2007.
36. Mark Lever in, 'Time-poor Britons shy away from charity work,' *The Independent*, 2 February 2004.
37. *WRVS Press Release*, 10 January 2008.
38. Interview with Dame Mary Corsar, 2008.
39. *Nella Last's War (2006)*, pp69 & 108. Elaine Smith to author, 2007.

PRINCIPAL SOURCES

WVS and WRVS documentation is available for consultation in several major archives. For day-to-day activities much information is contained in the organisation's newsletters which began as the handwritten then printed WVS Bulletin, before taking on new guises as *WRVS Magazine*, *WRVS Today*, *WRVS News* and ultimately *WRVS Action*. Copies of these are kept at WRVS Milton Hill, Abingdon, Oxfordshire, along with copies of Circular Notices and later annual reports issued from Tothill Street and Edinburgh. The archive at Milton Hill is the principal source for original records, photographs, memorabilia and ephemera. The WRVS website www.wrvs.org.uk is a useful start point for a historical overview of the organisation.

Scottish WVS News Reviews, minutes of meetings and reports for most periods are also held at the National Archives of Scotland. Documents relating to Lady Reading, Lady Balfour, the Scottish Office and Westminster Departments are also at the NAS: see, for example, GD1/171/1, GNC5/109 and HH61/698. These include internal memorandums, records of ministerial meetings and private correspondence. Collections of civil defence documents can be viewed at the Public Record Office (Kew) and the British Library. Individual archives relating to WVS and WRVS activities are housed in various Scottish institutions, including the National Library of Scotland. Where used, these are mentioned in footnotes. Reports and photographs are, as expected, to be found in numerous Scottish newspapers.

Two contemporary publications charted the history of WVS. The first was *Women in Green: The Story of the W.V.S. in Wartime*, by Charles Graves, written shortly after the war in 1948. A more colourful narrative and pictorial history was compiled by Virginia Graham in booklet form, and published by HMSO in 1959. Katharine Bentley Beauman then took the story up to 1977 in *Green Sleeves*. More recently (2002) James Hinton has carried out an academic study of the social leadership of WVS, but his research did not include Scotland.

BIBLIOGRAPHY

Andrews, Maggie, *The Acceptable Face of Feminism, The Women's Institute as a Social Movement*, Lawrence & Wishart Ltd, London, 1997.

Anon, (WRVS), Stella Reading, *Some Recollections by Her Friends*, London, 1971.

Anon (Ed. Pauline Fenno), *It's The Job That Counts: 1939–1953. A selection from the Speeches and Writings of the Dowager Marchioness of Reading*, private circulation, 1954.

Anon (Ed. Pauline Fenno), *It's The Job That Counts: 1954–1971. A selection from the Speeches and Writings of the Dowager Marchioness of Reading, Vol 2*, private circulation, 1972.

Bale, Bernard, *Aberdeen & The North East at War*, Black & White Publishing, Edinburgh, 2005.

Barton, Elaine, *What of the Women? A Study of Women in Wartime*, London, 1941.

Beauman, Katharine Bentley, *Green Sleeves: The Story of the WVS/WRVS*, Seeley, Service & Co, London, 1977.

Beveridge, Lord (William) and Wells A.F., *The Evidence for Voluntary Action*, George Allen & Unwin, London, 1949.

Boyd, William (Ed), *Evacuation in Scotland: A Record of Events and Experiments*, University of London Press, Kent, 1944.

Broad, Richard and Fleming, Suzie, *Nella Last's War, The Second World War Diaries of Housewife, 49*, Profile Books, London, 2006.

Chambers, Rosalind, 'A Study of Three Voluntary Organisations', in Glass D.V. (Ed), *Social Mobility in Britain*, Routledge & Keegan Paul, London, 1954.

Cox, Mary, *British Women at War*, John Murray, London, 1941.

Ellis, Jennifer (Ed), *Thatched With Gold, The Memoirs of Mabell Countess of Airlie*, Hutchison, London, 1962.

Finlay, Richard, *Modern Scotland*, Profile Books, London, 2004.

Fraser, Eugenie, *A Home by the Hooghly; A Jute Wallah's Wife*, Mainstream, Edinburgh, 1989.

Goodall, Felicity, *Voices from the Home Front*, David & Charles, London, 2004.

Graham, Virginia, *The Story of WVS*, HMSO, London, 1959.

Graves, Charles, *Women in Green: The Story of the W.V.S. in Wartime*, Wm Heinemann, London, 1948.

Harris, Paul, *Disaster! One Hundred Years of Wreck, Rescue and Tragedy in Scotland*, Archive Publications, Runcorn, Cheshire, 1989.

Hennessy, Peter. *Having it So Good, Britain in the Fifties*, Penguin, London, 2006.

Hetherington, S. J., Katharine Atholl 1874–1960, *Against The Tide*, Aberdeen University Press.

Hinton, James, *Women, Social Leadership, and the Second World War*, Oxford University Press, 2002.

HMSO, *Preparation for Heavy Attacks Next Winter*, London, 1944.

HMSO, *Protect and Survive*, London, 1980.

Jamison, Brian (Ed), *Scotland and the Cold War*, Cualann Press, Dunfermline, 2003.

Jeffrey, Andrew, *This Present Emergency, Edinburgh, The River Forth and South East Scotland and the Second World War*, Mainstream, Edinburgh, 1992.

Jeffrey, Andrew, *This Time of Crisis; Glasgow, The West of Scotland and the North Western Approaches in the Second World War*, Mainstream, Edinburgh, 1993.

Lewis, Peter, *The Fifties*, Wm Heinemann, London, 1978.

Lynch, Michael, (Ed), *The Oxford Companion to Scottish History*, Oxford, 2001.

McPhail, I.M.M., *The Clydebank Blitz*, West Dunbartonshire Libraries, 1974 (2000 edition).

Marwick, Arthur, *British Society Since 1945*, Penguin, London 1982 (2003 edition).

Mess, Henry, *Voluntary Services Since 1918*, London 1948.

Mills, J., *Within the Island Fortress: The Uniforms, Insignia & Ephemera of the Home Front in Britain 1939–1945. No 1, The Women's Voluntary Services (WVS)*, Wardens Publishing, Orpington, 2005.

Morris, Mary, *Voluntary Workers and The Welfare State*, Routledge, London, 1969 (1998 edition).

Nicholson, Mavis, *What did you do in the war, mummy?: Women in World War II*, Chatto & Windus, London, 1975.

Osborne, Brian and Armstrong, Ronald, Glasgow: *A City at War*, Birlinn, Edinburgh, 2003.

Partnership in Action, *WRVS Manifesto*, Milton Hill, 1999.

Readers Digest, Life on The Home Front, Readers Digest Journeys into the Past Series, London 1993.

Report on Evacuation of Tarbat Training Area, November and December 1943. (Submitted by Janet Douglas, Conon Bridge centre organiser, Ross-shire), December 1943.

Report on Ministry of Information action and on public behaviour during and following the Clydeside Raids – March 13 and 14, 1941. HM Government, 20 March 1941.

Robertson, Seona, and Wilson, Les, *Scotland's War*, Mainstream, Edinburgh, 1995.

Smith, Robin, *The Making of Scotland*, Edinburgh, 2001.

Smout, T. C., *A Century of Scottish People 1830–1950*, London, 1986.

Sweet, Leslie, 'Women's "Voluntary" Services, Some Comments on a New Organisation', in *Red Tape*, the magazine of the Civil Service Clerical Association, July 1938.

Titmuss, Richard, *History of the Second World War, Problems of Social Policy*, Chapter XV, 'The Attack on Ports and Provincial Cities', London, 1963.

Watson, Norman, *Dundee: A Short History*, Black & White Publishing, Edinburgh, 2005.

Women's Royal Voluntary Services at Work in Scotland, HQ Scotland booklet, undated (1973).

Women's Royal Voluntary Services, Rescue a Recipe, London, 1975. (A booklet compiled by WRVS organised meals department and containing 'regional and family recipes remembered' and sponsored by Hotlock Food Conveyors Ltd.)

Women's Royal Voluntary Service, WRVS Cook Book, Milton Hill, Abingdon, 2003. An updated cook book offering 'Favourite Recipes from WRVS Members and Friends', and compiled to celebrate the Golden Jubilee of the Patron, the Queen.

Women's Royal Voluntary Services, Historical Notes, WRVS Headquarters, Stockwell Road, undated (1988). This four-page document provides a timeline of the organisation's achievements from 1938 to the Golden Jubilee in 1988.

Women's Royal Voluntary Services, Emergency Welfare, London, 1967.

Women's Royal Voluntary Services Scotland, Golden Jubilee, Edinburgh 1988. A booklet commemorating the 50th anniversary of the Service in Scotland and listing activities of its regional centres.

Women's Voluntary Services, Community Feeding in War Time, London 1941. Booklet prepared by WVS for civil defence training purposes.

Women's Voluntary Services, Report on Ten Years Work for the Nation, 1938–1948, London, 1948.

Women's Voluntary Services, Report on Twenty-Five Years Work, London, 1963.

Women's Voluntary Services, Introduction, Administration and Organisation, Post War Development of Administration and Organisation, War Work and Post-War Developments, London, December 1948.

World War II, The Scottish Home Front, National Archives of Scotland, Edinburgh 2004.

GENERAL INDEX

TOPOGRAPHICAL INDEX